Matters of Substance

Griffith Edwards

Matters of Substance
Drugs—and Why
Everyone's a User

THOMAS DUNNE BOOKS
ST. MARTIN'S PRESS ⚏ NEW YORK

This book is dedicated to Sue, my wife, who tested its thought, typed it and generally helped make it happen, and to Dan and Rose who continue to help make Sue and me happen.

Contents

Part Three: Other Drugs Outside the Law

Part Four: What To Do About Drugs?

Preface

I buy a railway ticket on a summer afternoon and am temporarily mesmerized by the tattoos on the clerk's arms, revealed by his rolled-up sleeves. He says, 'Thirty years ago, you remember where we met, the hospital, I was a junkie. A wonderful family now, I didn't look back ever.' Life keeps crossing its own path, I think to myself. And I go off down the platform in a blur of rejoicing.

Drugs, licit and illicit, are used by many people without damage done at all. Drugs can also be dangerous, and in sum the harm they do today to the health, welfare and productivity of the world's people is appalling, and increases. This book will examine the history of human relationships with the vast array of mind-acting drugs that have at one time or another been used as medicines, in religious ritual or for the magical getting of wisdom, for fun and frolic, or for numbed oblivion. Drugs can properly only be understood in their historical, social and cultural context – they have no meaning in thin air. I will explore what multiple sciences can contribute to explanation of compulsive personal appetite for drugs, and why drug epidemics can so often run like fire across dry grass.

In the light of the history and the science, this book will make proposals for a more effective and rational public response to the drug problem – a handling that at present too often seems to involve a patching together of ad hoc remedies done in the dark. But the conclusions emerging from this analysis cannot be a set of simplistic answers to what are great perplexities. This is not a book that will crusade for an even bloodier and more punitive war on drugs, and neither will it press as miracle cure the legalization of all drugs.

Around 1880 one of my Victorian great-uncles was shipped off to America because of his scandalous drinking, but I doubt whether that had much to do with my career choice. In the 1930s, I grew up in a family that had relaxed attitudes to alcohol but there was not much alcohol around. On picnics, along with the spread of cold meat and pickles and gooseberry pie, there would be a bottle of Sunlight Ale, and the children might be given a sip or two to taste. When the vicar called at our cottage, the sherry decanter would be ceremoniously produced. 'Oh no, please no,' he would say, taking the second glass with a show of reluctance. But that was the lot, a third glass would have been unthinkable debauchery. Brandy was kept strictly for medicinal purposes, and when a racing pigeon, blown off course, flopped down on a windowsill, an attempt was made to pour a little down its throat.

Every Christmas, my mother was given a pack of twenty Gold Flake by a bachelor cousin. These were transferred to a lacquered box that stood on a table in the drawing room. That gradually crumbling stash lasted for a full twelve months. Years later, on going through the accumulation of ages (nothing was ever thrown out in that home), we found a tin which revealed on its label that it had once contained cocaine-impregnated throat lozenges. We bought our first radio, knew that the world was threatening, dug our air-raid shelter, but mind-acting chemicals were for us at that time no part of the world's threat.

So, from that background and baseline, I qualified in medicine and then specialized in psychiatry, and found myself in the 1960s treating patients with alcohol problems. In the late 1960s we were suddenly confronted by the appearance of dreadfully messed-up young men and women who were injecting heroin, and we had the sense of a storm blowing along our streets. Since then, storm has followed storm without let up or fair weather.

Along with those front-line clinical involvements, my colleagues and I were trying to research addiction. We were mounting some early treatment trials, conducting community surveys, trying better to understand what addiction *is*, the itness of it, what drives the compulsion. In 1967, I set up the Addiction Research Unit (ARU), at the Institute of Psychiatry, London, as the first specialized addiction research group to operate in the UK. In 1991, a natural evolution resulted in the establishment of the National Addiction Centre in London.

As for what took my career in its particular direction, I do not at all know why from a home so unworried about drugs I should have come to this speciality. But I do know what led me towards trying to make science of difficult material. When I was aged about five or six, my father, when walking back one evening from his veterinary research laboratory, chanced upon a baby hedgehog dangerously lost in the road. He gave it to me as a present, and we fed it with milk from a dropper. Every week my father then stretched it out, measured it with a metre rule, and entered another point on the growth curve which he pinned up in his office. That was my introduction to science.

I am very grateful that, by whatever play of chance and fortune, and from the background of distant picnics and a hedgehog, my life should have gone in the professional direction it took. It has been intensely rewarding to work with patients who so often, with immense courage, have pulled themselves out of the pit of self-destruction to make sense of their lives. People with substance problems are of us, deserve our compassion, should not be stigmatized. Some years into this career, I went to a party where everyone else present was a recovered skid-row alcoholic, and I had been told earlier that such people never recover. Research has brought another kind of fulfilment, and addiction science is for me an international friendship network.

There have been bad days, days when tragic things have happened to patients, days when research has seemed all dead ends and failure, and disappointments have come in their legions. But always at the core has been for me the sheer fascination of the subject itself. Addictions – all life is there and it is about the human play in its totality. I hope that this book can put on offer some sharing of that fascination.

Acknowledgements

My thanks are due to colleagues too numerous to list fully but whose ideas are reflected everywhere in this book. It would however be an unbearable oversight to leave unmentioned my indebtedness to Thomas Babor, Taha Baasher, Michael Farrell, Hamid Ghodse, Michael Gossop, Wayne Hall, John Hughes, Jerome Jaffe, Harold Kalant, Neil McKeganey, Juan Carlos Negrete, Vichai Poshyachinda, Peter Reuter, Lee Robins, Robin Room, Ole-Jørgen Skog, John Strang, George Vaillant and Robert West. Historians whose scholarship I have greatly relied upon include Virginia Berridge, David Courtwright, Jonathon Goodman, Sarah Mars, David Musto and Joseph Spillane. The library staff of the Athenaeum, the Institute of Psychiatry and the London Library gave me bibliographic assistance. Patricia Davis, Rose Edwards and Dan Edwards helped with electronic searches. To my editors at Penguin, Stefan McGrath and Helen Conford, and my copy-editor Monica Schmoller, I am grateful for exemplary editorial support.

Note

This book will at several points use personal case histories to make live its arguments. Patients, families and doctors are all absolutely true to life but invented.

Introduction: Understanding Drugs

Posturing, fixed positions, monotonous repetition of untested assertions, and all this with the facts of the matter ignored or trashed. Too often that is the flavour of what passes for the debate on drugs. The public is not offered a debate of the quality, rationality and subtlety which the subject deserves. Day in and day out, drugs provoke in the media a sustained, intense and, for the most part, science-free feeding frenzy. Here is a collage of the kind of headlines which are generated.

Monday Schoolteacher says Ecstasy causes zero harm and should be made freely available. Story that more than one in ten air passengers coming into Heathrow from Jamaica are 'mules' carrying cocaine. Research shows that children of mothers who smoke cigarettes during pregnancy have an increased risk of diabetes. 'Johnny is stoned on twelfth birthday' is the heading for a front-page tabloid splash.

Tuesday Judge calls for all drugs to be legalized – 'Prohibition has failed,' he declares. Survey suggests that women are drinking more than ever before and government adviser declares: 'Alcohol is a bigger killer for women than cancer of the cervix.' 'Cocaine the New Champagne' is the headline for a glossy feature on Penthouse Lifestyles.

Wednesday 'Give addicts the free heroin they need,' says Chief Constable. News story, 'Cannabis linked with cancer say scientists', 'Kids will visit bars alone under relaxed new licensing law'. Bishop says, 'Christians are too afraid of drugs.'

Thursday Revelation that tobacco industry has been priming the developing world's black market in cigarettes with its own branded products. Radio feature suggesting Swiss experiments on prescribing heroin to heroin addicts have achieved outstandingly positive results – 'On a free supply of their drug, addicts get back in to work and stop stealing.' Former Cabinet Minister says, 'Legalize all drugs.' 'Youngest Ecstasy victim dead at age ten' is another headline.

Friday. MP calls for Royal Commission to tell Britain 'how to liberalize drug laws from top to bottom'...'Prohibition always fails,' he says. Death of famous model in Hollywood by heroin overdose is extensively reported. Customs admit that they seize only 7 per cent of imported illicit drugs. Smoking costs British business £100 million each week.

Saturday Diaries of rock star who lost battle with heroin sold for £2.8 million. 'Drugs now "normal" in youth lifestyle,' claims probation officer. 'Gangland cocaine slayings reach new peak' is a tabloid headline. 'Ecstasy brings spate of deaths' reports another paper. Manchester has increased its licensed premises for alcohol by 240 per cent over a four-year period.

Sunday Rally organized by Sunday newspaper for legalization of cannabis. 'Prohibition has failed,' asserts the editor. Two-column-inch story tucked away towards back of a paper is headed 'Ecstasy kills brain cells, says new study'. 'Ancient Britons got to the beer before they found out about bread'. 'Drunken Muscovites on rampage after Japanese football win'. Psychologist claims that Ecstasy is safe. 'Cannabis is potential health disaster,' says doctor. 'Free cup of coffee voucher for each one of our readers' is a newspaper's offer. 'War on drugs is hypocrisy' is an item in letters column.

And come Monday, the headline 'Date rape drug to be banned' is not a reference to lager.

All those entries are based on true instances, although the timescale has been shrunk.

As a corrective to that frenzy, this introduction will offer an objective account of certain important facts about drugs, as a framework for the detailed consideration of different substances discussed in later chapters. With which drugs should we be concerned? How do drugs produce their effects on the brain? A fundamental question: why do people take or not take any drug? What is this thing called 'dependence'? What are the dangers in drug use? Why does the choice of route by which a drug is taken affect danger? What causes established balances in the population's drug use to break down and drug epidemics to break out? How, for instance, did society's relationship with cocaine come to switch from medicated lozenges to gangland murder?

For the present I will entirely hold back from discussing what society can do better about drugs, and will return to this question only in the final part of the book. By that point many facts will have been laid out, a great range of witnesses heard, diverse geographical territory will have been visited, all the way from the remote Andean uplands to the street corners of our modern cities; many historical miles will have been travelled. The book will be examining interventions which have been ineffective or have clumsily made the drug situation worse, and, in contrast, some actions which have had beneficial outcomes. To ignore the hard won store of experience and leap instead to partisan judgement makes no sense at all.

What is a mind-acting drug?

I once heard the question 'What is a drug?' put to William Paton, the then Professor of Pharmacology at Oxford, at a scientific meeting. His unhesitating answer was: 'A drug is any chemical which when injected into a laboratory animal will produce a scientific paper.' Perhaps one may, by analogy, claim that a mind-acting drug is any substance which, when taken by a human being, will result in a newspaper headline.

Drugs can be grouped according to their major modes of impact on the mind. Here is the system of classification that people who study drugs generally find useful.

- *Sedatives* Sedatives come as alcohol, as pills in the shape of barbiturates, or as minor tranquillizers such as Valium or other benzodiazepines, as anaesthetic gases and other volatile substances. What sedatives have in common is their capacity to down-regulate mental activity and produce a state of relaxation or sleepiness. In larger dosage they cause intoxication and perhaps unconsciousness. All these primarily sedative drugs can sometimes give rise to disinhibition and paradoxical excitement, hence the fighting drunk. These drugs also have the capacity to slow reaction time and impair coordination.
- *Stimulants* Members of this group include cocaine, amphetamine and caffeine. They have the capacity to up-regulate mental activity

so as to cause excitement and wakefulness. They can, however, easily move on to provoke agitation and anxiety. The more powerful drugs in this group can in higher dosage cause disruption of thought processes, extremes of excitement and hallucinatory illness.

- *Opiates* Opium is the father and mother of all opiates but there are synthetic drugs in this group which mimic the actions of opium. A person who is given an opiate or a sedative and not told which is which, may not be able to tell the difference. But opiates can produce euphoria of a special and intense kind which is different from the more crass type of effect engendered by sedatives. They also possess a wonderful ability to relieve pain.
- *Hallucinogens* Mescaline as a plant substance and LSD (Lysergide) as a synthetic drug are examples of hallucinogens. These drugs are capable of astonishingly complex mental effects. They can bend time and space and feelings, but the visions they give can rather easily tilt towards nightmare.
- *Drugs with mixed actions* Besides these four main types of drug there are quite a few substances which have actions of more than one kind. Examples include cannabis (sedative and hallucinogen), nicotine (sedative and stimulant), Ecstasy (stimulant and hallucinogen).

A simple scheme which seeks to bring order to the vast diversity of chemicals that act on an organ so multiple in its capacities as the human brain is likely to involve a little cutting of corners. That said, the scheme offered here provides a reasonably good mapping of the territory. Meet any new drug and if the researcher can place it in one or other of those categories, they will, through the family resemblances, know much about what to expect of it.

But beyond the scientifically based system of classification, one does well now and then to stand back from the science and acknowledge in awe that chemicals can, in extraordinary and varied ways, play with our perceptions of external reality and the experiencing of the inner world. They can send a witch riding on her imagined broomstick, allow the Inca's messenger to run the mountain tracks for days without sustenance, give the shaman contact with ancestral spirits, make a man or woman murderously drunk, ease the pain of terminal cancer, get a disco crowd loved-up, be the Sunlight Ale for the picnic.

What does that say about the chemical substrate of mentation, the arbitrariness of reality, the ceiling to consciousness, the fragility of sanity?

How drugs produce their effects on the brain

The physical effects of drugs on the brain can only be understood within the context of the body's own system of chemical messengers such as serotonin, dopamine and GABA (gamma-aminobutyric acid), which are constantly helping to conduct signals across the nerve tracts. Each drug will have its own pattern of interaction with these work-aday chemicals: it may act as a mimic, selectively block activity or enhance the action of a natural transmitter. These transmitters are chemical keys, each with their own designated keyhole, which are the various types of receptor sites found on the surface of nerve cells. A drug may be able to key into one or more kind of site. At times, the chemical complexities within the drug–brain interaction begin to look like the swirling of a thick, stirred soup. Over recent years, there has been an enormous increase in the understanding of the nerve pathways and transmitter substances involved in the actions of drugs on the brain.

But the processes involved in a drug's actions usually go beyond the mechanical key-into-keyhole analogy. The psychological expectation that a person has of a drug will bear strongly on the way in which it is experienced. Someone who expects to find pleasure in a cigarette is likely to feel the next puff pleasurable, but not so the person who cares nothing for nicotine. The way in which a drug is experienced is enormously influenced by what the peer group and social mores propose as being the drug's effects. Thus, an opiate taken for pain-relief will be experienced as a pain-reliever; taken as a street drug, exactly the same chemical will give the euphoria of a 'high', while consumed by a romantic poet it might help build the pleasure-dome of Kubla Khan. A lot of what drugs do to the mind is in the mind.

To illustrate the fact that drug effects are usually much more than the mere mechanical, same-for-all-comers consequence of a chemical reaching the brain, we can turn to an experiment which manipulated the effect of morphine on the eye. It is well known that morphine produces contraction of the pupils, which may be narrowed down to pin-point size. However, put the subject through a conditioning process so the next drug they expect to receive will dilate the pupil, slip them morphine instead, and the morphine will dilate the pupil. Learning processes can profoundly influence drug effects.

Use, misuse, abuse and recreational use

The phrase 'drug use' has transparent meaning and is free of moral judgement: all use is use, and the term embraces drug taking both of a kind society approves and of a type or degree that is disapproved. The cut-off point that determines when use shades into misuse is largely in the eye of the beholder. 'Misuse' is the term likely to be favoured in Britain when the behaviour is deemed by the state to be problematic, while in America the rather more pejorative 'abuse' is in those circumstances the favoured label. 'Recreational use' implies non-harmful, non-compulsive use within a leisure lifestyle.

Drug choices

By 'drug choice' I mean the decision to use a particular drug, or mix of drugs, within a defined pattern of dose and regularity, or the decision perhaps to quit; but also and importantly the choice not to use at all is contained within the idea. The question of why individuals use (or do not use) drugs has no single answer to fit everyone. Reasons for starting are often different from the reasons for continuing.

Take the adolescent's starting point as he or she moves from being more or less drug-free to experience with a variety of licit drugs, quite probably an involvement with some widely available illicit substances, and, less probably, through to the use of more destructive illicit drugs. The following factors may contribute to initiation and that young person's early steps along the drug pathway.

- *The drug is physically available* The most basic fact affecting any adolescent's drug choice is that in their individual environment this or that chemical may be more or less physically available. No one ever uses a drug which is not within their arm's reach.

- *The drug is psychologically available* The drug may theoretically be there for the stretching out of the arm, but because of religious or other social or family prohibitions the drug is psychologically not available. This kind of barrier may affect choice more than any legal prohibitions.

- *Choice and temperament* Some young people break rules and kick over conformity more easily and often than do others. There is no unique personality type which might guarantee drug taking, but the constitutional risk-taker is more likely to break through the barriers of legal constraint or moral dissuasion and take drugs than the conformist.

- *Liking for the actual drug effect* The reason why a young person chooses to use a drug lies in part with their finding that, with the initial aversion overcome (many drugs are unpleasant on first experience), they like what the drug does for them. It is their way of dealing with anxiety or depression, their liking for the mellow feeling or the high, or their enjoyment of the trip to the mental fairground, which motivates the drug use. The positives they will find in the drug effect are often in some measure genetically determined but never entirely programmed by their genes.

- *Personal image and peer-group approbation* The drug is a badge and entry ticket to a young peer-group world redolent with all sorts of symbols. Take that drug and become one of us. It will make you cool, aesthetic, sophisticated, sexy, conformist, rebellious, punk rotten, and ensure every other wish-fulfilment of your adolescent dreams.

But some years along the individual's drug pathway, their self-image, ambitions, relationships, responsibilities, friendship networks have changed, and within that nexus of change their drug-use choices will have consolidated, escalated or dropped off. One will have to look very closely at the individual adult to understand why they do whatever drugs they choose to do, and at the particular dosage. Symbolism is still operative, even if transmuted, peer groups will still support or negate the habit, but for the heavy user the drug itself often, over time, becomes the dominant reason for the reinforced drug choice. Smoking the first cigarette at fourteen and a pack a day at the age of forty may be choices made by the same person but within different fields of force.

What is addiction?

Scientists prefer 'drug dependence' to 'addiction', but this book will not be purist and will use the terms interchangeably. Here are people talking about what to them characterized the inner experience of being dependent:

Male actor, aged 51 They have that saying at Alcoholics Anonymous meetings. First the man takes the drink and then the drink takes the man. That rang a loud bell for me when I first heard it. I had been taken by the drink for at least ten years.

Woman teacher, 31 Cannabis, funny, most of our friends have given up but me and my partner are still using it regularly and I can feel quite uncomfortable without it. Feel I ought to give up but don't make it.

Woman doctor, 46 OK, I smoke thirty cigarettes a day. Know it's amazingly stupid. My kids hate it. Yes, filthy, but I can't stop.

Unemployed man, 26 I was in prison eighteen months. Stayed pretty clean at first when I came out. Then I started using a bit of H, nothing too heavy. It was when a mate moved in to my flat who was a dealer that the habit once more took over. I mean, I know when I'm hooked again, right back where I started from sort of thing. When I'm not shooting up the H I'm wondering where the next fix will come from. I call it an obsession when it gets like that, no space for anything else in my mind, it takes over mind and body.

Male executive, 38 They told me sniffing cocaine was not addictive. To begin with I could take it or leave it. But Christ, it became for me all night and day.

The common thread found running through these statements is of dependence experienced as an impairment of an individual's power to choose, a state of inner duress, something alien. In contrast, the touchstone for not being addicted is the retention of the capacity to 'take it or leave it'. And it is worth noting that, contrary to the common belief that potentially addictive drugs must all lead precipitously to addiction, many people will for a longer or shorter time use them without becoming dependent. Nothing about dependence is inevitable.

Woman poet, aged 60 Yes, I used heroin when I was younger. And I can tell you exactly how often I took it. Seventeen times and then I stopped.

Any attempt to understand dependence (addiction) must start with this sort of listening to what people say, the reaching for an understanding of what it really feels like, the realization that in its being and essence dependence is felt as an altered power relationship between person and drug. As regards the scientific basis for this altered state, the mechanisms are both psychological and biological. Addictive drugs have in common the capacity to be *rewarding*. They lead to a release of chemicals which act on specific areas of the brain to induce pleasure. The repeated experience of the reward builds up the drug-seeking habit. In the simplest terms, dependence is a strong, learnt, drug-seeking habit. It is not all-or-none, but may exist in various degrees of strength.

There is often a further layer to dependence in terms of a social role which is entered.

Female heroin addict, 23 I tell you, I grew up as no one, an abused child, dirt. When I became a heroin addict then I became someone. Being an addict, you're important, feels good, yes. TV cameras and that. You tell a bloke and it's like saying to him, 'Oh I've got this important job.' Respect, sort of, and the drug gives you mates who are doing the same thing, all one big club.

Dependence has a chemical and psychological substrate but to understand it one needs to enter other people's worlds.

Dependence syndromes

Over the last twenty-five years, much scientific effort has gone in to the identification of the core features of the drug dependence syndrome. The search started in the 1970s to identify the criteria that could define the graded, multi-layered condition which is dependence on a drug. The proper question becomes not 'Is he or she addicted to drug X?' but 'How far along the path of dependence on drug X has this person progressed?' Whatever the drug, give or take a little, the following criteria provide the template for defining the presence of a drug dependence syndrome. I will talk the ideas through in relation to alcohol.

- *The subjective awareness of a changed relationship with a drug* The AA member's admission that alcohol had become the controller offers an example of that kind of experience.
- *An acquired brain tolerance to the drug's effects* A given dose of the drug will have a smaller effect on the dependent than on the naïve user. Hence the 'hardened drinker' who dangerously takes pride in their ability to drink others under the table.
- *Withdrawal symptoms* The range and intensity of withdrawal symptoms that can be produced by different drugs varies from the evident and catastrophic to the subtle and not very obvious. Withdrawal symptoms from alcohol can range from mild shakiness on waking to convulsions or the life-threatening illness of delirium tremens.
- *Taking the drug to relieve the withdrawal symptom* Hence the morning drink.
- *Increased salience of the need for the drug over competing needs and responsibilities* Paying for the drink becomes more important than paying the rent; time spent drinking takes precedence over time with the family; sooner drink and drive than not get to the pub.
- *Narrowing of the drug-taking repertoire* The severely dependent drinker no longer varies their intake by the day of the week, by work or holiday or festive season, or in the presence of a visiting teetotal aunt. The drinking will be timetabled by the need for drink and will end up in a machine-like, drink-driven pattern.
- *Reinstatement after abstinence* If a severely dependent drinker is abstinent for a year and then attempts to return to social drinking, it is likely that within days they will be back to an intensity of withdrawal experience which had previously taken many years of drinking to develop. Dependence has a memory.

Pick and mix these elements, shrink or intensify their expression, see them change over time, have them shaped by personality and context, do not expect the alcohol dependence of the French café owner to look exactly like that of the New York stockbroker, and one will find a way of appreciating the underlying sameness in the vastly diverse degrees and types of addiction. Dependence is the trap in the drug experience waiting to be sprung.

Having emphasized the subtleties of dependence and the fact that the difference between being and not being dependent has no single marker, I will try to give a one-sentence answer to the question 'What is addiction?'. Dependence, addiction, call it what you will, is a state of duress where the individual's freedom of choice over their drug has become impaired and the drug has begun to take control over their drug taking.

To be certain in any instance as to whether dependence is or is not present can be difficult at the early stage, but see it fully developed and it will have become an evident and crushing reality. We need to be much more alert to those early stages rather than believing that only the later stages rate. Late can be too late.

Why dependence can be bad news

There is nothing necessarily bad in having a habit – a chewing-gum habit is commonly viewed as innocent by the person concerned and by their friends, especially so in North America. In the present age, if the gum happens to be a pharmaceutical product loaded with nicotine, friends and family will accept and even applaud the gum habit as a substitute for cigarettes. There is no evidence that nicotine-impregnated gum taken within a normal schedule is likely to damage the user's health, and unlike cigarettes it does not pollute the atmosphere. Gum provides an example where drug dependence is not bad news.

Dependence on a drug more often carries with it threats and burdens, as this case history shows.

Sally, aged twenty-six, had grown up in a small town where all drugs were taboo. Having broken with her family she took a job a hundred miles north, in Chicago, as a hostess in a club. There, drugs were readily available, and before long she was dependent on crack cocaine, with her control over the drug near zero. She would have binges lasting several days at a time. The only way for her to raise the money needed was to sell sex. If her clients wanted sex without a condom and paid the price, that was business. In this chaotic drug-induced state, she had no care for herself and became infected with HIV. Her parents found her and tried to take her home, but she would not accept their rescue. She wanted to stay where she could get the crack.

That woman's HIV infection and later AIDS were a direct consequence of her dependence on cocaine. Dependence drove her to consume at a high level and made the need for the drug salient over health and survival. Two different types of control are in such circumstances generally lost or impaired.

- *Self control* is impaired and the user will persist in taking their drug when they know the dangers and even when their rational self wants to stop. The cigarette-smoking doctor showed that kind of malign consequence stemming from her nicotine dependence.
- *Responsiveness to external controls* is likely to be weakened. The person's drive to take the drug will negate the controls ordinarily exerted by good manners, what the family expects, and the expectations and sanctions of society. Caught in the thrall of her nicotine dependence, the doctor smoking her thirty cigarettes a day was immune to the pleadings of her children, and the need for crack easily overrode the tearful pleading of that cocaine-addicted young woman's desperate family.

And with those two vital and complementary types of barrier weakened or knocked down, the road is then open for the forward march of drug taking with no care for the pains which litter the way. Thus, the prime reason why dependence is often bad news for the individual is its capacity to drive forward heavy and persistent drug use through every kind of red light. Dependence powers the creation of drug problems. It is also bad news because withdrawal symptoms can be unpleasant and dangerous, and because it is personally uncomfortable to feel oneself controlled by a drug. The alien sense of the monkey on the back is something which addicts often put high on the list of what is unpleasant and humiliating about dependence.

Although nicotine gum is an interesting instance of a benign dependence, dependence is much more often bad news all round.

The routes by which drugs are taken into the body

Look again at the references made above to cocaine. The Inca messenger's energizing chew of coca leaves, and that sort of traditional and rather benign use of cocaine, continues in the Andes to this day. I have instanced the executive who was told that sniffed cocaine was non-addictive and who ended up addicted. Then there is the crack-smoking young woman caught in a devastating compulsion. These varieties of experience may suggest that headlines which categorically declare that a particular drug is or is not 'addictive' are likely to be simplistic. The necessary question is not whether a drug is dependence-inducing in some absolute way, but the likelihood of dependence occurring when it is taken by any given route within a particular frequency and intensity of use. Dependence risk is a more nuanced affair than the headlines propose.

There are often several different techniques available for getting any one drug into the body. Chewing the drug and absorbing it through the lining of the mouth, swallowing with absorption by the stomach, smoking with absorption through the lining of the lungs, snuffing the powder up the nose and injection are the most commonly favoured routes. Some drugs can be taken by only one route (alcohol), but frequently there are a range of route choices: cocaine, opiates and tobacco all having multiple potential ways of being taken.

Routes bear on danger in a number of ways. The learning of a habit, which is the psychological process underlying dependence, is influenced by the time interval between the act of drug taking and the drug's rewarding impact on the brain. Make the interval too long and the psychological connection is not made, the habit receives no reinforcement. But make the interval brief and the drug-taking habit is boosted. By analogy, if a dog is offered a rewarding biscuit five minutes after it has come when called, it will not build up a habit of coming when called. Have the biscuit ready and waiting the moment the hound bounds up to the owner, repeat the sequence with some frequency, and soon Pongo will have a strong come-when-called habit. So it is with the learning of drug habits: giving the drug by mouth with slow absorption is not as effective a reinforcer as getting it to the brain quickly by smoking or injection. The route options considerably modify the dependence liability of any drug. Here is an example of learning theory coming through to operate at street level.

Jeff had as a lad grown up on a housing estate where everyone used drugs all the time, he told the Project's staff. Aged twenty, he was introduced to smoked heroin – no needle, no blood, no fuss, that seemed a breeze, very acceptable. For the best part of a summer he would smoke a bit of heroin, 'No big deal, I didn't have a habit.' But by September he was smoking enough heroin to be running himself short of cash. 'Why not try fixing, more cost effective in management speak,' one of his mates suggested. 'I was hooked bad by my birthday in October,' Jeff recalled.

Jeff's progression not only shows the pathway followed by one young heroin user, but the experience of many other young heroin users in British inner-city areas in the 1980s.

Besides the relation with dependence, the choice of route is likely also to bear on the type and level of the accompanying health risk. For instance, injection carries the danger of virus transmission, the products of a drug which is smoked may damage the lungs, while alcohol taken by mouth can cause cancer of the gullet. Injection, because it is the readiest way of getting a lot of a drug very quickly into the user's body, is also a common cause of death by overdose.

Use patterns and the risk of dependence

The risk of dependence on a drug is influenced not only by its intrinsic properties and the route of use, but also by the extent of the individual's exposure to the drug. Start cannabis at the age of fifteen, use a high-potency preparation several times a week, move in to a group which supports that kind of use, keep at it for five years, and the risk of dependence is much higher than for the student who uses cannabis casually a few times at university. Flood the inner city with cheap heroin and there will soon be a significant count of dependent heroin users: increased access enhances use level and that in turn pushes up the likelihood of dependence.

The dangers in drugs

Having dealt with routes of use as one element to be considered when assessing drug dangers, one needs also to take in to account more broadly what can make a drug more or less dangerous to its user. The truth of the matter is that nearly all the substances discussed in this book carry no absolute guarantee of danger.

Thomas, a one-time classics scholar now in his eighties, had started on amphetamine to keep him awake on night-watch when he was a naval officer during the Second World War. He continued to take these tablets in civilian life, assisted by a sequence of doctors whom he tended to outlive. When I last saw him socially, he told me that he was still taking the drug, which is controlled under Class B of the British Misuse of Drugs Act. He took one tablet on a few days each week 'to help the gardening', but he might go weeks without in winter when the garden had been put to bed.

There are people who have taken cocaine or clean, prescribed heroin for decades and who have suffered no physical harm. Just as sitting in the corner of many a pub is the notorious boozer and heavy smoker defying all prognostications, at least so far.

With drugs, nothing is always. Their use does not carry a guarantee of danger, but neither is their safety guaranteed. What one needs to ask about any substance is not whether in absolute terms it is 'safe', but rather the degree of risk which may attach to its use. Alcohol provides an example of how that question should be put. No matter how sodden the man in the bar sitting with his sixth pint of the evening, his drink is not 100 per cent guaranteed to give him alcoholic cirrhosis. The relationship between quantity drunk and risk of alcoholic cirrhosis is exponential, but there is no level at which the risk will inevitably be cashed in as the sad actuality.

For a number of other physical drug-related dangers, the risk can be neatly graphed with longer-term and heavier use carrying with it greater accumulated risk of a nasty outcome. For other types of problem, the risk can come along much more randomly: the tenth evening out on Ecstasy may kill the teenager, the very first injection of heroin may infect the user with the hepatitis C virus that will kill them twenty years later, a person tragically drowns when swimming too far off the beach at the barbecue where they had drunk what passed at the party as a social quantity of beer.

Drug use may carry risk to different aspects of life: the threat may be to physical or mental health, educational and social function, to self, or to the safety and welfare of other people. The damage done may be major or minor, one off or chronic. The victim often says, 'I did not think it would hit me,' while the family is apt to say: 'We never expected it to happen.' Risk is uncertain, that is the essence of the thing. Let's not ever exaggerate the dangers in drugs, but equally no one should trivialize or deny those dangers with absolutist statements on safety.

Lenny, aged twenty-four, came from Barbados. His brother, who brought him to the clinic, limped into the room and said, 'I want you to do something about this boy's habit before crack does for him what it did to me.' The brother had credibility. His limp was due to a cocaine-induced stroke that had occurred a few months previously – unexpectedly.

The relativities question

The media tend to be confused in their positions taken on the relative dangerousness of different drugs. Sometimes the line is that *all* drugs, licit and illicit, are essentially on the same level, and should therefore without differentiation be made legally available. The assertion is, however, also commonly made that illicit recreational drugs, and in particular cannabis and Ecstasy, are safer than alcohol and tobacco. And at other times, a distinction is assumed to exist between 'hard' and 'soft' drugs, with the terms never defined. The law meanwhile seeks to operate a control system grading drugs by their dangers, but with alcohol and tobacco forgotten. The answers to the relativities question thus tend to be somewhat confused.

A comparison between cannabis and nicotine may serve to illustrate the difficulties inherent in any such exercise in comparison. In Britain, at present, about 120,000 people die each year of tobacco-related illness. Very few (not zero) die probably as a result of cannabis-induced cancers, or car crashes caused by cannabis. That on the face of it might be read as overwhelming evidence that nicotine is more dangerous than cannabis. Add to this the fact that nicotine is much the more dependence inducing of the two substances, and what reasonable person could doubt that the licit compared to the currently illicit drug is as plague to a head cold in terms of killer potential?

Pause! Are like conditions of human exposure to the two drugs being compared fairly? Cigarettes are licit. Many people's lives still allow them to smoke during every waking hour, they can start young and go on for a lifetime, at a pack or two a day, until their lung cancer kills them. In contrast, very few people will achieve a daylong, lifelong, high-dosage exposure to cannabis of the sort which is the norm for tobacco. What the cannabis and nicotine comparison points up is that although drugs may carry different degrees of dependence potential and different degrees and types of danger, their capacity to turn potential into actual harm will depend enormously on dosage and duration of use.

Besides degrees of lifetime exposure and route of use as the dominant factors bearing on the development of risky potential into nasty actualities, there are a range of other modifying influences that may need to be taken into the reckoning. Immediate circumstances of use will often modify the degree of danger, as with drunk driving. Two or three whiskies downed before getting behind the steering wheel carry different implications than the same quantity at bedtime in the drinker's own easy chair. The danger of one drug can be exacerbated by taking another at the same time: alcohol with tobacco is a greater cancer threat than either drug used alone. And genetic predisposition influences many drug outcomes.

There are two linked answers to the relativities question. First, some drugs have intrinsically greater potential than others to cause dependence and certain types of harm. Second, from those starting points, the way in which the potentials develop will depend on a host of factors besides the intrinsic. That is a more complex truth than the simplistics of the chat show.

Controls on drugs: their variety

As already emphasized, this book will seek to throw light on questions around how to control drugs as well as on many aspects of drugs per se. Some definition of what is meant by control is needed.

Drug controls can be informal or formal. By informal controls we mean the manners, customs and social prohibitions which have already been briefly mentioned under the 'Drug choices' heading above. Informal controls have no police to enforce them, but they can exert tremendous if invisible restraint on the individual. They will differ across cultures and subcultures, and by age and gender. Deviant drug-taking groups will have their own codes and expectations even if these are abhorrent to the wider society: on skid row, drinking to the point of gross intoxication is the polite norm and the shared expectation, but the cider bottle must be passed fairly around the gang rather than guzzled by the person who provides it.

Formal controls on mind-acting substances are, in contrast, intentional measures deployed by government to control who uses drugs, and the level and circumstances of use. This is legislature coming in and taking a hand in the business of control, rather than its being left to manners. A different control mix is applied to licit and illicit drugs. With licit drugs, a lot is still left to manners despite government taking a hand. The range of measures which governments have at one time or another deployed in the licit arena is, however, extensive. Pricing, restriction on sales outlets or hours or days of sale, prevention of sale to minors, curbs on advertising, are examples of what traditionally has supported formal control of licit substances. During the First World War, Sweden introduced a rationing system for alcohol based on the number of people in the household, which seems in the event to have rather too often resulted in the head of the household consuming the maidservant's share. The control formula has over its history shown many inventive variations in its provisions and a time-honoured parallel ingenuity in its floutings.

The criminal law can be used in some circumstances in support of licit control, as occurs with drunk driving or the prosecution of tobacconists who are caught selling cigarettes one at a time to school-children.

But with formal controls of illicit drugs, the criminal law is, in contrast, absolutely centre stage. Supply of drugs, and also their possession, are both subject to criminal sanctions. In some jurisdictions it can be an offence to be found with an opium pipe; a criminal conviction for a drug offence may, as a secondary penalty in some countries, result in loss of welfare benefits; and the cocaine-addicted mother may be prosecuted in the US for the risk to which she has supposedly exposed her foetus. Criminal controls have as their titular intent the elimination rather than the amelioration of drug use; the goal is widely recognized as unreachable. Crude or subtle, the criminal law as instrument for control of illicit drug choices is an undertaking which can often become a problem in its own right and inflict intense damage of its own kind. I will come to consideration of this kind of problem in Chapter 19.

This book will attempt as far as possible a rational analysis of what control measures work, to what degree, in what circumstances and for what substances. Control itself is the suitable case for study. A science of drug control is beginning to evolve but more in relation to alcohol and tobacco than the proscribed chemicals.

Drug-use ecologies: delicate balances which can easily fall apart

With the aid of satellite pictures, population surveys and international intelligence systems, it should be possible to construct, for any moment, a map of the world's production, trade in and use of mind-acting drugs. It would be a map, however, of that moment only. Come back some few years later and the multinational drinks industry has put its capital in to establishing breweries in developing countries, so as greatly to enhance the consumption of commercial beer in communities that previously only knew the weak, home-brewed product. Meanwhile, Alcopops have been launched across the developed world, and this will steeply put up drinking in the youth market. One area of opium cultivation has faded and another opened up; Colombia not the Golden Triangle is now feeding New York its heroin. Crack cocaine has made its entry and Ecstasy has become a dance drug. Even a ten-year-old map will be considerably outdated, but compare two maps made a century apart and they will not look like pictures of the same drug globe.

Intense changeability is the order of the day. Here is a picture of a balance overthrown, a drug epidemic raging, the view from Lord Lonsdale's coach as he drives through the streets of London in 1743:

In every part of this great metropolis, whoever shall pass along the streets, will find wretchedness stretched upon the pavement, insensible and motion-less, and only removed by the charity of passengers from the danger of being crushed by carriages or trampled by horses, or strangled with filth in the common sewers; and others, less helpless perhaps, but more dangerous, who have drunk too much to fear punishment, but not enough to hinder them from provoking it . . . No man can pass a single hour in public places without meeting such objects or hearing such expressions as disgrace human nature – such as cannot be looked upon without horror or heard without indigna-tion, and which there is no possibility of removing or preventing, while this hateful liquor is publicly sold . . .

I quoted Lord Lonsdale in my earlier book on alcohol, but he is so cogent a witness that I must call him again. This is a picture of London in the grip of cheap gin, the days of drunk for a penny, dead drunk for tuppence, all the straw the collapsed drunkard could want for thrupence. Neither the streets of that city a century earlier nor two hundred years later looked like that. The epidemic came and went, fuelled by the gin and taking root in the social terrain of the Industrial Revolution. No one driving through London in 1643 could have imagined the kind and the scale of drunkenness lurking around the corner of a century later.

So here is a plea to those who today proffer instant remedies for 'the drug problem'. Please grasp the fact that drug-control policies have as their target not a mass of mutually isolated individuals, but a dynamic, population-based ecological system. Hit that system with a swingeing intervention of one sort or another, an intensive tight-ening of control or an abrupt relaxation, and the impact will judder across the balances, unbalance the system and perhaps do much harm. And our well-meant manipulations, contrived and intentional, are only a small part of the total flux of influences bearing at any moment on the stability or otherwise of the drug ecology. Suddenly there is an influx of labour to the cities, a new urban underclass is created, terrible living conditions are rife, cheap gin is poured in. There can be no one explanation for the street scene of 1743, but then there is seldom any single explanation for a drug epidemic. The gin epidemic burnt across a landscape, and the landscape mattered as much as the gin. Come that kind of disaster, there is no single, certain, immediate way of extinguishing the fire.

Drug use seen as an ecological issue is central to the perspective which will be developed in this book. And that ecological view is not meant as mere metaphor. On the contrary, only the ecological model can represent the realities of the intensely dynamic system which determines a population's choice, use and mix of mind-acting substances and the ways in which the map changes before the spectator's eyes. To give the matter formal definition, what is meant here by a *drug ecology* is the system (physical, social, cultural and economic) which mediates the drug use and within which it is embedded. The term *drug epidemic* is used as an up-front description of a rapid increase in a population's drug use, while *endemic use* refers to a more or less steady state.

Seven ways to create a drug epidemic

On the evidence of history, there are seven common ways in which to destabilize a drug ecology and create a drug epidemic. Each wrecking tactic has been tried and tested in the field, and comes with a warranty. Read the evidence the other way round and we have here a pretty reliable set of ideas on how to protect the drug ecology from bad happenings.

1. Submit the fabric of the intended target population to an intense strain of a kind to damage family and social relationships, fragment that society and create sectors of great poverty and contrasting wealth, destroy the old community gods and build no new values, leave youth adrift, create the soil for the epidemic and the wind is likely to blow in the seed to take root.
2. Make your chosen epidemic substance, whether it be licit or illicit, intensely available, have it on sale at every grocers, keep the price

low, abolish all controls, leave drugs to the free play of the market and treat them like every other consumer commodity.

3. Build a climate of acceptance. Persuade people that everyone uses the drug and non-users are deviant. Secure a massive advertising budget, and if that is not possible for illicit drugs, count on the endorsement of opinion leaders and the support of the media to market these substances. Associate alcohol with images of sport, cigarettes with Grand Prix motor racing and cocaine with the penthouse lifestyle, it's all the same game.

4. There can be a special benefit in getting the medical profession to take up the drug, prescribe it with abandon, declare it to be non-addictive and leak the drug to the streets. A century or so back this greatly helped to create a favourable image for alcohol, but doctors have also been very helpful in the epidemic spread of many other drugs – opium, heroin, cocaine, barbiturates, amphetamine, LSD, benzodiazepines. It is an amazing roll-call of medical intemperance.

5. Look out for innovative opportunities to market a new drug in a more dangerous form or by a new route of use. Get the population to believe that sniffing cocaine is safe and then slam them with crack, have them drink a little laudanum and then pull a syringe loaded with morphine from behind your back, let them get used to their snuff and cigars and pipes and then bowl them clean over with the deadly cigarettes.

6. Embed your operation as far as is possible in a mutuality of greed. For licit drugs, count on a complicity between the manufacturers and the tax-taking state, for illicit drugs find infinitely replaceable poor people to fill the lower ranks in the distribution chain and the top cats will grow ever fatter on the profits.

7. Try to ensure that the media portray drug taking as lying entirely with the individual: 'their flawed genetic make-up', 'addictive personality', 'woeful moral bankruptcy'. Keep the discourse at this individual level, and at the same time screen from public perception any awareness that drug misuse is in part caused by social environment.

The book: purpose and main themes

This book is written with one purpose running through every chapter. It attempts, plain and simple, the enlightenment of society's understanding of the pervasive fact of drugs in our midst. Only when we understand drugs better can we hope to deal with them better. My purpose is not mere abstract erudition, but knowledge in aid of a more effective and less damaging response to an enormously important, complex, costly and worrying set of happenings. The aim is to upset myths, discomfort spurious certainties and help build a climate of rationality where irrationality has previously too often clouded the debate. This is not, however, a tract to trade new bogus certainty for old false absolutes. There is still much about drugs which is not understood and part of any new rationality must be a modest admission of the limits to present knowledge.

With the central purpose declared, there are then a number of core thematic arguments to be identified, which will recur and be developed as the exposition unfolds. The framework set out below seeks to order, recapitulate and emphasize key facets of the positions taken in this Introduction and will constitute the themes to be varied and developed across the chapters which follow.

1. *Drugs are chemicals but they are also potently symbols.* We need to understand how drugs produce their effects on the brain, but, whatever the chemical, it is likely to find itself dressed up by society with symbolic meanings, packaged as a social construct, and made into a good and cherished, or evil and hated, object. The physical reality of these drugs is manifest, but the symbolism which attaches is also a potent and sometimes toxic reality which is likely to colour the policy choices.

2. *Differences but commonalities too.* Drugs differ enormously in their actions, dangerousness and dependence risk. Yet they all are still mind-acting substances and in that sense one universe. Understanding drugs is about their differences but also about a productive cross-referencing. Whether they are illicit or licit, weak or strong, ancient or modern, society's experience with drugs is a variation on common themes. A shared language for the

understanding of drugs has to be built up which is one language with many dialects, not the multiple tongues of Babel.

3. *The need to understand the dynamics of the drug flow.* Whatever the drug, its ecology can only be understood as the result of the dynamic, multiple field of shifting forces bearing on the drug-taking behaviour of the population. Drug use is more like flowing water than a still lake, and what may make for drought or flood are, by analogy, the questions for anyone who wants to understand the flow of drugs. Controls which are blind to the complexity of the underlying dynamics are likely to be rendered null and void before the ink is dry – controls must be intelligent.

4. *The danger in drugs is never a quantity fixed for all time.* Unpredictability, a sense of a game of hazard, most often typifies the danger in drugs. It is complacency which is the chronic danger and the following chapters will reiterate, Cassandra-like, dreadful instances of disastrous incaution leading to dire drug consequences.

5. *Experience, experience and experience.* Chapter by chapter, this book will argue that there is across time and culture a vast and rich store of experience with drugs on which to build, if we care to mine and sift it, and we are willing to learn. The rise and fall of epidemics and ecologies tipped out of balance, dangers exaggerated or blithe incaution the order of the day, control responses abjectly failing or producing at least some benefits: there is no shortage of drug and drug-policy experience to serve the cause of enlightenment.

So much then for a summary statement of core purposes and an identification of five main themes. There are other threads also to be drawn out as the story proceeds, but, across time, national boundaries, chemical choices, and across much ebb and flow, these will be the strong, main themes.

Part One

Licit Drugs

1

On the Drink

Alcohol: the play's the thing

I want to start this chapter with the everyday image of a drinker whom we might encounter any evening in our lives.

Johnny, the young man leaning against the piano and well on the way to being the life and soul of the suburban party, is a fellow who, as the saying goes, likes a drink. Watch him as he proffers his glass for the third ample refill in a short time. How are we to understand what makes Johnny stretch out his hand again – and again and again? By the time he leaves this neighbourly get-together, he will have tipped back the equivalent of two bottles of red wine. Noisy good-night, big hugs and kisses, some fumbling with the latch at the front gate, he staggers into the night. Lucky he is not driving, for his blood-alcohol level is now at three to four times the statutory limit.

That is a banal image, which poses extraordinarily echoing questions.

The immediate question that will come to the minds of most people who witness this scene will probably be of the kind, 'What is it about Johnny which makes him drink this way?' Within that perspective, the personally rooted reasons for the individual's drinking are the focus. Certainly, some part of the explanation for Johnny's drinking will be found in him as a unique being and his genetics. But beyond that individually directed line of enquiry, there are questions needing to be explored about why any given population drinks in the way that it does. This latter perspective invites Johnny's drinking to be viewed as behaviour carried along by the population's use of alcohol, and it is that which has to be understood, rather than just any one person's glass refilled.

Take that broader focus and the question becomes, 'What is the spectrum of drinking behaviours which are invited and enabled by the population to which Johnny belongs?' Society in the shape of the party was very tangibly inviting guests to drink that evening, and to focus all the explanatory attention on Johnny, while forgetting the invitation given to him, would be half blind. The play may put the spotlight on one actor, but to understand why he drinks we will also have to look at the nature of contemporary drama, who directs the play, the script, and at the other actors on the stage. The questions will spread out to the drinking habits in the hinterland of class and suburb, to gender roles, to what drink costs and the money in people's pockets, and the way in which the nation in general is drinking at this time. It is quite a broad stage that Johnny is tripping across.

The influence exerted by the silent, unnoticed but ever-present contextual factors which shape the individual's drinking, is immensely powerful. In *Alcohol Policy and the Public Good*, a book sponsored by the World Health Organization that was published in 1994 with sixteen international scientists and myself as joint authors, data is given on cross-national differences in rates of cirrhosis mortality. Cirrhosis can have causes other than alcohol, and there are many ways of dying of drink besides contracting alcoholic liver damage. National cirrhosis death rates are, however, a good indicator of levels of alcohol-related health harm within a country. One of the tables in the WHO report shows the spectrum of cirrhosis death rates that existed across Europe. This shows that over roughly the same period of time, different European countries were experiencing startlingly different degrees of alcohol-related health harm. At the top of the league was Hungary, with an index of 55 (55 cirrhosis deaths annually for each one hundred thousand adults in the population), and at the bottom was Ireland coming in with an index of 3. Undoubtedly, that eighteen-fold difference between the two countries is not on the lips of most party goers across the globe, but is highly relevant to understanding why Johnny drinks. The data makes it evident that an attempt to understand the individual's drinking behaviour cannot be divorced from their historical, social and economic context – the play on the wide stage. Drinking in Hungary and Ireland carries very different health risks. This is not because the people are genetically different or the drug is different, but because alcohol is much more available and cheap in Hungary than in Ireland. By reason of history, the place of alcohol within the culture and its cost, the two countries give drinkers different intensities of invitation to hold out the glass for a refill.

Hungary is a wine-producing country and was at the time of the WHO publication beginning to experience disruption caused by its transition to free-market economics. Ireland, despite the popular stereotype, had at the time a generally rather light-drinking population with over 20 per cent of adults being abstainers. Heavy beer-drinking countries such as Germany and Czechoslovakia were high in the cirrhosis league, and the Latin wine-producing countries were vulnerable also. The UK recorded a little over one third the French cirrhosis rate and less than a quarter of the Italian rate.

So this chapter offers at the start two counterpoised images: the individual standing drink in hand and the statistical abstract from the World Health Organization report. What is to be learnt from society's long experience with its favourite licit drug, that great source of pleasure, profitably tradable commodity and, for some people and families, the cause of misery or disaster?

Alcohol, the drug

Alcohol in pure form is a colourless liquid which is astringent to the taste buds, and which only the desperate would want to drink raw. To make beverage alcohol palatable, it has to be diluted and have flavouring added. The impurities (congeners) derived from the brewing or fermentation process, or brought over with the distillation when spirits are prepared, provide the flavour. It is the dilution and the congeners which make an intrinsically noxious chemical into a fine ale, a vintage wine, a brandy or whisky to have the connoisseur swooning. Vodka is the nearest thing that beverage alcohol comes to alcohol in pure brute form. The alcohol concentration of beer is usually at about 4 per cent absolute alcohol, wine 12 per cent and spirits 40 per cent. Whatever the label on the bottle, so far as the body is concerned alcohol is just alcohol. No beverage type is intrinsically more dangerous or beneficent than another.

Once the drug has been absorbed through the alimentary tract, alcohol is rapidly distributed throughout the body's tissues. When alcohol reaches the brain, there are no specific alcohol receptor sites waiting for the molecules to dock. This is a substance which exerts its effects by manipulation of the brain's natural transmitter systems. Alcohol seems to interact in one way or another with a wide range of chemical transmitters, including the serotonin, dopamine and GABA systems.

Through these interactions, alcohol can produce several types of impact on brain activity. It can impair and slow down many aspects of the brain's functioning, and act as a sedative. Paradoxically, it can, at least transiently, act as a stimulant. It can cause impaired judgement, detachment from ordinary responsiveness to what other people expect of the drinker's behaviour, and a degree of disinhibition. Whatever the mix of impacts on the brain's functioning alcohol brings about, the consequence is likely to be subjectively interpreted by the drinker as pleasurable, at least up to the point of staggering, vomiting and overdose.

But to comprehend alcohol's actions fully, that phrase 'subjectively interpreted' needs to be understood as pointing to the vital psychological mediation which links the chemical impact with the subjective experience. We learn from the world around us, our family and friends, our culture and society, the party, to expect good things from the glass filled again. A party is about having a good time, and alcohol has the capacity to mix in with, and multiply, all those good feelings. Expectations psychologically transform the physical impact of the chemical into experiences which may include intimacy, elation, laughter, sexuality, fearlessness, creativity, a myriad good feelings, and then on the downside anger or rage, gloom, or even suicidal despair. The physical impact of the drug invokes and stirs all those possibilities but it is the individual's psychological interpretation of the impact that paints the colours of what then happens. Let the drinker take their alcohol in a medicine glass while holding their nose and sitting companionless in an empty room, and the effect will be of few mood colours painted.

There is anthropological research to show that people in different cultures can react in very different ways to alcohol. Some South American people will still be smiling and paying each other compliments up to the point when they drunkenly pass out, while in another culture fiesta drinking will routinely result in knives drawn and homicidal violence. A compliment or a fatal stabbing, that is the extent of the influence which psychological expectation, the surrounds, the shaping influence of the culture, can have when alcohol physically impacts on the brain.

Alcohol is exemplar, but what is being said here about the capacity of this particular drug to produce a physical impact on the brain, which is then transmuted by many kinds of factor into a felt experience, is true also for every other kind of mind-acting substance.

Alcohol esteemed

As mentioned in the Introduction, all drugs acquire some sort of gift-wrapping with the popular image, and the image, negative or positive, may frequently get in the way of objective appraisal of the drug's dangers and benefits. At the negative pole lies heroin, often popularly seen more as devil than drug, and with the user viewed as an alien to be cast out from society. At the extreme positive pole stands alcohol, as exemplified by the rhetorical question posed by the Reverend Sydney Smith a couple of centuries ago: 'What two ideas are more inseparable than Beer and Britannia?' he asked, and looking at a contemporary crowd of football fans in celebratory mood, Smith's judgement still seems as apt as ever.

The esteem in which alcohol is held in a drinking culture means that any citizen living in that environment will have their assessment of the pleasures of alcohol endlessly enhanced, and perception of the threats constantly down-played. The packaging invites them to drink and drink up, and neutralizes warnings of danger as nanny talk. Who would want to welcome to the party the person who drinks our health only in chlorinated tap water?

Let's sketch the pattern of this packaging using literature as a source (slang, jokes, the lyrics of popular songs are equally valid material as the WHO and science when trying to understand why people use drugs). Here is a pastiche which relies on my dog-eared *Penguin Dictionary of Quotations*:

Set my pugging tooth on edge; for a quart of ale is a dish for a king
    (Shakespeare, *The Winter's Tale*, IV.2)

If all be true that I do think,
There are five reasons we should drink;
Good wine, a friend, or being dry,
Or lest we should be by and by;
Or any other reason why

(*A Catch*, Henry Aldrich, 1647–1710)

'I drink for the thirst to come'
(*Gargantua*, François Rabelais, *c.* 1492–1553)

He said that few people had intellectual resources sufficient to forgo the pleasures of wine. They could not otherwise contrive how to fill the interval between dinner and supper.

(Boswell's *Life of Johnson*, 1772, Samuel Johnson, 1709–84)

Not drunk is he who from floor
Can rise alone and still drink more;
But drunk is he, who prostrate lies,
Without the power to drink or rise.

(*The Misfortunes of Elphin*,
Thomas Love Peacock, 1785–1866)

These are only a few of that dictionary's many drink-related entries, but they are sufficient to confirm that the intangible wrapping in which alcohol is got up is more ancient and pretty than the tissue paper wrapping the next bottle purchased at the neighbourhood off-licence. Champagne is packaged as celebration, warm beer is wrapped metaphorically in the Union Jack, pints of lager are laddishness incarnate, or the female equivalent of that state, fine wines are wrapped as social sophistication. Alcohol is an adjunct for every rite of passage from christening onwards because people have been persuaded to believe that without it the occasion will be lesser, incomplete, barren. A bottle of sherry for Aunty on her birthday, a present of whisky for the man who helps cut the lawn, a bottle or two of Chardonnay for the office at Christmas: alcohol is the standard gift for all occasions. Alcohol provides a wonderfully rich case study in the image which can be created around a drug.

Alcohol, the poisoner and ensnarer

The alcohol drunk by Johnny, who opened this chapter, was probably a substance viewed by all present as the 'good creature of God', to borrow a phrase from Increase Mather, a New England preacher of the seventeenth century. Anyone who had dared to ruin the convivial atmosphere of the party with a diatribe on alcohol as the angel of death would have had their fellow guests move quickly out of earshot. The downside of alcohol is not talked about in polite company, is not cocktail party gossip, and is usually covered up by the gift wrapping.

But by sheer bad luck, this highly esteemed substance, with its pleasure-giving potential, has an innate capacity to cause harm. The negatives cannot just be ignored by dismissing the potential problems as rare or trivial. An American survey has shown that about 24 per cent of male and 4–5 per cent of female drinkers will encounter a significant drinking problem at some point during their adult lives. Here is some of the damage feeding these overall statistics.

- *Alcohol is a poison which can damage the body* Either as a consequence of its direct toxic effects, or because of the dietary and vitamin deficiencies which often accompany heavy drinking, alcohol can harm the body. It can damage the brain with, at worst, dementia the result. The nerve supply to the limbs can be impaired with numbing and pain (peripheral neuritis). The liver can be the prime site of alcohol poisoning, with cirrhosis the outcome. The pancreas can become inflamed, with painful and potentially lethal consequences. The limb muscles can be weakened. Alcohol is often viewed today as good for the heart, but the heart muscle also can be damaged by drink (cardiomyopathy). Hypertension can be caused by heavy drinking with stroke a consequence. Add these various possible medical complications together, and the result is the consistent finding that about 20 per cent of patients on a general hospital ward will have been admitted because of an illness caused in part or entirely by their drinking. And the mother's drinking can damage the unborn baby (foetal alcohol syndrome).
- *Alcohol is a chemical which can cause cancer* Exposure to alcohol

is a direct cause of certain types of cancer of the mouth, pharynx and oesophagus (gullet). In addition, and by less direct mechanisms, alcohol makes a causal contribution to cancer of the female breast. There is a question mark over whether it may sometimes be implicated in cancer of the colon. In a heavy-drinking nation such as France, about one third of all cancer deaths are alcohol-related.

- *Alcohol as cause of injury* As a result of alcohol's effect on reaction time, coordination and judgement, it can multiply the risks for accident. In America, about 40–50 per cent of road traffic fatalities are alcohol related. What is not so commonly realized is the strong connection between drinking and fatal accidents of various other kinds: something around 34 per cent of drownings, 47 per cent of death by fire and 28 per cent of deaths by falls were found by Cheryl Cherpitel, an American researcher, to have had alcohol as a contributing cause. Heavy drinking increases the risk of suicide. Getting drunk is very bad for personal safety.

- *Alcohol contributes to crime* The spectrum of crimes to which alcohol contributes goes all the way from petty public-disorder offences, where it is a big contributor, to murder, where in some countries 30–40 per cent of those convicted of homicide will have been drunk at the time of the offence. People who are intoxicated not only have an enhanced likelihood of committing violent offences, but are themselves also at heightened risk of being robbed or assaulted. The drink-crime connection is however complex: drinking is sometimes central to the offence, can be part of a causal network, but may be merely coincidental.

- *Drink can impair many aspects of social life* The contribution which drink makes to social problems is more difficult to quantify than with physical illness. But alcohol contributes to family problems and family breakdown, job loss and unemployment, financial problems and homelessness.

- *Alcohol is a drug which can snare the drinker* Alcohol is made more threatening by the fact that it has a subtle but dangerous potential to enmesh its users in a drug dependence. To set up a dependence on this drug will take at least some years of use, and will often require twenty or thirty years on the drink before morning shakes appear. The popular cultural package does not carry warning of the dependence risk. People tend to think of the addicted drinker as a person not like us, someone who 'can't hold their drink' and has let the side down, a skid-row drunk, not anyone ever to be found with their glass held out at *our* party. Those misconceptions serve only to exacerbate the danger. The truth is that in America about 6 per cent of men who drink will develop dependence on alcohol to some degree, and perhaps 2 per cent of women; the rates in Britain are similar.

It is easy to dismiss the facts set out above as the mournful litany of the temperance lecture, or the sermons and soda water of the morning-after scold. Together those facts do, however, amount to considerable pain and trouble, sometimes wreckage, for the individual who finds the good creature turns bad on them. And very large troubles and costs accrue for society when all those negatives are put together and seen in terms of the total population impact. It is a misreading of the situation to suppose that the bulk of the harm is borne only by a small minority of heavy drinkers, or by so-called 'alcoholics'. A large proportion of the total damage is contributed by the few who drink heavily, but a bigger percentage contribution comes from the large sector who drink in the high middle range.

Blindness to the reality that our favourite drug can rather easily begin to mock us, is of course the intended consequence of the popular mythologizing, of Beer and Britannia and the drug wrapped in the flag of British patriotism. Here is a contrasting literary view as given by Jack London in his 1903 *The People of the Abyss*. He was an American writer who changed into second-hand clothes bought at a pawn shop and went out to look at what the city streets painfully and starkly had to tell, in this case in London's East End.

The English working classes may be said to be soaked in beer. They are made dull and sodden by it. Their efficiency is sadly impaired, and they lose whatever imagination, invention, and quickness may be theirs by right of race. It may hardly be called an acquired habit, for they are acquainted with it from their earliest infancy. Children are begotten in drunkenness, saturated in drink before they draw their first breath, born to the smell and taste of it, and brought up in the midst of it.

Pitifully, this author was in due course himself to be destroyed by alcohol.

Alcohol as medicine

Alcohol can decrease the danger of heart disease (myocardial infarction) but if Johnny wants to find comfort in that argument he will be deceiving himself. This benefit is operative only in the age group which is significantly at risk of experiencing that kind of heart trouble, namely men over forty and post-menopausal women. No more than two to three drinks per day should be taken for optimum health benefit and beyond that point more harm than good is likely to be done. Despite Johnny's penchant for red wine and the widespread magical belief that red drink will thin the blood, any alcoholic drink will do as heart medicine. Alcohol may also help prevent the type of stroke that is caused by a clot. But giving up smoking, weight reduction, sensible exercise and half an aspirin per day will be at least as beneficial as alcohol taken for prophylaxis against heart attack or stroke. It would be an incautious doctor who advised a previous abstainer to take up drink in middle age as the best way to protect the heart.

More drink, more danger

The progressive, stepwise risk of health damage from alcohol as intake levels increase is a repeated research finding both for individuals and for populations. With the only exception relating to the cardiac protection from light drinking discussed above, for the individual a rise in weekly intake will mean more risk of alcohol-related illness or accident. Very heavy drinkers will on average shorten their life expectation by about ten years. Research also shows that a population's average annual per-capita consumption of alcohol will go hand in hand with population indices of alcohol-related harm. If a population increases its annual per-capita consumption by one litre of absolute alcohol, middle-aged males will as a consequence suffer a one-year reduction in the average life expectation. This is a summary statistic: 'more drink, more danger'. I will consider the policy implications in Chapter 20.

This overall conclusion relating to alcohol applies also to most of the other drugs with which this book will deal. If a drug carries any kind of risk, the damage it inflicts will be related to the level of its use.

Alcohol, the commodity

Alcohol is a drug with the double-edged capacity to give good cheer and inflict damage, but seen in another light it is a commodity, something else on the supermarket shelf and with a couple of dollars or a pound off you can get two bottles cheap in this week's promotion. Beverage alcohol is tradable goods around which mega millions change hands every year in the process of cultivation of raw materials, manufacture, distribution, trade and advertising. The alcohol and the entertainment industry are enterprises that are horse and carriage, and provide a vast source of employment. In rich countries, the drinks multinationals take a large slice of the profit, while in poor countries the village women make a little money to support their families by selling home-brewed beer.

In many countries, taxes will be imposed on alcohol, both by local government and at the national level. The total tax take on liquor in the USA, with state and federal taxation combined, runs at around $18,000 million annually. In developing countries, alcohol taxes are likely to account for about 5 per cent of revenue. In Britain, the Chancellor of the Exchequer has traditionally made his annual Budget speech before Parliament with a glass of whisky close to hand. A government can put a few additional tax pence on a bottle and enjoy big takings, in another year freeze or reduce the tax level and win instant political popularity. The individual may be on the drink, the population drinks en masse, but the truth of the matter is that, in their own way, governments are drink-dependent because of their reliance on the tax. So far as international trade agreements are concerned, alcohol is just a commodity among commodities and no special pleadings from health interests will be allowed. Poor countries, so far as the drinks barons are concerned, are 'emerging markets' rather than vulnerable populations.

Messages in the bottle

Alcohol provides a case study of how societies can live with the legally sanctioned presence in their midst of a substance which, on any objective reckoning, is a dangerous drug.

One way of interpreting this case is to read it as cogently supporting the argument for relaxing controls on currently illicit drugs – if we can coexist with a substance as dangerous as alcohol, why not go in the same sensible direction with heroin and cocaine, or at the very least with cannabis and Ecstasy? That poisonous, accident-inducing, reeking-of-addiction stuff called alcohol, we have managed largely to de-demonize it and accept it as a taxed and traded commodity, rather than defining it as a drug. No policeman at our drinking elbows, no busts at the neighbourhood party for possession or supply. Alcohol drunk in our homes and in all manner of public places, the stuff consumed on every imaginable occasion, from football match to cele-bration of the Holy Eucharist, alcohol as the young person's dance drug and a tot of whisky by the fireside to comfort old age, the vintage claret delicately sipped and beer bought by the crate for the orgiastic booze-up; we are having a great party.

But the alternative reading is entirely opposite. It is that society has bought a load of trouble with alcohol and that controlling a dangerous drug only by good manners and increasingly lax licensing laws leaves far too many people dead or injured while the party goers celebrate. 'Good creature' – a sham some would say. On this latter reading, the alcohol case study can lead only to the conclusion that here is a cautionary tale rather than a universal model for drug control.

What message can be taken from society's experience with the bottle? The current level of licit controls allows much damage to occur. Because of the drug's legal status, its reassuring packaging and its status as a commodity, there are strong pressures to ignore the poisoning and celebrate the pleasure. An open-minded reading of the story is thus likely to offer something far more mixed, contradictory and provisional than any one-sided decipherment of the record. One does not need the exotic shores of a desert island for the message in the bottle to find its landfall. The puzzling, worrying, two-sided message can be found in any of the empties left scattered around when the guests have gone home after the party, when Johnny has fumbled the gate shut, and the WHO report on the statistical outcome for the great international drinking party has been put back on the shelf.

2

Tobacco

A plant brought home

On the second day of November 1492, a detachment of men who had landed with Christopher Columbus in Cuba reported back to their Captain a strange happening. They had come across a group of Indians who were holding tubes of loosely rolled burning leaves to their mouths and 'eating the smoke'. Here is the first recorded occasion of an outsider seeing the act of tobacco smoking, a widely disseminated practice at that time across the Americas but unknown to the rest of the world.

The New World was stocked with many plants strange to European eyes. These constituted great potential riches as sources of medicinal products, or as spices to be sold on the home market. Among the plants was *Nicotiana tabacum*, which in its native setting was often employed in shamanistic ritual, and at such intense dosage as to produce hallucinations and putative contact with the spirit world. Yet by 1600, tobacco was in use not only across all Europe, but had also gained a foothold in Asia and Africa, and was being grown in all three of those continents. Although *Nicotiana* had at an early stage been used for medicinal purposes and had been recommended as a cure for cancer, by this point in the history of the relationship between tobacco and human populations it was for the most part being used as what would much later be called a 'recreational drug'.

Track forward for five centuries from the day on which those Spaniards stared curiously at a primitive form of cigar smoking and we arrive at today's situation where, according to a recent World Bank Report, one in three adults – a total of 1.1 billion people across the globe – is a smoker of tobacco. That plant was no doubt plucked from the New World with no insight at all as to the likelihood of the later triumphal mass penetration of society by the drug it contains. Drugs are packages which carry a surprise.

There is not a country on the modern map where a latter-day landing party would venture for more than a minute or two up any street before seeing a tube of burning tobacco in someone's mouth, stub ends in the gutter, a tobacconist shop, and in most countries the alluring advertising of the product. Tobacco is a cash crop of great importance to many countries, a tradable commodity from which the manufacturers accrue their multi-billion-dollar profits, a taxable product making a huge and welcome contribution to treasuries. There is at present a fall-off in smoking in developed countries but a rising uptake in poorer sectors of the globe. The World Bank's projection is that by the year 2025, the 1.1 billion figure will climb to 1.6 billion for the world's smokers.

Tobacco has over all those centuries been imbued with a myriad images in the culture of its times. Such imagery – the long-stemmed clay pipe of the seventeenth-century tavern, the dandy's jewelled snuffbox, the sailor chewing his wad, cigarettes in the 1920s as a symbol of female emancipation, early movies and the curl of smoke as a backdrop to romance, the smoked-filled room a habitat for the political fixers, the man with the briar epitomizing the solid citizen, the Marlboro man and smoking to feed macho fantasies, branded American cigarettes a harbinger of modernity in Africa and Asia, the Havana lit after dinner, my mother's twenty Goldflake given to her every Christmas.

The previous chapter used a dictionary of quotations to portray the esteem in which alcohol has been held over the ages; with smoking one can also pick up the evidence scattered everywhere. 'The use of tobacco has vanquished humanity and will continue to reign until the end of the world,' wrote Louis Lewin, a German pharmacologist, in his book *Phantastica*, first published in 1924. The extended story of those five hundred years of tobacco's dissemination might be no more than intriguing social history were it not for another kind of statistic, also to be found in that World Bank publication. The report projects that by the year 2030, about 10 million people will be killed worldwide by tobacco each year. Half of all long-term smokers will eventually die from their habit. These figures cannot be downplayed by the specious assertion that smokers mostly die in later life, when their state pensions are a drain on the exchequer, so that their deaths may in economic terms be a cost saver: half those fatalities will be occurring among people who are in productive middle age. Here is a telling example of the astonishing capacity of a drug to spread across a population, win acceptance and insidiously start to cause terrible harm. Who stowed that plant into the hold of a sailing ship, not knowing how the voyage would end?

Tobacco, a substance brought to Europe as a herbal medicine, has by sheer bad luck turned out to be a cause of death on an apocalyptic scale. In the face of such manifest dangers to health and life, why is it that the habit is still pervasive and spreading? Why is it that adolescents are still so likely to take up smoking? Why do most adult smokers stay with the habit until parted from it by premature death?

Those are among the questions this chapter will tackle.

Nicotine, the drug

The fact that nicotine is a drug of dependence is central to the understanding of why its use has spread like wildfire across the world and become so embedded, and also why the user finds it so notoriously difficult to stop and stay stopped. We have here a mind-acting substance that is dream stuff for the machinations of the apprentice devil who was mentioned in the Introduction. Before continuing with an account of the twists and turns in mankind's encounter with this weed, I want to profile some features of the drug contained within it.

Nicotine is a drug that can induce acute nausea, and the novice's first experience with it is frequently none too pleasant. However, with repeated exposure, tolerance to the negative effects soon develops. Thereafter, the experience of nicotine is usually reported as pleasure all the way – or at least until the smoker begins to fear or encounter tobacco-related health damage, or discover with dismay that although wanting to give up the now unwelcome habit, they cannot at all easily do so because of a drug dependence.

The nature of the pleasure is likely to include a feeling that the drug makes the smoker calm and relaxed, anxiety is relieved, and in some gentle and pervasive way the drug is a comforter to the nerves and a buffer against life's stresses. As well as having a tranquillizing effect, nicotine also appears, paradoxically, to have a capacity to act as a stimulant and help concentrate the mind. Many smokers will say that this mix of positive effects is as reliably present after, say, thirty years with tobacco, as at the beginning of their smoking careers. Unlike the experience of nausea, no tolerance develops to the positives and age does not stale the pleasures. Robert Louis Stevenson personified the drug as 'My Lady Nicotine', and his smoking was a love-affair with the lady.

Recent research shows that there are several different types of nicotine receptor found in the human brain. Nicotine has the capacity to act on dopamine pathways, and, like cocaine and other stimulants, it can cause this transmitter chemical to be released in areas of the brain which subserve the experience of pleasure. Exposure to steady, low concentrations of the drug can deactivate rather than activate receptor sites, and hence the drug's sedative effects. A drug or any combination of drugs that mixes both sedative and stimulant effects is likely to be especially attractive to the user.

Until the 1960s, the view among researchers was that cigarette smoking was driven and maintained less by the drug than by the associated rituals, by the pleasure of putting something in one's mouth or having an object to fiddle with between one's fingers, or by the pleasant reverie of watching the smoke float. Since then, evidence of many kinds has come together to demonstrate that nicotine is, by any and every reckoning, a drug with the capacity to induce a dependence syndrome. There is indeed a case for rating nicotine as an even more powerfully dependence-inducing substance than cocaine or heroin – a conclusion at a great distance from the former psychoanalytical talk of the cigarette habit as oral fixation.

Some of the lines of evidence that support the contention that nicotine is a drug of dependence are as follows:

- Only about 5 per cent of people who smoke cigarettes are able to go on smoking in a take-it-or-leave-it kind of way; in contrast, the great majority of smokers will escalate quite soon into what is for them a fixed personal intake of, say, twenty to thirty cigarettes a day. They will experience great difficulty in sustaining any reduction, and even greater difficulty in stopping and staying off.

- Approximately 50 per cent of people who have stopped smoking will be back on their cigarettes within one week, and despite repeated efforts only about 50 per cent of smokers eventually succeed in quitting their habit long-term before the age of sixty. Thus if an adolescent starts to smoke at fifteen, there are even odds that they will still be smoking forty-five years later, despite mounting personal worries about the habit and the scoldings of friends and family, and in spite of medical advice. Even after sustaining a myocardial infarction or developing angina, only about 20 per cent of smokers who receive counselling to help them stop smoking will a year later have succeeded.

- Many smokers will want to have their first cigarette of the day with breakfast or even perhaps light up before they get out of bed. That looks very like the dependent drinker's 'hair of the dog' or the heroin user's anxious reaching for the syringe.

- Withdrawal symptoms occur when nicotine-dependent subjects allow their blood level of the drug to fall overnight, or when they attempt to give up the habit. The symptoms reach a peak about three days after smoking has stopped and include restlessness, anxiety, irritability and strong craving for restoration of the drug. Much of what smokers believe to be the intrinsically soothing property of the drug is in fact no more than the relief of intermittent, low-grade withdrawal by the next fix. Withdrawal symptoms commonly continue with diminishing severity for up to four weeks after the smoking has stopped, and that is a longer duration of withdrawal distress than occurs with most other drugs. No wonder it is difficult to stop smoking and stay stopped.

A book by Seebohm Rowntree and G. R. Lavers published in 1951, with the title *English Life and Leisure*, devoted a chapter to smoking. At that time rather over 80 per cent of men and 42 per cent of women aged over sixteen were smokers. Rowntree and Lavers did not use the term 'addiction' when they wrote about smoking, but they remarked that 'Time after time we have come across cases in our investigations, where men and women admit that they cannot do without tobacco.' They offered some acutely observed case examples:

Artisan in factory. Age 35. Smokes 20 cigarettes a day. Cannot afford so many because he is married with two children, but cannot do without. Has tried several times to give up smoking, but becomes so irritable that home life is impossible and his wife begs him to start smoking again.

A middle class housewife . . . used to smoke about 50 cigarettes a day but with difficulty has cut the number down to 25. She keeps as many of her daily 25 as she can for the evening so that she shall not be irritable when her husband is at home.

A clerk aged 21 . . . spends 5s per day on cigarettes. By the middle of many weeks he is so short of money that his breakfast of tea and toast is the only meal of the day. He says, 'Lots of times I've gone without food for a smoke but never without a smoke for food.'

Each of these vignettes timelessly captures a facet of nicotine dependence.

Smoking and the harm to health

In 1896, a polemic written by a Mr Frank Ballard appeared as 'The Smoking Craze: an Indictment with Reasons and an Appeal to Christians'. It was one among many anti-smoking tracts to be published in the latter half of the nineteenth century, and it is of interest as showing the kind of material that anti-smoking campaigners were at that period likely to use as ammunition. They believed that smoking would ravage physical health, yet when it came to evidence to support that contention there was precious little on offer other than a flow of alarming but unsubstantiated statements from eminent physicians. Here are a few examples of the medical opinions which Mr Ballard used to bolster his case:

Dr Trask says, 'I can specify on sound medical authority, more than fifty diseases that either spring from this vile narcotic or which are really intensified by its use.'

Dr Spoor, of New York, an eminent man, says he is prepared to show that *delirium tremens* was unknown prior to the use of tobacco, and is much more due to this than to alcohol.

It is said that in some of the examinations undergone by the volunteer soldiers [Americans volunteering for the Spanish American War] fully 30% have been rejected on account of defective heart action caused by cigarette smoking.

According to Ballard's witnesses, not only did tobacco lead with near inevitability to physical wreckage, but it was also a prime cause of moral degeneracy and crime: 'Prison statistics show that almost all criminals use tobacco; definitely 97% of male convicts thus began the downward career.' A Mr Horace Greely supported that case strongly: 'Show me a genuine blaggard, one of the boys and no mistake – who is not a lover of tobacco in some shape, and I will agree to find two white blackbirds.'

A century later, it is easy to laugh at the absurdity of Ballard's claims, with his confusion between association and cause, all mixed in with a good dose of moralism as a substitute for the evidence on the harm done by tobacco. The fact of the matter is that investigative techniques to allow objective exploration of these kinds of question were at the time not available, so rhetoric filled the gap. Over and over again, including the present day, in the history of society's encounter with drugs one finds rhetoric filling the gaps in knowledge.

During the early decades of the twentieth century, medical opinion firmed up on the conclusion that smoking could cause cancer of the mouth and larynx. It was believed that heavy smoking could cause a rare type of blindness, tobacco amblyopia. It also seemed likely that smoking could exacerbate peptic ulcers or delay their healing. But doctors themselves smoked in large numbers, some of them might recommend the habit as helpful to their more highly-strung patients, and the *British Medical Journal* and the *Lancet* saw nothing wrong in carrying advertisements for tobacco products. Scientifically, it is difficult to establish a causal link between a drug and its consequences when linkage is not inevitable, when multiple other factors may impact on the connection, and where the interval between exposure and harm may be many years.

Crucial evidence to link smoking to major health damage began to emerge only in the early 1950s. The stimulus for the research was the intense public-health concern provoked by the astonishing increase in deaths due to cancer of the lung. In the UK, the annual number of deaths per hundred thousand living, recorded as due to cancer of the bronchus, was below five cases each year up to 1930. A steep increase then occurred, and for the five-year period 1946–50 the average annual mortality from this cause was running at a little over a hundred. Five years later, the 150 mark had been reached. Similar trends were being seen in the US and in many other countries. No cancer epidemic of such scale and suddenness had ever been encountered previously.

Many hypotheses were put forward to explain the upsurge in lung-cancer deaths. Perhaps, for instance, it was caused by the tarring of roads or atmospheric pollution, or maybe the figures were due to more accurate death certification. On both sides of the Atlantic, research was funded to explore these possibilities, but also to test what many saw as the outside wager that cigarette smoking might be implicated.

The technique that the American and British researchers employed was the so-called 'case-control method', which had by then become established as a medical investigative tool. Essentially, this involved interviewing, over a stated period, consecutive patients admitted to collaborating hospitals who were diagnosed as suffering from lung cancer, and enquiring into their smoking habits and what were deemed to be other potential causative factors. At the same time, a control subject who was not suffering from lung cancer was recruited to match each lung-cancer victim, and that person's risk factors were recorded in exactly parallel fashion. With all the data to hand, the researchers could then determine whether the lung-cancer patients were, on average, people who had experienced any hypothesized risk factor more commonly than the controls. The findings obtained by both research groups were closely similar. The risk of contracting lung cancer was strongly related to cigarette smoking, with no other factor found to be significant.

The American investigators, E. L. Wynder and E. A. Graham, published their results in 1950, and the British researchers, Richard Doll and Austin Bradford Hill, published their findings in the same year but a few months later. The historical importance of these reports cannot be overstated. This body of work did not, at a stroke and beyond all doubt, establish that cigarette smoking causes lung disease, and the investigators themselves were well aware that even a strong statistical association did not by itself prove cause. That smoking was a cause of lung cancer was, however, a plausible lead explanation for the findings. Many years later, when discussing his recollections of that research, Doll stated that every now and then a patient who had been put into the lung-cancer group was, on further investigation, found not to be suffering from cancer and would have to be excluded from the study. Doll began to notice that such patients were always non-smokers. At the beginning of the project, he had not believed that cigarettes were implicated as a cause of cancer, but suddenly he was seeing things happening before his eyes that made him change his mind.

The British government's acceptance of the significance of the research was slow in coming. According to Charles Webster, who has chronicled the story of the British government's response to Doll and Hill's 1950 report, it was not until June 1957 that a Ministry of Health spokesman gave support in the House of Commons to these researchers' conclusions. On that day, local authorities were for the first time instructed by the Ministry to inform the public that smoking was dangerous.

Stimulated by that early work on smoking and lung cancer, from the 1950s onwards, a mass of high-quality international research was published which confirmed smoking as the dominant cause of lung cancer, and researchers soon went on to explore its contribution to other types of disease. Cigarette smoking is today in Britain calculated as being responsible for 84 per cent of all lung-cancer deaths, 84 per cent of deaths due to emphysema, and 17 per cent of all deaths due to heart attack. The true human scale of the problem is identified in a recent report from the Royal College of Physicians. It concludes that smoking is responsible in the UK for 117,400 deaths annually: 'This annual mortality translates into an average of 2,300 people killed by smoking every week, 320 every day and 13 every hour.'

The material from cigarette smoke which is most damaging to the smoker's health is the tar. This contains a variety of cancer-inducing chemicals which, with every inhalation, are sprayed onto the lining of the air passages. Aspects of the way in which the tobacco is prepared and cured, the high temperature of the combustion, and the year-after-year exposure to these dangerous, inhaled chemicals, conspire to make cigarettes more harmful to health than any previous way of delivering nicotine. Tar is not the only dangerous product of the combustion: the nicotine itself carries some health risks, particularly for the heart and blood vessels, and the inhaled carbon monoxide is likely to be damaging.

Furthermore, it is now well established that smoking can have adverse health impacts on people other than the smoker. A non-smoker married to a smoker is at a small but significantly enhanced risk of lung cancer, compared with someone whose spouse is not a smoker. A person working in a smoke-laden environment will encounter similar risks. Children of smoking parents are at greater risk of chest infections, and having two smoking parents is almost twice as bad for the child as having just one of them smoke. The unborn baby will be disadvantaged by the mother's smoking, with the likelihood of decreased birth-weight.

As for the health costs to the state resulting from the need to treat smoking-related illnesses, this burden is, in the UK, currently running at about £1500 million annually. A recent report suggested that, in total, smoking may cost Britain about £100 million a week, if account is taken of time for smoking breaks and the petty distraction of looking for a light or cadging a cigarette from a friend, in addition to all the time off work for illnesses caused by smoking. There may be some saving in the paying of pensions. But even a public inured to a financial balance-sheet perspective on health issues is unlikely to accept death and suffering on the scale caused today world-wide by tobacco as a matter only for the accountants.

Routes of use

The importance of route of use as a factor influencing and potentially destabilizing drug ecologies, is a theme which will in this book recur in relation to many different drugs. Nicotine over the centuries has provided a powerful example of this factor in action.

In the London of the 1600s, it was the clay pipe that ruled supreme. This was the scene as observed in 1618 by a visitor, Horatio Busino (this quotation is taken from Jordan Goodman's *Tobacco in History*, which I will use extensively as a source in the historical account which follows):

It is in such frequent use that not at every hour of the day but even at night they keep the pipe and steel at their pillows and gratify their longings. Amongst themselves, they are in the habit of circulating toasts, passing the pipe from one to the other with much grace . . . gentlewomen moreover and virtuous women accustom themselves to take it as medicine, but in secret . . .

At the beginning of the 1600s, England was importing around a quarter of a million pounds weight of tobacco a year from the Spanish colonies in America, but by the end of the century that figure had increased to about 38 million pounds. Thus by 1700, plenty of tobacco was available for the Englishman's pipe, and for the Englishwoman's secret enjoyment laced with a medical cover story.

However, as a technology for delivering nicotine to the brain, the pipe had both advantages and limitations. As regards advantages, Busino's observation that the habit could be of such intensity that the pipe might be smoked not only 'every hour of the day' but in addition kept by the bedside, suggests that this sort of smoking could make nicotine available in a dosage sufficient to set up dependence on the drug. It is likely that devotees learnt to inhale the pipe smoke without too much coughing and choking, despite the fact that the tobacco available at that time was a crude product. The pipe was also capable of being embraced by social ritual, as Busino reported. The downside of this mode of use was that preparing, lighting and smoking a clay pipe set a series of little demands, which meant that it could never be an altogether casual habit. Furthermore, billows of pipe smoke were sufficiently unpleasant to people in the smoker's environment as never to be acceptable in polite circles: pipe smoking was a taproom rather than a drawing-room technology. Lastly, the number of bits of broken pipe stem still to be dug up in many country gardens hints that the utility of those elegant long-stemmed pipes acting as cooling device was offset by their considerable fragility. Pipes were in their time popular but they did not take the world by storm.

During the eighteenth century, the chewing of tobacco provided an alternative to smoking, but appears never to have become very popular, at least with the British. With this technique the nicotine is absorbed through the lining of the mouth. For optimum transfer, the saliva needs to be rendered alkaline. But European chewers of tobacco seem never to have hit on the idea of adding an alkalinizing agent to their wad as coca chewers do in South America. Chewed tobacco cannot give the same rewarding instant impact on the brain as when smoked. Chewing induces salivation and the ensuing spitting must have been even less attractive to polite society than the pipe. However, sailors of that period favoured chewing: on wooden ships it was free of fire hazards and compatible with work on deck or up the rigging in a high sea. So, up to the eighteenth century, the major choice for mode of tobacco use lay between two not altogether satisfactory alternatives.

In the seventeenth century, the fact that priests in Spain had taken to using snuff whilst celebrating Mass had become cause for scandal. But during the eighteenth century, snuffing made an impact on the tobacco habit in many European countries, as a highly popular way of delivering nicotine to the brain. Powdered tobacco was sniffed up the nose (a finger held delicately against the opposite nostril); the technique allowed nicotine to be absorbed rapidly through the nasal lining, achieving high levels of the drug. The powdered tobacco was often mixed with rose petals or other pleasant additives. A little sneezing would be seen as polite and good for the health. Gone was the need for pipe or fire, noxious smoke and spitting were obviated, and snuff could be taken into the drawing room.

Here, in 1773, is Dr Samuel Johnson grouching about what the advent of snuff had done for the acceptability of the pipe.

Smoking has gone out. To be sure, it is a shocking thing, blowing smoake out of our mouths into other people's mouths, eyes and noses and having the same thing done to us. Yet I cannot account why a thing which requires so little exertion, and yet preserves the mind from total vacuity, should have gone out.

And 'Smoaking' had undoubtedly gone as a direct result of snuff coming in. The ritual was now not a shared pipe but the offer to a friend of a pinch from one's snuffbox. Snuffboxes became a status symbol and, according to Goodman, Lord Petersham claimed to have a different box for every day of the year. Snuff never eradicated the pipe, and patterns of use varied across time and countries and social strata, but snuff was not just a habit of the upper classes.

Then came a further transition. The records show that at the beginning of the nineteenth century over half tobacco consumption was in the form of snuff, but by the end of that century snuff accounted for a mere 1 per cent of the tobacco market. The cigarette had arrived and had virtually driven out snuff. As a nicotine-dosing device, the cigarette was an innovation that surpassed all previous methods in effectiveness. It is easy to draw the cigarette's relatively mild smoke into the lungs. A smoker will puff ten times or more on a cigarette, and on each occasion absorb a shot of nicotine through their lungs and send it along their blood vessels to impact sharply within fifteen seconds on the brain. The heroin user will inject one dose of opiate as 'a hit' and will then wait some hours for the next dose, but the technology of the cigarette offers hit after hit after hit. An experimental pharmacologist who was searching for a drug-delivery system likely to ensure that the user developed a quick and almost inevitable dependence on nicotine, would be likely to regard the cigarette as the perfect answer to the problem. And of course the smoker will not only score ten or more hits with one cigarette but will carry a pack in their pocket for the day's multiple hits. Combine an intrinsically very dependence-inducing drug with that technical innovation, and you have the potential to sweep the world.

But to turn the potential into a marketing reality required much more than the mere discovery that tobacco could be rolled up in a thin bit of paper. Cigarettes in the first half of the nineteenth century had some currency in Europe and America. However, even as late as the 1870s, they were a hand-rolled product, fitted perhaps with an individual bamboo holder. A clutch of technical innovations and marketing strategies then came together so that the potential for this mode of delivery was made actual, and cigarettes become king.

At the technical level, the innovations that were to give cigarettes primacy included the introduction of mild Virginia tobacco of the so-called bright-cut variety, which derived from *Nicotiana rustica* rather than from the traditional *Nicotiana tabacum*. Developments in ways of harvesting, the introduction of pesticides, and new methods of curing and preparing the harvested leaves, were also important: cigarettes required a much more refined product than would have done for the churchwarden's pipe or the sailor's wad. A further hugely important and indeed revolutionary innovation came with the introduction in 1885 of a machine which could roll the cigarettes. This was the Bonsack machine. According to Jordan Goodman, to whom I am again much indebted, the total US production of cigarettes stood at 16 million annually in 1870 but by 1895 it had climbed to 42 billion.

Many other minor technical advances played their part in furthering the burgeoning success of cigarettes and included the invention of safety matches and the flip-top box as packaging for the output of Bonsack's machine. But whatever the clever inventions, the product still had to be sold, and the story here is about marketing innovation. That the twentieth century became, in terms of tobacco, the century of the cigarette, was in large measure because it also became the century of marketing, advertising, branding and the rise of the multinational corporation. Cigarettes not only were carried forward by but themselves helped make and nurture these new forces. The pace at which cigarettes gained dominance over other tobacco products did, however, vary between different countries, and the Americans for a long time still had a fondness for chewing tobacco.

The struggle to curb the harm

Attempts to curb the harm done by cigarettes began not long after the first demonstrations of the lung-cancer link. Sadly, despite these efforts, during the years following publication of the research, people in their millions have continued to smoke and die of tobacco-related disease. Research which demonstrates the lethality of a drug will not by itself do much to curb the mass use of the pleasurable agent. That said, there have over those same years been some incremental gains in understanding what might be the necessary elements within an effective Public Health counter-attack. This must start with multiple and sustained efforts to educate the public. Progressive taxation is an effective strategy for reducing economic access to tobacco. Making work and leisure space smoke-free and banning smoking on public transport; enforcing the law on under-age purchases: these strategies are not only effective in curbing physical access, but they serve also by a knock-on effect to further educate the public. Bans on advertising are a necessary component of a health strategy, and in a secondary way a further underlining that society is taking the smoking problem seriously. In New York, smoking has recently been banned from all bars and restaurants, and that kind of move must feed through to a sea change in the way people think about and react to smoking.

Tar levels in most branded cigarettes have been substantially reduced over recent decades, but it is impossible to get rid of all the tar without making the product flavourless, and that also sets the limit to what can be done with filters. If the nicotine content is reduced, smokers will draw more heavily on each cigarette, smoke further down the butt, or smoke more cigarettes – such are the imperatives of the drug dependence. It is possible to remove most of the cancer-producing substances from chewed tobacco, and the Swedish experience with so called Snus (tobacco that can be sucked in sachet form) is seen by some experts as encouraging. Theoretically, a mass movement away from cigarettes and back to an oral form might be pro-health, but the real world consequences of any attempt to engineer a movement in that direction are very uncertain.

Attempts by individual smokers to sue manufacturers for the damage done by the products have over the years met with little success. More recently, individual American states have sued the manufacturers successfully for health-care costs. Damages of that kind must at the very least serve to curb the overweening confidence of the tobacco companies, who for long believed that they had the power to get away with anything. Tobacco is rooted in a widely international commercial enterprise. The response to the problem needs to square up to this fact, with strengthened international collaboration to combat the trade. WHO is currently developing a Framework Convention on Tobacco Control. How then to advance further on the smoking front? That is a question to which I will return in Chapter 20.

Dominant themes

Running through all the twists in the plot, there have been three dominant factors scripting this story's development. One has been the innate fact that nicotine is a dependence-inducing drug: the basics of the pharmacology greatly matter in shaping a drug's relationship with society. The second has been the stepwise, trial-and-error development of increasingly effective and socially acceptable nicotine-delivery systems. The third influence has been that tobacco is a tradable and hence a taxable commodity. None of these factors if taken alone can explain what happened, but put them together and there is the explanation for the triumph of tobacco. Tobacco is a failure in licit control of a dangerous drug writ hideously large.

3

Little Comforters

Valium was launched as a medicinal product by Roche in 1963. By 1978 it had become the best-selling pharmaceutical in the world. It was marketed as a drug for the treatment of anxiety (an anxiolytic), but anxiety is a concept with uncertain boundaries. Here is a passage taken from a report published in 1979 by a Canadian researcher, Ruth Cooperstock. She was exploring the meaning of tranquillizers, using taped interviews with women. This is a Valium user talking about what the drug meant for her:

I take it to protect the family from my irritability because the kids are kids. I don't think it's fair for me to start yelling at them because their normal activity is bothering me . . . So I take Valium to keep me calm . . . Peace and calm. That's what my husband wants because frankly the kids get on his nerves too. But he will not take anything . . . He blows his top . . . When I blow my top I am told to settle down. And this I have resented over the years, but I've accepted it. I'm biding my time. One of these days I'm going to leave the whole kit and kaboodle and walk out on him. Then maybe I won't need any more.

How's that for blurred margins? A popular term for Valium became 'Mother's little comforter'. In many countries it was twice as likely to be prescribed to women as to men.

The benzodiazepines are a group of chemicals to which diazepam (Valium), chlordiazepoxide (Librium), nitrazepam (Mogadon), lorazepam (Ativan), temazepam (Euhypnos), triazolam (Halcion) and flunitrazepam (Rohypnol), and a wide range of similar products all belong. From the ecological angle, what is especially interesting is that these drugs all have some dependence potential, they enjoyed an extraordinary global success as medicines, and in due time leaked on to the streets as one would inevitably have expected. But they did not then proceed to leak enormously, their use did not fuel a vast global street epidemic. The benzodiazepines are in that respect a negative case, the exception which proves the rule. Arthur Conan Doyle wrote a story in which Sherlock Holmes solved a murder when he noted that a dog did not bark in the night, and from negatives much positive can be learnt.

Many of the drugs and drug classes that are the concern of this chapter have been used as sedatives to treat anxiety, but they have often also been employed as hypnotics to induce sleep. Sedatives and hypnotics are near allies, and their capacity to dampen nervous arousal is their common feature. Like alcohol, they are 'downers' in contrast to 'uppers' such as caffeine, amphetamines and cocaine.

Anxiety and its fuzzy edges

Every human being will throughout life taste anxiety as part of the normal range of emotional experiences available to them. Learning to cope with anxiety rather than being overthrown by it is part of maturity. Some degree of anxiety will usually enhance performance. The tennis player, who is fighting their way through a difficult set, needs a sufficient charge of anxiety to fire their game, but not so much as to make their play fall apart. That kind of normal anxiety is characterized by alertness, excitement, butterflies in the stomach perhaps, and some racing of the pulse. But it is not sensed as unduly unpleasant or alien.

Anxiety becomes abnormal when it reaches an excessive intensity, or when it is provoked inappropriately by cues which would not normally be expected to stimulate extreme degrees of unpleasant emotion. People may, for instance, become intensely anxious or phobic in response to heights, open spaces, closed spaces or crowded situations, or the presence of a spider. Some unfortunate persons may develop panic attacks of searing intensity, either spontaneously or precipitated by what for them is a familiar trigger. Consumed by a sudden awful storm of anxiety, they may, for example, have to rush out of the supermarket, and with heart pounding and head bursting collapse against a wall. There are sufferers who will all their lives experience phobias and panic attacks of fluctuating and sometimes crippling severity.

But let's look again at what that Canadian woman related to the researcher's tape recorder. She did not actually use the word 'anxiety' at all. She said that she was irritable and sometimes felt like yelling at her children. She dreamt of the day when she would escape from family life. That was not a woman who was ill with anxiety, but she was stressed and not finding it easy to cope. And the Valium could do the coping for her. She talked about the children's 'normal activity', and it was in fact normal life that was getting her down rather than any unusual or appalling adversities. The pills were not being prescribed to treat an abnormal mental state but were being used to neutralize a woman's complaint about her life space. The margins of what is to count as anxiety are very fuzzy, and so are the criteria which legitimize the writing out of a prescription for an anxiolytic. Sometimes the prescribing can look more like social control than legitimate medicine.

Valium arrived in the early 1960s, but the benzodiazepines lie in a centuries-long line of drugs that has been employed to treat sleeplessness and anxiety and the margins of anxiety, back to the ancient world. Prior to Valium, or even today, that woman or her husband might have used alcohol as a drug temporarily to dissolve their discontents. Gin was 'mother's ruin' long before Valium was 'mother's little comforter'. For much of the eighteenth and nineteenth centuries, man and wife could have expected to dose themselves with any one of a huge variety of opium-containing medicines available at the grocer's shop, and they might have administered an opium-containing 'quietening syrup' to their normal children. The edges between the recreational use of a drug, its use as nerve medicine, and its deployment to ease the human condition or shut out complaining, have always been blurred.

How the pharmaceutical industry made its entry on the anxiolytic market

Alcohol and opium were the time-honoured remedies for anxiety and insomnia, but towards the latter part of the nineteenth century the pharmaceutical industry began, for the first time, to market a variety of synthetic substances for the alleviation of these conditions. Then, as now, the potential profits were beckoningly huge if a drug could be found as comforter for the masses.

One such synthetic was chloral hydrate. It was introduced in the 1880s as a sedative and sleeping draft. Chloral has a simple organic (carbon-containing) molecular structure, based on acetaldehyde but with three chlorine atoms substituted for three hydrogen atoms. It does not attach to a specific receptor site and is alcohol-like in many of its actions. More than a hundred years later, chloral still retains a place in modern pharmacopoeias, despite its dependence potential and the danger of fatal overdose if it is swallowed in too large a dose with alcohol. Its unpleasant taste when taken in liquid form limited its popularity, but pharmaceutical ingenuity has made a pill form available. Chloral and alcohol are together the traditional constituents of the eponymous Mickey Finn, a knock-out draught originating in the shadier reaches of Chicago.

In 1889, Norman Kerr, a founding British contributor to the study and treatment of addiction (I will refer to him again later), was reporting on cases he was beginning to encounter of 'chloral inebriety'. Kerr considered chloral as 'a most valuable medicinal remedy', but at the same time he warned of the dangers attached to the burgeoning prescription of sedatives and hypnotics he saw going on around him, as doctors started to move away from the old, opium-based remedies. He offered some alternatives to the use of these drugs:

I always try to do without a narcotic. With some patients immersion of the feet in warm water at night succeeds. With others, a good sized towel wrung out of hot water, applied to the epigastrium [pit of the stomach], and covered over with folds of warm flannel tightly bound with a bandage round the body, answers well.

But with that advice given on homely alternatives, Kerr slipped inexorably towards a prescription.

Potassium and sodium bromides are preferable to an opiate. They may advantageously be combined with henbane. In many intractable cases, the addition of chloral hydrate renders the remedy more effectual.

Sedatives symptomatically work and doctors like giving drugs that work, especially for conditions where the symptoms are intractable and the patients demanding.

Enter the barbiturates

Chloral and the bromides were among several popular precursors of the benzodiazepines, but they were never more than pharmaceutical bit players compared with the central role played during the twentieth century by the barbiturates. Barbitone, the first drug in this class, was introduced in 1903. The barbiturates have a complex molecular structure but do not attach to a specific receptor. They have been used to treat epilepsy (phenobarbitone) and as an anaesthetic (thiopentone), for treatment of anxiety (amylobarbital) and for sleep (nembutal). As sedatives and hypnotics, barbiturates were highly effective and became widely favoured by the public and the prescribing doctors. There was a booming barbiturate bonanza long before the benzodiazepines came over the horizon. Unfortunately, these drugs not only worked but were extremely dangerous. Death from intentional or accidental barbiturate overdose became a shockingly common tragedy: that was how Marilyn Monroe died. Barbiturates were dependence-inducing beyond anything experienced with chloral or those other proto-tranquillizers. Withdrawal could cause fits or a condition resembling delirium tremens. But in my young days as a house physician (intern) in the 1950s, every patient admitted to the wards was routinely written up for a clutch of barbiturates, and nembutal brought round on the evening medicine trolley was as routine as the milky drink.

Following their introduction, there was a rapid worldwide spread in the use of barbiturates. By 1946, annual sales in Britain were estimated to be a staggering 71,500 lb (32,500 kg), which worked out at one tablet daily for a million people. In the same year it was calculated that 5 million Americans were taking a tablet of this type every day. By the 1950s, about 5,000–7,000 cases of barbiturate overdose were being dealt with each year in the UK, and in 1967 over 2,000 deaths due to barbiturates were recorded in Britain.

Barbiturates in many countries became available as part of the stock of the illicit drug scene. William Burroughs, author of *The Naked Lunch*, that cult work of the beat generation, in his time engaged in almost every imaginable type of drug taking. He wrote thus to the then editor of the *British Journal of Addiction*, Dr J.

Yerbury Dent, in a communication vaingloriously headed 'Letter from a master addict', dated August 1958 and posted from Venice:

> The barbiturate addict presents a shocking spectacle. He can not co-ordinate, he staggers, falls off bar stools, goes to sleep in the middle of a sentence, drops food out of his mouth. He is confused, quarrelsome and stupid. And he almost always uses other drugs, anything he can lay hands on . . . Barbiturate users are looked down on in addict society: 'Goof ball bums. They got no class to them.' The next step down is coal gas and milk, or sniffing ammonia in a bucket – 'The scrub woman's kick'.

The description of barbiturate dependence given by Burroughs is sadly true to life.

The extent to which barbiturates were being used as street drugs varied over time and from country to country. In the USA of the 1960s, barbiturates were used as a common adjunct to heroin. About 20 per cent of drug takers admitted to the federal narcotics hospitals (the main drug-treatment centres of that period) were dependent on barbiturates as well as an opiate.

In Britain in the 1960s, it was estimated that 100,000 people were dependent on these drugs. Many of them were middle-aged citizens who had become dependent because of careless medical prescribing. Doctors at that time were familiar with the patient who appeared to be drunk on walking into the consulting room, but who had no smell of drink on their breath. On physical examination, burns on the chest might be revealed where lighted cigarettes had been dropped, and bedsores could occur as a result of prolonged, stuporous uncon-sciousness. The plight of these patients was pitiful and a reproach to the medical profession.

In the late 1960s, the problems caused by illicit use of barbiturates in London took a new and nasty turn. Injecting heroin use had only recently emerged when addicts hit on the idea of grinding up barbit-urates and injecting the dissolved product intravenously. A heroin-intoxicated person is likely to be passive rather than giving rise to public disorder. But someone who is instantly and grossly intoxicated by a barbiturate injection may become fighting drunk and cause mayhem. Such barbiturate injectors for a brief period caused terror among the staff of Accident and Emergency departments in London. This form of injected-drug misuse frequently resulted in death by overdose.

Over many decades, the response evoked by the barbiturate problem was, on both sides of the Atlantic, sanguine. Governments were not very worried and it was opiates that were centre stage for the enforcement agencies. The public liked barbiturates, and no popular outcry against them arose. Doctors were happy to go on prescribing barbiturates in generous quantities to their patients and thus assist high levels of spillage into illicit use. It is likely that medical attitudes towards the therapeutic value of barbiturates were coloured by the fact that doctors were, through personal experience, aware that these were drugs that worked. Here is a medical pharmacologist, Professor J. H. Burn, hinting in 1956 at exactly that kind of mindset:

There can be no doubt that as in the case of alcohol, the introduction of the barbiturates has been of very great value to mankind. About alcohol there is little need to remind ourselves that it has played a large part in rendering life tolerable. For the many people who spend their day in work which is uninteresting and fatiguing alcohol taken in the evening makes the world look a more cheerful place, and helps us to find the outlook attractive and even gay. In the words of Laurence Housman

> Malt does more than Milton can
> To justify God's ways to man.

As much as this cannot be said of barbiturates, but they are, nevertheless, a boon, though in a minor degree. To those who have to travel, to sleep in trains or in hotel bedrooms overlooking a noisy street, or who need to be fresh the next day after an exciting evening, barbiturates are of the greatest value.

Who can doubt that Burn was speaking from personal experience of the good night's sleep granted to the academic traveller by the grace of nembutal?

Barbiturates eventually began to wane in fashion because of public and medical concern about overdose deaths, and mounting awareness of the dependence risk. In the 1950s, a drug called meprobamate (Miltown) enjoyed brief popularity as a supposedly safer alternative to barbiturates and with less dependence risk, but those hopes were disappointed. What in the end put paid to the barbiturates was the arrival in the 1960s of the benzodiazepines as the new universal comforters. It was to be goodbye to nembutal and a hallo to Mogadon, which would thenceforward be the sleeping pill for the itinerant professor in need of a good night's sleep.

The benzodiazepines take off

Launched in the 1960s, thirty years later the annual world sales of the benzodiazepines were exceeding $2 billion in value. That was quite some rags to riches story for a class of chemicals that had been discovered in 1891, and had for long lain around without an obvious therapeutic application. Benzodiazepines were to enjoy success beyond any previous comforter.

The story of how the benzodiazepine class of drugs came to be developed is a tale of happenstance. In the 1930s, Dr Leo Sternbach was a junior chemist working at the University of Cracow in Poland. Motivated entirely by theoretical interests, he synthesized a number of benzodiazepines – science for the sake of science. He then left his native country and in 1954 was working in the New Jersey laboratories of Hoffman-La Roche. In New Jersey, he was screening previously unconsidered chemicals for their possible pharmacological actions almost with a bran-tub type of approach: research of this kind is not led by science but works on the principle of lucky dip. In the course of this work he turned back once more to look at the benzodiazepines. For Sternbach, their attraction was that their therapeutic potential had not up to that point attracted the attention of other drug firms. He took the chemistry a little further and synthesized forty new derivatives, but all to no avail so far as therapeutic potential was concerned. He gave up on this line of work, but eighteen months later he found one leftover derivative, coded Ro 5–0690, on the laboratory shelf, which had not been assayed for pharmacological effect. He sent it off to a colleague for testing, and a note came back to say that when given to experimental animals it was a potent sedative. Thus, by a lucky dip, was discovered a drug later to be given the name Librium. Clinical trials rapidly confirmed effectiveness on human subjects.

Librium and Valium were both Roche products and more than twenty-five benzodiazepines were subsequently marketed by various pharmaceutical companies. Some were long-acting and others shorter acting. Much of the product development became what industry scientists dismissively call 'me-tooism' or a matter of slight alteration in a drug's chemical structure so as to outflank a rival's patent. The plethora of heavily advertised and competing drugs, all promising wonders, probably helped further to drive upwards the total sales and profits. It was gold rush time, with plenty of drug-firm chemists engaged in the panhandling.

Whatever the brand name, the way in which all benzodiazepines exert their effect is primarily through their interaction with the transmitter chemical GABA (gamma-aminobutyric acid). GABA is sedative in its actions and produces exactly the opposite kinds of effect to dopamine, the stimulant transmitter involved in the brain's reward system and in the actions of stimulant drugs. Benzodiazepines bind to receptor sites so as to enhance the sedative action of GABA and dampen down the experience of anxiety.

Tolerance develops quickly to benzodiazepines and a high degree of tolerance can occur. As to the question whether dependence is possible on these drugs, despite initial denial by the manufacturers and the blindness of some researchers, the answer is unequivocally 'yes'. I will return to the dependence question shortly.

Benzodiazepines were marketed overtly as day-time sedatives or as sleeping tablets, but with the covert subtext often being that they were a cure-all for life's discomforts of precisely the kind Ruth Cooperstock's subject was encountering. They were also used medically for relief of muscle spasm and for their anti-epileptic properties, and they were useful in anaesthesia. But it was primarily as comforters that they had their market triumph.

The reasons why benzodiazepines replaced barbiturates are several. The newer drugs were more acceptable in the treatment of anxiety because they relieved symptoms at a dose which did not make the patient slurred and uncoordinated, and they did not so readily cause the kind of torpor that went with the barbiturates. They were less dependence inducing and vastly safer so far as risk of fatal overdose was concerned. It is almost impossible to commit suicide with even a bottleful of Valium, although benzodiazepines mixed with alcohol can be fatal.

As for the follow-through of these various comparisons to the bottom line of market share, between 1965 and 1970 the number of prescriptions dispensed annually in England and Wales for barbiturates fell from 20 million to 5 million. Over those same years, prescriptions for benzodiazepines showed a mirror-image trend, rising from 5 to 20 million. The market over this period voted with its feet: patients were happy, doctors delighted, the scourge of barbiturate-related deaths was ameliorated, and the sale of benzodiazepines climbed ever upwards. By 1970, every tenth night of British sleep was benzodiazepine induced. There were about a million people in the country who were taking benzodiazepines in the long term, often for a year or more without interruption. The marketing success was similar in most developed countries, and in the developing world there were instances of health-service budgets giving the purchase of Valium priority over saline transfusions. Worldwide, the benzodiazepines became the most highly prescribed drug of any sort, and all that as a result of Dr Leo Sternbach's bran-tub draw.

The tranquillization of society begins to be cause for anxiety

In Britain, a backlash against the mass tranquillization of society began to develop in the 1970s, although the Americans tended to be less worried by the cocooning of their people by benzodiazepines. The causes of the backlash were of three sorts.

● *The feeling that mass tranquillization is in itself unacceptable* Leaders in the medical profession in Britain began to point to the absurdity of the situation where, if the prescribing trends were allowed to continue, very soon every citizen would be tranquillized by benzodiazepines all day long, and zonked out by them every night. Sir William Trethowan, a senior British psychiatrist, in 1975 denounced benzodiazepine prescribing as an 'out of control juggernaut'. Professor Malcolm Lader, a British authority on the use of drugs in psychiatry, expressed similar views in a scientific article published in 1978.

The indications for these drugs are being insidiously widened and the boundaries between normality and illness increasingly blurred ... It is much cheaper to tranquillise distraught housewives living in isolating tower-blocks with nowhere for their children to play than to demolish those blocks and to rebuild on a human scale, or even to provide playgroups ...

But it was not only the doctors who in the 1970s began to rail against this juggernaut. Something in the spirit of the times meant that people were less willing to be medically drugged out of their minds, more questioning of doctors and less trusting of the pharmaceutical industry, and keener to take their health into their own hands. Benzodiazepines became an issue for the Women's Movement. For an increasingly consumer-oriented society, the question of what prescribed drugs were to be consumed became a focus of concern.

- *Evidence that long-term use of benzodiazepines is likely to do more harm than good* From the 1970s onwards evidence accumulated to suggest that the long-term consumption of benzodiazepines could cause psychological side effects. Depression and anxiety could be caused by withdrawal if the dose was decreased. Symptoms that the drug was supposed to make better could be made worse. Confusion was another common side effect. Patients often only realized how psychologically unwell the drug had been making them when their prescription was stopped. The frequent complaint was that in retrospect the patient had been 'living in cotton wool' and robbed of normal emotions during their drugged years. Amnesia could be part of the picture: a woman who had been for a long time on a benzodiazepine might afterwards complain that with her feelings blocked out and her memory impaired, she had totally missed the experience of motherhood and having her children grow up. Someone who had been put on benzodiazepines to quell their grief at a time of bereavement (a common reason for GP prescribing of these pills), might subsequently discover that the drugs had covered up the rightful pain and denied them the possibility of working through their grief.
- *Benzodiazepines: the dependence risk* Roche originally marketed Librium and Valium as dependence-free, although even in the early 1960s there was contrary evidence. When cases of dependence began to be reported they were dismissed as freakish, and as occurring only among patients with an underlying personality disorder or a drinking problem. There are always some patients who will give a good drug a bad name, it was argued. To play down or

deny the dependence danger was vital to the continued marketing success.

In 1984, a monograph published by Hannus Petursson and Malcolm Lader provided evidence on the dependence potential of the benzodiazepines. It was conclusive. They showed experimentally that when patients taking benzodiazepines in no more than a normally prescribed dosage were withdrawn from their drugs after twelve months or more of dosing, they would suffer very unpleasant withdrawal symptoms. These symptoms included anxiety, which might sometimes not have been withdrawal related but the recrudescence of a complaint for which the patient had originally been put on the drug. But there was also evidence for a wide variety of unusual and even bizarre symptoms specifically due to withdrawal: a metallic taste in the mouth, for instance, hallucinatory smells, numbness, a sense of objects in the room moving.

The accepted view is now that addiction to benzodiazepines can happen in two distinct circumstances. First it can occur as a so-called 'normal dose dependence'. In such cases there is no demand by the patient for an escalated dosage level, little evidence of compulsive drug seeking, probably no subjective sense of dependence, but when the drug is stopped the patient becomes ill. It is the normal dose aspect of this problem which makes it so insidious. Probably about 40–50 per cent of patients who have been prescribed benzodiazepines for three to six months or more will on cessation experience withdrawal. Perhaps 10 per cent of those will experience major and protracted withdrawal distress lasting, at the extreme, up to one year. The second type of dependence is the rarer problem seen where the patient has escalated their use to a high level, and drug taking has become chaotic and out of control. Withdrawal from high-level dependence can cause fits or delirium, and deaths have occurred.

Benzodiazepines abhorred

From the early 1980s onwards, the media took off with warnings against the dangers of being 'hooked on the happy pill'. Negative images were portrayed of doctors who 'pushed pills', and personal accounts were published of the 'hell' of benzodiazepine dependence and the misery of withdrawal. Taken from an analysis by Dr Jonathan Gabe, a medical sociologist, of the newspaper coverage of benzo-diazepine dependence, the following illustrate that type of press treatment:

Ada has been 'to hell and back' with Ativan. While taking it she became a near-zombie slumped on the settee of her Nottingham home, unable to do anything. (*Star*, 3 May 1988)

Marian Dinwoodie is a junkie . . . Marian is an Ativan addict – hooked on a tran-quilliser designed to keep her calm. A drug which turned, and now produces the very symptoms it was supposed to control. 'I would have been better on heroin', she said in a flat unemotional voice. (*Daily Record*, Glasgow, 30 May 1988)

I'm told it is harder to kick than heroin. (*Evening Echo*, Bournemouth, 4 May 1988)

Benzodiazepines became a high-profile media topic. The impact of such sustained public outrage on patients' wariness of these drugs and on GPs' prescribing habits was considerable. The reflex reaching for the prescription pad for the treatment of anxiety and its margins was no longer acceptable. Not only were the media achieving public education but they were beginning to impact on the training given in medical schools.

Lawyers were soon in on the benzodiazepine act and doctors were being sued in large numbers for alleged careless prescribing of these drugs. At one time, some hundred litigants in the UK banded together and attempted to sue the manufacturers, but this was unsuccessful.

Operating in conjunction, the groundswell of awareness that the juggernaut was unacceptable and had to be stopped, the realization that numbing people with benzodiazepines could ruin their quality of life, the discovery that happy pills could hook people and produce very unhappy dependence: all this turned the climate of popular and medical opinion radically against the slap-happy handing out of these comforters. Today, the advice to doctors on benzodiazepine prescribing is not to go beyond two weeks, and many practitioners will avoid these drugs altogether. Sales have greatly declined.

More recently, medical enthusiasm for the antidepressant Prozac (Fluoxetine) has, at times, been a little indiscriminating. It is a substance in an entirely different drug class than the benzodiazepines, and with minimal or nil misuse or dependence capacity. Media criticism of potential over-prescribing developed quickly. Prozac is not, however, the benzodiazepines story over again.

Benzodiazepines as drugs of misuse

Benzodiazepines have, for the last twenty or so years, contributed at times to the array of commonly available misused drugs. A pill or two may be casually swallowed by the clubber on a night out, a person with a bad alcohol problem may add in some Valium, the street user who is involved with multiple drugs may use benzodiazepines as an ad hoc supplement, with the tranquillizers adding to the risk of overdose. Ground up tablets are sometimes injected. In Britain, a vogue developed for injection of temazepam, which could be drawn out by a hypodermic needle direct from a proprietary capsule. This type of misuse is associated with unpleasant injection complications and the possibility of gangrene. Benzodiazepines can be taken as snuff, but that route has never gained popularity. Their street status, however, remains that of minor contributor to the circulating stock, rather than their ever winning a dominant market share. There are few habitués of the drug scene who take benzodiazepines for joy.

Messages from the medicine bottle

The bottles, which in this instance are found washed on the long, metaphorical shores of the world's experience with mind-acting chemicals, are of a kind less likely to be remarked on than the discarded containers for alcohol or the cigarette packs that feature in the flotsam. But comforters have important insights to offer towards the broad understanding of drugs. The theme of packaging comes through again and this time the mind-acting chemicals are wrapped fuzzily as medicines. Profit features once more as a driving force, with the pharmaceutical companies ladling the huge profits. Dependence features, but with comforters the new and distinct theme to enter is the notion that the drug supply can be controlled and

rationed by the prescription pad. The recent story with benzodiazepines seems to be of the people turning against medical incaution, the doctors gaining wisdom, and a bad situation turned largely
around over a relatively short time.

4
Deadly Vapours

Mention was made earlier of Lewin's *Phantastica*. Here we have him giving an illustration of what is today usually called VSA or Volatile Substance Abuse. The popular term 'glue sniffing' is too restrictive because many products other than glue can be sniffed.

A girl suffered from disagreeable disturbance of sight due to a central scotome [blind spot]. According to the report of her mother, who cleaned gloves for a living, she had had for some years the habit of smelling at a rag soaked in benzene or of holding the petrol bottle to her nose. Especially before bedtime the craving was so violent that neither punishment nor entreaty was of any avail, and although the mother attempted to lock up her store of benzene the girl had her own supply that she always replenished from a hiding-place in the garden. The girl bought more of the liquid as soon as she had collected a few pence. She was removed from home and placed in a convent. According to the evidence from the nuns, she was not able to indulge in her old habit, although during the first few days she did everything she could to obtain petrol.

Glove cleaning has become a rare trade. But VSA remains a problem in many countries as the furtive sniffing of this or that cheap, licit and widely available household or industrial product. It is a down-market, juvenile habit, from which most adolescents will pull out before they have left school. VSA, compared to injected heroin, might seem to be no more than a banality. Unfortunately, it is a banality that randomly kills.

VSA is a stigmatized behaviour, but it is based on the misuse of legally available substances which are being diverted to mind-acting purposes. The sniffing of solvents, their possession, sharing them with young friends, are not arrestable offences. Perhaps to some people's surprise, VSA has its place under the licit drugs heading.

This chapter will identify the products involved, describe how they are used and the acute effects they produce in the user, their potential for physical harm, their capacity to bring about dependence, and how they kill.

The products involved

What these abusable chemicals have in common is that they are organic substances which give off vapour that can be readily inhaled. Toluene and butane are the commonest chemicals involved, but many other substances can also be employed in this way. They are found in what constitutes a list of ordinary consumer materials: aerosol propellants of many types, although safer chemicals are often now being employed for this purpose; petrol; balsa wood cement, contact adhesives and cycle tyre-repair adhesives; dry-cleaning and de-greasing preparations and domestic spot removers; fire extinguishers; fuel gases including those used in cigarette lighters and camper stoves; paint-strippers; nail-varnish removers. These substances are ubiquitously present in every home, workshop and garage. They are not products easily locked away in a cupboard, banned, or made subject to control by the criminal law.

How volatile substances are inhaled and their immediate effects

Fashion and imitation can make one mode of use more popular than another in a particular locality. Substances may be sniffed directly from a can, a squirt of the liquid can be directed into the back of the mouth, or, as with the glove cleaner's daughter, a fluid can be poured onto a rag and inhaled. Cement and some other substances are often poured into a plastic bag that is held over the user's face.

'Glue sniffing' is usually a group activity conducted on a stairwell of a city housing block, in a park or derelict building, by a canal or in some other public space, but young people will also engage in this behaviour secretly at home.

The immediate effects of inhaling a volatile substance are likely to be the thrill of a sudden intoxication, and the abrupt change in mental state is probably the major attraction of VSA for young people. Rather than the relatively slow intoxication to be obtained from, say, a shared bottle of Bacardi, VSA offers something nearer to the precipitate 'high' of injected heroin. Inhalants quickly go from the lungs, to the blood stream, and to the brain. They then act on cell membranes rather than having receptor sites, and are rather anaesthetic-like.

Within the VSA-induced experience is a component similar to sudden alcohol-induced drunkenness, with uncoordination, staggering and mental confusion. Coughing, sneezing and vomiting may occur. The intoxication can sometimes progress rapidly to an acute delirium in which the person becomes disoriented and is assailed by vivid and often frightening hallucinations. Here is a description of such an instance as given by a fifteen-year-old boy.

I was round at my mate's place, his parents were away for the day. In the garden shed, and we had a can of something. He said you first. Sat down, took it at the back of my mouth. I knew straightaway something funny was happening this time. The air going all shaky, never had that before. Sounds zooming. Then suddenly, snakes everywhere. I saw snakes crawling over the lawn and up on the wheelbarrow. I was screaming, terrified out of my life. Ran to escape over the wall, fell off, Jim came to calm me down, suppose it was twenty minutes before I knew where I was.

This is a typical account of an inhalant-induced delirium, but most users, most of the time, will experience only the intoxication and perhaps a little perceptual distortion at the edge.

Can volatile substances lead to a dependence?

Mostly the use of these substances by young people is intermittent and not within a schedule likely to set up a dependence. At seventeen, the previous inhalant users will typically be in the pub or sharing a pack of take-home cans of beer with their friends; experimentation with volatile substances will have ceased. However, in a small percentage of users the habit can persist and take on a compulsive quality. In such instances, it is likely that dependence of a rather alcohol-like type has been set up. There are 'glue sniffers' who are still sniffing at the age of twenty or thirty, usually in a solitary and unhappy kind of way.

VSA and social deprivation in the UK

Most use of solvents is concentrated within a fairly narrow age band. Such experimentation does not necessarily imply major personal deviance or carry risk of progression to other types of drug misuse. It can exist in settings of rural idyll as well as in run-down urban areas, and there can be outbreaks in private schools as well as in schools struggling to meet the educational needs of poor communities. That said, in many countries VSA is predominantly a problem associated with social deprivation.

Dr A. Esmail and his colleagues studied the connection between VSA deaths and social deprivation in the UK over the period 1985–91. They made use of a national register of deaths from VSA, which is updated annually by workers at St George's Hospital, London. The register provided the researchers with information on 775 deaths that had occurred over the six-year period. They were then able, in each instance, to link place of death to census data that gave information on the degree of social deprivation present in the locality where the death had occurred. In effect, VSA deaths were projected on to a national map on which deprivation had been coloured in.

The researchers found a startling variation in rates of mortality from VSA across counties. These rates were reported in terms of so-called age-standardized mortality ratios (ASMRs), which make allowance for the size and age structure of any population. They identified, at the high end, the industrial conurbation of Tyne and Wear as having an ASMR of 289, or almost three times the national average of 100. In Scotland, the Lothian area, including Edinburgh and its environs, gave an ASMR of 253. In contrast, the predominantly rural county of Cornwall came in with an ASMR of three, and the Shetland Islands at zero.

Having established the fact of wide regional variation, the team looked for an explanation. And this is where the mapping of deprivation became illuminating. Using a composite index to measure the local ward level of deprivation, the score was found to average 0.2 in localities where VSA deaths had not occurred over the given period, and 2.8 where at least one such death had been recorded. The nineteen-fold difference was far beyond anything that could be explained by chance. In a rich country which has within it a patchwork of wealth and poverty, VSA mapped rather sharply on to the contours of deprivation.

VSA in Mexico City

Turn from a developed country's experience with VSA to a different scene, the sprawling metropolis of Mexico City with its little patches of wealth, some comfortable suburbs and vast areas of squalor. What we have in this instance is not a statistical analysis but a street-level picture of the relationship between poverty and solvent misuse, as given by Dr Ramon de la Fuente, a Mexican psychiatrist.

The regular inhabitants ... have almost no contact with the inhalers but if their paths cross the inhalers are ostracized since they are regarded as depraved. Within a group the adolescent uses the child to obtain food and money, and seeks the protection of the young adult, whose business it is to obtain and distribute the inhalant ... For a child to be taken into a group he undergoes a series of tests such as putting up with having his money or some of his clothes taken away, or being beaten ... The child inhaler then seems to develop certain characteristics. He has a practical type of intelligence ... He is self-sufficient and avails himself of the resources in his environment to satisfy, after his own fashion, his vital needs. He is understanding and does not criticize his comrades when they cry or grieve over some recollection or deprivation ... he puts considerable trust in members of the group but not in outsiders. He is a rebel rejecting every kind of authority. He plays on people's feelings, lying and weeping to arouse their pity so that they give him food and money.

In this picture of Mexican street life, the solvent abuse is deep in the culture of deprivation, and is a phenomenon proposed and made by the social conditions of the young people's lives. It becomes normal rather than deviant behaviour and helps form bonds rather than being a maladjustment.

Many other examples can be found from around the world where

VSA shows a similarly close relationship with deprivation. For instance, in the USA the problem is rife among adolescents and young people living in Native American communities. In Australia, petrol sniffing is endemic among Aboriginal people but there affects adults as well as the young. But whether it is Tyne and Wear, a slum in Latin America, the Australian outback or any other landscape, what the reports generally reveal is that where young people feel themselves excluded from mainstream society at an age when they do not have the buying power to lay hands on alcohol or illicit drugs, they will rather easily join with others to make solvent use a part of the group's definition and cohesion. VSA provides powerful confirmation that the genesis of an individual's drug use is often as much determined by environmental factors as by the properties of the drug or by characteristics of the individual. VSA provides a good illustration of an important general truth.

The nature of VSA deaths

In Britain, VSA deaths were, in the mid to late 1980s, running consistently at over one hundred a year, peaking at 152 in 1990. They have since declined, but there are still about seventy fatalities annually. At the age of fifteen to sixteen, VSA is in Britain a commoner cause of death than leukaemia. Suddenly, what may have seemed to the young people involved to be a little adolescent larking around, has someone dead on the floor. What is often so distressing to the parents is that this death is the first they knew of their child's inhalant use. 'How could I have stopped it happening?' is the question left hanging agonizingly in the air.

VSA can kill abruptly in a number of ways. Many fatalities are due to the direct toxic effect of a chemical on the circulation or on breathing, starving the brain of oxygen. Inhalation of vomit can cause death. Falls and unintentional injuries contribute to the toll. Deaths can happen as a result of fire or explosion, as someone lights a match in a vapour-laden atmosphere.

When VSA leads to tragedy, the death usually occurs within minutes. No young companion is likely to be competent to give first aid. By the time an ambulance crew arrives, all they will be able to do is confirm the fact of death. VSA fatalities tend to be stark and comfortless.

VSA and physical damage

There are reports suggesting that VSA can, in the long term, cause harm to the user's body. Damage to the brain, peripheral nerves, kidneys, liver, bone marrow and lungs have been described. Research on this topic is not at present well developed and little is known about the real level of risk that may result from any particular intensity or duration of exposure. But taking these substances repeatedly into the system is likely to be risky. The blindspot in the glove cleaner's daughter was probably a consequence of damage to the retina or the optic nerve.

VSA deaths: what can be done to mitigate the problem?

The fact that VSA deaths in Britain declined in number over the last decade or so could reflect no more than random variation, or at worst a readier access to other and more dangerous substances. But the mix of preventive measures that were put and held in place by the authorities in response to what was widely seen as a very unacceptable situation, is likely to have contributed to the so far sustained improvement.

The measures have been of three sorts. First, manufacturers are being encouraged to make their products intrinsically safer: the removal of a dangerous solvent from typewriter correction fluid provides an example, as does the introduction of safer aerosol propellants (the latter change was driven more by European environmental regulations than concern for health). Second, there have been attempts to limit, so far as possible, the physical access of young people to dangerous products: for example, the stricter enforcement of the law that makes it a criminal offence for a shopkeeper knowingly to sell quantities of, say, cigarette lighter refills to an adolescent who is likely to be misusing the product. The final element has been the attempt to enhance the climate of awareness on this problem, as it may affect young people, parents, schools, social services, the caring professions, the police, shopkeepers, the community in general and the media. No measures will ever produce a solvent-free environment in a world in which consumers want the products and where manufacturers and retailers profit from the legitimate supply, but between them these strategies are better than neglect.

Doctors and dentists who sniff gases

Laughing gas, or nitrous oxide, was first used as an anaesthetic as long ago as 1844. Accounts of its misuse soon followed. Anaesthetics have provided great blessings but they have given rise to occasional professional misuse. The typical story today is of a doctor or dentist who turns on their modern gases early in the morning 'just to have a sniff and test the machine'. The odour is agreeable, the sensation pleasant, and testing escalates into a habit that is damaging to the reputation of the professional concerned, and threatening to the welfare of their patients. Professional regulatory bodies see a trickle of these cases and are likely to react with great stringency when a case is brought to light. Sometimes the anaesthetic gas is the only misused substance involved in the story, but enquiries often reveal that it was the presenting symptom for a deeper and long-standing drug and alcohol problem.

Vapours

The misuse of anaesthetic gases by the man or woman in a surgical gown is a different social phenomenon than adolescent inhalant misuse in areas of social deprivation. At a deeper level, a commonality between these seemingly different behaviours does exist. Both of them are outcomes of a play between multiple, personal and environmental factors that predispose to any kind of drug use. Yet only one point of one per cent of exposed professionals will ever misuse their anaesthetic gases, while perhaps as many as 10 per cent of young people in the deprived inner city will have misused their readily available solvents. Physical access is a precondition for use of these inhalants, whether for the glove cleaner's daughter, the lad who saw snakes, the Mexican street children, or the doctor or dentist 'testing' their machine. But what the VSA story cogently demonstrates is that the mere fact of access may not by itself provide a sufficient explanation for how a drug problem is distributed across a population. Here we see clearly how social deprivation can become a mediating factor shaping a drug's ecology. That kind of poverty connection is not an axiom for all time or all drugs, but there is a theme developing here to which I will return in Chapter 20. The very general point made by VSA is that when thinking about drugs, one should often think about the landscape. Poverty impairs self-protective responses to access; the privileged professionals with a career at stake and a regulatory body watching are less likely to succumb to ready availability than the poor and dispossessed. Physical availability matters, but what vapours tell is that the impact of availability will be modified by other forces. Volatile solvents are equally available to the rich and poor, but the mortality rates are not distributed evenly over the map.

5

All Sorts

Caffeine

Coffee came to the Western world from the Middle East, towards the middle of the seventeenth century. In England the first coffee house was opened in 1650, in Oxford. So greatly did this institution recommend itself to the population that twenty-five years later 3,000 coffee houses existed the length and breadth of the land, with a concentration in London. Coffee houses were centres for social intercourse, business, politics and the literary life. The authorities became concerned, not due to any perceived danger lurking in the beverage, but because of the fear that these places might become centres for anti-state agitation. In 1675, Charles II impetuously banned coffee houses, but two weeks later had to rescind an unpopular measure. The imperial powers were before long establishing coffee plantations in their colonies. As a result of that history, parts of Africa, Latin America and the West Indies, to this day, have huge areas of land devoted to the cultivation of coffee. In the US, 80–90 per cent of adults are regular coffee drinkers with an average intake of two and a half cups each day. The British notch up only about 70 per cent of the US per-capita intake. The world champions are to be found in Scandinavian countries, where citizens exceed the American personal intake by at least twofold.

Next to crude oil, coffee is in cash terms the world's most traded substance. That is quite a triumph for a drink which a few centuries ago was limited in its distribution to parts of Arabia. Coffee is today a household commodity in every country, and public consumption goes on in ever-increasing numbers of outlets with no whisper of a banning proclamation. Instant coffee was a brilliant marketing invention which helped spread the habit, while cappuccinos and espressos and other latter-day inventions help keep coffee in fashion. Besides the coffee cup, the world gets its caffeine in a myriad of soft drinks, in cocoa and in chocolate, in the kola nut, and as a constituent of medicines and over-the-counter remedies.

The market also offers the drug to all comers through the medium of that other great caffeine-containing beverage, tea. Tea came to Europe from China, arriving shortly after coffee. It was at first a luxury, but soon achieved common popularity. Here is Dr Samuel Johnson admitting in 1757 to his gargantuan tea drinking in a confessional self-portrait:

A hardened and shameless tea-drinker, who has for twenty years diluted his meals with only the infusion of this fascinating plant; whose kettle has scarcely time to cool; who with tea amuses the evening, with tea solaces the midnight, and with tea welcomes the morning.

Vin Mariani, a coca wine, later had the blessing of the Pope (see Chapter 13), but an endorsement for the tea from Dr Johnson would surely have done well for any Protestant family. As mentioned in Chapter 2, he was keen also on his tobacco but in later years he gave up alcohol because it was getting too much of a grip on him.

An average cup of coffee contains about 100mg of caffeine, while a cup of tea has in it 50mg, and a can of soft drink 30mg. Tea and cola drinkers often seem to forget that their beverage is, in pharmacological terms, weak coffee with a few minor constituents added and a different flavouring. Yet, at least in the UK, coffee is viewed as a rather strong and perhaps even dangerous drink, with tea seen as water with some leaves dropped in. The UK and Ireland are top of the international tea-drinking league, with the US coming in low, at only about one eighth of the British per-capita level. The drinking of green tea is largely restricted to China and Taiwan. Black tea, where the raw leaves have been allowed to ferment slightly by enzymatic action, is preferred elsewhere. The tea plantations of India and Sri Lanka (Ceylon) derive from the nineteenth-century British attempt to establish a cash-saving alternative to the Chinese tea imports.

The explanation for tea's being favoured in some countries while coffee takes first place in others lies partly in previous colonial relationships, geographic access and pricing differentials, but cultural traditions also play a part.

The English love of tea drinking provides an example of a beverage adopted as a national symbol, perhaps even more wholeheartedly than beer and Britannia. Tea is written into the metaphor and usage of the English language in an extraordinary number of ways. There are teaspoons, teacups, tea-kettles, tea cosies, tea trays and tea rooms, and the teapot is a symbol of decent, feminine-dominated domesticity, be it the simple enamelled tin variety or a fine piece of antique Georgian silver. 'Will you be mother?' is an invitation to accept a prestigious responsibility for the pouring. Every office used to have its tea lady come round even if she serves out coffee. Tea leaves may be read, a storm in a teacup should be avoided, and if we don't trust a person they are not quite our cup of tea. In the British vernacular, a cup of tea is a cup of char, from a Hindi word of Chinese derivation. A tea party is an occasion where teacakes may be served and the teaset afterwards dried with a tea towel. A woman who is much given to tea and gossip with her cronies was, in my mother's day, a tea biddy. The list if fully stated might even put in the shade the richness of American drug slang (see Chapter 9), but the tea language is fond and frank rather than an underworld argot. Polly put the kettle on and we'll all have tea.

Pharmacologically, caffeine is classed as a mild stimulant, but its mechanism of brain action is not fully known. Although the taste of tea and the taste and aroma of coffee must have much to do with why consumers so greatly favour their chosen beverage, the drug effect is also likely to reinforce the habit. This is more probable with coffee than tea or soft drinks because of the relative caffeine contents, but step up the intake of the weaker preparations and this differential is soon overcome.

Caffeine in moderate doses of up to, say, 200mg (2 cups of coffee) will produce alertness and an enhanced sense of energy and well-being. At higher doses the effects can shade into jitteriness, anxiety, pressured talk and an unpleasant feeling of over-stimulation. Caffeine, notoriously, can disturb sleep, but that as well as other reactions vary between individuals because of personal differences in rates of the drug's clearance. Pregnant women clear caffeine more slowly; cigarette smoking can intensify the action of caffeine by delaying its clearance.

With caffeine, a stimulant drug which has been shown to be capable of encouraging drug-seeking behaviour in experimental animals, one would expect to see a human caffeine dependence syndrome. Some people drink more tea, coffee and caffeine-enriched soft drinks than do others and a few drink these beverages in oceanic quantities: ten or twenty cups of coffee a day is not unknown. Yet until recently, most authorities took the view that caffeine is too mild a stimulant to set up addiction in any real clinical sense.

Recent research does, however, suggest that the conventional view needs to be revised. A number of studies employing a double-blind design (a research strategy where neither subject nor experimental observer knows whether the subject is on caffeine or a placebo) have shown that there are in the community coffee drinkers who, on stopping their intake, experience distinctly unpleasant withdrawal symptoms. Commonly reported consequences of withdrawal include fatigue, anxiety, depression and headache. These symptoms can in vulnerable individuals occur on the cessation of a relatively low level of coffee intake, such as two or three cups a day.

And caffeine withdrawal experience can be of a far from trivial intensity. For instance, a study by Eric Strain, published in 1994, found caffeine withdrawal to carry with it such behaviours as screaming at the children, missing work, going home early, 'sat in office awake with lights off and head down', and a child's birthday party cancelled. Caffeine-withdrawal headaches can be excruciating.

Tolerance can also be demonstrated, but there are caffeine drinkers who are aware of a compulsiveness in their coffee drinking: they urgently need that first cup of coffee in the morning, will feel anxious if coffee is not served quickly at the 9am office meeting, and throughout the day will want to see the cups regularly coming. Caffeine is not in the same league as amphetamine or cocaine, although the evidence suggests that it is a stimulant drug with dependence potential. Perhaps 10 per cent of its regular users will become dependent. The alluring aroma of fresh-ground coffee invading the street as one nears the coffee house is wonderfully inviting in its own right, but in psychological terms it may also be a conditioned cue priming the desire for a further experience of the drug.

No one would suggest that being coffee dependent implies the need for referral to a Drug Dependence Unit. Most people will know when they should cut down or cut out their caffeine consumption, and they will manage their problem by their own devices. But the fact that caffeine has a dependence potential needs to be more widely known, so that people can recognize the origin of the otherwise rather easily misattributed symptoms. Some people may need explanation and support from their doctor in dealing with a caffeine problem.

In addition to the debate over whether caffeine can cause dependence, there has been discussion over many years as to whether it can cause any serious kind of harm. Victorian physicians were fond of denouncing the evils of tea drinking. Here are the views of Dr Benjamin Ward Richardson, as given in his 1883 *Diseases of Modern Life*.

Some functional nervous derangements are excited by fluids commonly consumed with, or as foods. *Tea* taken in excess is one of these disturbing agents . . . The symptoms which indicate injurious action of this article of food are sufficiently characteristic. They are, intensely severe headache . . . flatulency, and unsteadiness and feebleness of muscular power, and, not unfrequently, a lowness of spirits amounting to hypochondriacal despondency. In poverty-striken districts, amongst the women who take tea at every meal, this extremely nervous semi-hysterical condition from the action of tea is almost universal.

Richardson believed that tea-induced nervous disorders had more recently become prevalent in the moneyed classes as well, with the victims then dosing themselves with alcohol to calm the nervousness which tea had brought on, 'thus one evil feeds another which is worse'. A section in Richardson's book dealt with diseases resulting from too tightly laced corsets, and there was a minatory chapter on 'Disease from sloth and idleness'. His and other denunciations of the tea-drinking habit have usually been seen by modern commentators as evidence of preposterous Victorian moralism. In retrospect, Richardson should perhaps be recognized as rather an astute clinical observer of the caffeine-dependence picture, even if he drew exaggerated conclusions.

As for what modern medical science has to say about health dangers which may lurk in caffeine consumption, there is agreement that both use and withdrawal can lead to psychological disturbance. But there is no persuasive evidence of an association between caffeine consumption and cancer, heart disease or stroke, although heavy intake can probably contribute to a raised blood pressure. There is no evidence that the mother's coffee intake will damage the foetus. An as yet unidentified caffeine-related evil may one day walk towards us from around the corner. But on present evidence, caffeine, although an enormously widely used drug with a dependence potential, does little harm to the population's health.

A mildly reinforcing drug, not much harm done to the devotee, a substance which is tradable and pleasurable, a drug which has never gone over to use by injection or smoking, no wonder the coffee house was a gateway to a giant habit.

Ether drinking epidemic in Ulster

Ether was patented as an anaesthetic in 1846 by William Morton, a dentist who had his practice in Boston, Massachusetts. His right to the patent was disputed by other contenders, and he was not the first person to have exploited the anaesthetic properties of the substance. But whatever the rows over precedence, ether anaesthesia was gratefully received as an invaluable innovation in the aid of surgery of all types. Outside medicine, ether had, and has, a place in various trades as an industrial solvent.

Ether has the chemical formula $(C_2H_5)_2O$, with two ethyl (C_2H_5) radicals joined up by the bivalent oxygen. At room temperature ether is a liquid, but it easily vaporizes and the vapour is the anaesthetic gas. Ether can be taken by mouth, but, at least in the uninitiated, its immediate effects are likely to include a very unpleasant burning sensation, nausea and much belching of fumes as the liquid heats up in the stomach. Ether vapour is inflammable; mixed with air it can explode.

Ether is similar to alcohol: it does not attach in the brain to a receptor site. It can, however, produce rapid intoxication. Indeed, from the imbiber's point of view, ether can be viewed as having an advantage over alcohol in that it is possible to get drunk more quickly, with a rapid subsequent sobering up. The police were reluctant to arrest an ether drunkard out on the street because the offender would probably have sobered up by the time of arrival at the police station. A high degree of tolerance can occur on repeated use. Evidence on the dependence potential is scant but the habitué can develop craving, and withdrawal symptoms probably do occur. Ether abuse predated the era of exact clinical science, and little is known about the toxicology, although various types of bodily damage can occur with chronic use. Overdose can be fatal.

Soon after ether's entry on to the medical scene as an anaesthetic, doctors who had started to sniff their own anaesthetic gas occasionally came to notice. Experts in inebriety encountered a few patients, besides these medical casualties, who had taken to ether sniffing. Young people were reported as sometimes getting together for 'an ether frolic'.

If the problem had remained at the level of frolic and a few casualties engendered by the sniffing of the gas, there would have been no great cause for alarm. But with the increased production and distribution of this substance to meet medical and industrial needs, reports began to come in that people had discovered that ether was good stuff to drink, and a remarkably cheap way of getting stinking drunk.

In the nineteenth century the vogue for ether drinking took off in many countries. Louis Lewin, that ever-diligent chronicler of drug history, reported that 'etheromania' had spread from England to Germany and France. He believed that in some parts of Germany, and especially in the Lithuanian communities, 'the drinking of ether has become an epidemic'. He offered the following picture of a sort to have one leaping to the ditch:

On market days the smell of ether exhaled by the drinkers is noticeable at every turn. When, on the road between Heydekrug and the neighbouring villages, a carriage with noisy inmates drawn by a madly galloping horse which the intoxicated driver is unmercifully beating, passes the wayfarer, a strong smell of ether can be ascertained in the rush of air.

He also reported the habit as prevalent in Russia and in Norway. As for the English experience, Lewin's two cited cases were restricted to the titled classes – a baronet who used morphine and ether concurrently and 'an etheromaniac earl'.

However wide the geographical spread of ether as a cheap intoxicant, the epicentre of nineteenth-century ether drinking was a small area of rural Ulster. Around the market towns of Draperstown and

Cookstown, the railway carriages were heavy with the telltale odour. The habit was first introduced to the area in the 1840s, and was well established by the 1860s. In the 1890s, it was alleged that one person in eight who lived in the locality had become an ether drinker.

Norman Kerr gave a detailed account of the ether problem then rampant in Ulster in the 1894 edition of his textbook. He believed that ether drinking was a side effect of Father Mathew's famous temperance campaign of the 1840s.

Between 1842 and 1845 a local medical practitioner, in response to a request from a few newly pledged abstaining converts for something, the taking of which would not violate their vow, gave them a drachm of ether in water. So far as I can ascertain, this was the *fons et origo mali* [the source and origin of the evil] . . . The practice spread in and around Draperstown till there was a shop for the sale of ether, in one town, to every twenty-three of the population.

Father Mathew, a charismatic Catholic priest, had over a few years converted half the Irish adult population to abstinence. He reduced the spirit revenue to one sixth of its previous level and rendered 20,000 publicans bankrupt. As a result of this epic and unlikely triumph, the door had certainly been opened for a substitute drug should one come along.

Kerr stated that small farmers and agricultural labourers made up 'the bulk of the ether tipplers', and women were well represented.

Sturdy Irish lads and beautiful Irish lasses, brimful of Hibernian wit, as well as '60-year-olds' of both sexes, are slaves to ether drunkenness . . . schoolmasters have detected ether on the breaths of children from 10 to 14 (or even younger) on their arrival at school.

A popular calumny had it that one could tell a man's religion by his breath, but ether drinkers were equally common among Protestants and Catholics. In this small area of Ireland, the habit grew over a few decades to permeate society. There were cases reported from other parts of Ireland, from Scotland and from rural England. But no other locality ever saw such an intense and concentrated outbreak as occurred in Ulster, and nowhere else in Britain did ether drinking reach a level to constitute public scandal.

In 1965, K. H. Connell, writing from the Queen's University of Belfast, provided a detailed account of this strange episode in the history of inebriety. Putting together the information given in his report, Kerr's earlier observations and accounts to be found in the medical journals, it is evident that besides the ether-prescribing doctor as *fons et origo*, there were other and multiple causes which contributed to the ether epidemic. Bulk supplies were readily imported from England and Scotland. The product was cheap, and especially so when in the 1850s the supposedly non-drinkable methylated ether was introduced for industrial purposes and rapidly diverted for drinking. A novice could get drunk on a pennyworth of this solvent. Controls over retail selling were nil. Local people of small means could profit from their place in the distribution chain: an itinerant beggar woman would sell a nip from her bottle at a cottage door or barter for an egg. The building of paved roads in previously isolated country areas had made customs enforcement easier and was driving out the traditional distilling of poteen (an illicit spirit). Thus did forces conspire, and in a quiet corner of rural Ulster ether drinking became scandalous.

To the modern drinker, it may seem surprising that such a nauseous substance should have ever won popular acceptance as a way of getting drunk. Contemporary accounts describe, however, the manner in which hardened ether drinkers would throw the stuff back without even a swig of water, and there was a high degree of tolerance to the aversive effects. As Kerr put it:

More 'seasoned casks' have a higher capacity, many topping off half a wine-glassful as unconcernedly as an average Englishman would drink a glass of claret, or an average American a glass of champagne.

The economic imperative can overcome distastefulness in the poor person's pursuit of intoxication. Coal gas bubbled through milk, shoe polish cooked up for its solvent, methylated spirits drunk on skid row, all provide examples of the potential strength of the economic influence when people want to get drunk cheaply.

What is more difficult to understand is why, in the nineteenth century, this cheap and enormously available intoxicant did not spread more readily to other areas of Ireland. Country communities perhaps at that time were more isolated than we imagine today. A corner of Ulster seems to have constituted an ether-favourable microclimate.

The way in which this epidemic was brought under control provides a classic example of the importance of the supply side. Preaching from the pulpits on the evils of ether was largely ineffective. And yet, as Connell put it, ether drinking 'was all but stifled by the first restrictive legislation'. That measure was the scheduling of ether in 1891 as a poison within the meaning of the Pharmacy Act. The number of sales outlets was drastically reduced and access curtailed; retail sales fell immediately by 90 per cent. A tail end of the problem continued into the 1920s but the glory days of ether drinking in Ulster were by then long over.

What this story also offers is an illustration of the general fact that different people, in different cultures, can get different things out of an experience with the same drug. According to Connell:

The erotic appeal of ether was stressed more by continental than by Irish observers. Elsewhere, men hoping for 'strange voluptuousness, were rewarded by visions of lascivious situations' and 'beautiful women'; but in Ireland . . . the drinkers' dreams were said to be 'light' and 'refined'.

Seemingly, Hibernians were chaste and God-fearing even when etherized.

Khat

Abdullah is a Yemeni merchant in a good way of business. He lives at the edge of the city in a large, flat-roofed house that has on the second floor a chamber known as the Room of Peace. It is furnished with expensive carpets and comfortable cushions. Water pipes (hubble bubbles) adorned with brightly coloured tassels are clustered at the centre of the room.

Come Thursday, there is jostling and commotion at the market as the fresh supplies of khat arrive by truck from the Northern Highlands. The vendors have tied the twigs into little bundles, and they spray water on them to keep them moist and cool. Abdullah's servant pushes his way to the front and makes a purchase.

The party in the Room of Peace starts at about 3pm. There are greetings – Allah is merciful, praise be to Allah, Allah is great. Abdullah's guests are other merchants, a schoolteacher, a lawyer, a senior policeman, all of them wearing traditional dress. There is a smell of incense from the brazier hanging from the ceiling. Salutations and friendly laughter are heard.

The guests have taken off their shoes and are seated on the cushions. Everyone has brought their own contribution of khat. Each person takes a quantity of the plant material into their mouth and begins to chew the mixture of stalks, leaves and leafy buds. The tannin in this material dries the mouth and a servant hands round coffee and a tray with glasses of water. This is a Muslim country and no alcohol will be served.

At this party it is the conversation and the intimacy which matter, and the khat helps the talk to flow freely. An edge of excitement and exuberance is felt as the chewing continues; the drug blood levels rise in each participant. The juice is swallowed and the plant residue packed into the chewer's cheek. A few latecomers arrive. Abdullah leads the group into a discussion of politics and city affairs, poetry is read, there is singing and jokes are told. After three hours, the party atmosphere is at its apogee, with the sense of trust, contentedness and wisdom fusing with the smell of incense. Thereafter, the mood goes downhill. Personal problems emerge. A couple of guests become argumentative, irritable and over-excited. After five hours the party is breaking up. No one will sleep well that night and in the morning they will admit to exhaustion and low mood. But next week the gathering in the Room of Peace is certain to reconvene.

The use and cultivation of khat has for centuries been restricted largely to Yemen and some East African countries, including Ethiopia and Somalia. There are numerous variations in the name by which the plant material is known: khat, kat, qat, quat, quatt and mira or marae among others. The source is the shrub or small tree *Catha edulis forrskal*, named in honour of the eighteenth-century botanist Peter Forrskal, who first brought news of it to Europe. Khat is nearly always taken by chewing, but it can also be consumed in a tea-like infusion or smoked.

The identification of the active ingredient in the twigs for long defeated chemists. Because of the instability of cathinone, by the time a sample got back to the laboratory, the cathinone had vanished. It is now accepted that cathinone and cathine are the principle active ingredients. These substances are amphetamine-like in their actions. Cathinone and cathine have, respectively, about 50 per cent and 10 per cent of the potency of amphetamine. Although the vast majority of the market's customers are visitors like Abdullah's servants wanting to buy the drug for social use, the usual shading of boundaries between pleasure drug and medicine exists. In Ethiopia, khat is credited with 501 medicinal benefits.

Khat has been chewed recreationally in goat-like fashion within its circumscribed geographical areas of use for longer than anyone can remember. Watch a goat nibbling at any scrubby little tree, and the comparison is evident. The drug is usually consumed in the party situation, but solitary use does occur. Men are generally more frequent users than women and in a khat-chewing region 80–90 per cent of men will be regularly dedicated to the habit. Women have to set up their own single-sex parties if they want to indulge.

In a Muslim country which forbids alcohol, the availability of this weak stimulant is welcome. Khat is accepted and viewed as more or less trouble free in its indigenous territory. Custom and manners control the level of consumption on any one occasion, and set expectations as to how the individual will behave when under the influence. Consumption is also limited by supply and it may be difficult to get enough of the fresh material to the market before the cathinone has degraded. The French and British colonial powers tried banning it, without success. When the Yemeni government attempted to prohibit the drug, the adverse response came near to popular revolt and the banning order was soon rescinded. Saudi Arabia is the only Arab country which currently outlaws its use.

In the midst of the traditional, cultural acceptance, there have however been concerns. Khat is relatively cheap, but a family at a marginal level of subsistence may spend 25 per cent of their scant weekly income at the khat market. Multiply up that level of spending, and where khat is imported there is the making of a national balance of payments problem. There have been rumours of khat's causing mental illness and crime, and some anxiety about the possible adverse effects on physical health. But the use of khat in its limited indigenous base looks set to stay, although no one would expect this bulky and easily decomposing source of a weak stimulant to spread out to the Western world, where pleasure may more conveniently be packaged in various types of pill or bottle.

No one would expect khat to spread, but it has now happened.

Every week an astonishing seven tonnes of khat are flown licitly into Heathrow. Such is the efficiency of the operation, that the twigs which are on sale in London will have been picked a mere twenty-four hours previously in Ethiopia; the store holder in a Yemeni market cannot offer fresher produce. Some of the khat arriving at Heathrow is for quick onward shipment. Most of it will, however, be consumed by Somali and other refugee communities that have become established over recent years in the UK.

Khat has thus followed its people. As for patterns of use, there are groups of men assembling for khat parties in exactly the same manner as they previously did at home. A Room of Peace can be re-created in an alien clime. But the majority of these immigrants are not in work, life in London is for many of them difficult, and in addition to the old culturally approved and restrained modes of khat taking, there is evidence emerging of a new kind of heavy use.

A report on khat chewing among the Somali population in London, published in 1998 by Paul Griffiths (a researcher at the Addiction Research Unit), revealed that one user out of every five interviewed was spending over £100 each week on khat. About one in ten was showing signs of dependence. Many short-term, minor mental-health problems were occurring as a result of the drug, including anxiety and panic attacks. Rather more than 10 per cent of these subjects had at some time experienced 'severe hallucinations'. Solitary use was going on as well as the traditional group use. Women were becoming heavier users.

Griffiths was properly cautious not to over-interpret results from the one study of 200 subjects, but the overall picture which emerges is of a drug becoming somewhat more problematic than in the home situation. Khat may be beneficial in that it continues to give cultural identity and social cohesion. But for the immigrants, there is a negative side as unpleasant amphetamine-like effects begin to show through, and as the old cultural controls on level and pattern of use become weakened. There have been a few reports appearing in British medical journals over recent years of khat-induced psychosis, with the symptoms remarkably similar to amphetamine psychosis.

Another drug-containing plant product, traditionally geographically limited in its distribution, is betel (areca nut). A familiar sight in India is the railway platform stained a splattered red as the crowds chew and spit. Betel chewed alone, or with tobacco or spices, is an enormously widespread habit in Asia as source of a mild stimulant. With Asian immigration, streets in British cities now show the familiar stain. Chronic use can give rise to oral cancer. In certain islands of the Pacific, drinking of yet another stimulant, kava, was previously associated with a religious cult. The substance was prepared by volunteers (preferably virgin boys), who chewed the root and spat it into a bowl of water for the group's drinking. The missionaries disapproved of the heathen ritual. Unsurprisingly, kava drinking is a practice which has faded rather than spread, and there are no accounts of kava use outside its native islands.

But back to khat as a case study of a drug with historically limited distribution, and which for centuries has been given a value and meaning by certain societies. Culture has supported and controlled the experience, and in turn the drug has helped make the culture. Here is khat adulated by J. C. Carothers, a British doctor, writing in 1945:

The chewing of this weed induces a happy and mellow friendliness and an increase in intellectual vigour and activity, thought tends to rise to a higher plane, desire for war and women ceases, and conversation tends to concern itself with 'the affairs of God' and the accumulation of wealth by peaceful trade.

That was perhaps always too cosy a view of the drug. Take khat to the poor areas of a Western city and before long the medical services will have to meet the treatment needs of people who have become dependent on an amphetamine-like drug. Maybe if treatment had been available back in the Yemen, even some of Abdullah's friends might have been seeking help.

Going bananas

Here is the story of a crazy and brief fad, but one that can reveal an important truth. Some time around the late 1960s, the news came out of California that if fibres from the lining of banana skin were dried, rolled up in cigarette paper and smoked, the result could be a good high and perhaps a hallucinatory experience. Mellow Yellow had been born. This promised the ultimate cheap dope and no hassle from the cops. One can't be busted for possession of bananas. There was an instant run on supermarket stocks and shelves were emptied.

Who originated this craze, and whether the person was deceived by their own imagination or was a joker, will never be known. A website gives precedence to a certain Gary 'Chicken' Hirsh as the discoverer. He was on his way to play a gig in Vancouver when he set the band to preparing banana reefers. The roadies had already made available a jar in which they had dissolved a hundred tablets of LSD, and the band sipped at this psychedelic experience freely between acts. But when they got back to the Bay area, it was to find that they had launched a craze amongst the West Coast hippy communities.

There was never a nanogram of anything mind-acting in smoked bananas, as the Federal Drugs Agency soon confirmed on urgent analysis. If the findings had gone the other way, the result would have been an unimaginable crisis for drugs control, with desperate attempts at denial, and damage limitation emanating, no doubt, from the banana industry.

But the headlines went sour, people started to refer to 'the great banana hoax', and Mellow Yellow was forgotten other than as the title of Donovan's song, and he had had no connection with that prankish episode in the Summer of Love.

The important truth? One needs a drug to make a drug epidemic run and any old rope won't do.

More and yet more

There are many other substances that could be added to this variegated bottle. Horse dealers used to put a temporary sparkle into broken-winded nags by dosing them with arsenic. Considerable tolerance develops when this poison is taken in small repeat doses; arsenic in the nineteenth century became a habit with prostitutes who believed it could restore the bloom of youth. Anabolic steroids, widely used by bodybuilders, can produce euphoria, tipping over into irritability, aggression and rage. The keen user will inject steroids in large and escalating doses, and may feel bad when the drugs are stopped. Nutmeg, that well-known Eastern spice, has been used as a hallucinogen. Overdose with nutmeg can produce very unpleasant symptoms and fatalities have been reported. So on and on, and the candidates for a place in this miscellany queue to the mind-acting horizon.

Time to stop up the bottle. But there is one more item to which I must give a place or be left with a drug on my hands. In the Amazonian jungle, the Indian people sun-dry the seeds of a species of acacia, and then grind them in a mortar to make a snuff called parica. At festivals, everyone can be expected to get drunk on copious quantities of crude rum. People then pair off, each person propelling with a blow pipe a quantity of the parica up the nostrils of their partner. An orgiastic state of hallucinatory excitement is rapidly brought on. For days, drunkenness and parica madness mix and alternate, until the party is over.

The All Sorts party is at an end so far as this chapter is concerned but it is a party in full and licit swing around the whole world.

6

Licit Drugs and the Man from Mars

One may sometimes do well to stand back from the ordinary to see how truly extraordinary commonplaces can be. Look at the account of society's experience with licit drugs given in the foregoing chapters, and my personal feeling is that what is going on here, if seen with clear eyes, is truly extraordinary. Society is coexisting with a range of drugs, some of which are very damaging and others much less so, but they have in common the fact that control is left to non-criminal regulation, manners and the good sense and responsibility of the citizen. It is a massive hands-off act.

Does it work well? Well enough with caffeine, but take alcohol and tobacco as other leading fruits of laissez faire, and between them they cause such havoc as to make all illicit drugs rolled up together look pallid in comparison. Massive hands off, massive damage, no war on these drugs; stand back and it does look extraordinary that in some ways we do so well with the hands-off formula. But change focus slightly and it can look like licit carnage.

Mundane but extraordinary drug happenings are going on all the time, everywhere. I want at this juncture to try the device of seeing how it might all look to the fresh eyes of a Martian.

Our Martian is on a fact-finding mission to understand how this planet handles licit drugs. Says the visitor to the welcoming delegation: 'Thank you for arranging this intriguing chemical tour. My conclusions are twofold. Licit regulation, aided by informal control, seems to me on the basis of what you have shown me at times to achieve almost miraculous success. I mean, those people sipping white wine on the lawn, an astonishing taming of a dangerous drug, and the tour took in those pitiful meths drinkers in the park too.'

'Yes,' says the spokeswoman. 'Your first conclusion is shrewdly observed and incontestable. Please continue, we are grateful for this feedback.'

'Well,' the Martian says, 'secondly, and with equal confidence, I conclude that to continue with this system you have to behave like the herd of antelopes I saw when flying over Africa. They go on grazing when a lion pulls down one of their members and enjoys his breakfast. The price of peaceful coexistence with licit drugs is a rabid complacency.

'No offence intended,' continues the Martian. 'But your formula for licit control seems to me to be fuddle and muddle, coloured all too often by hypocrisy, venality, mendacity, stupidity and blind denial.'

Uneasy silence from the delegation.

Part Two

Opiates

7

Opiates Introduced

Why focus on opiates?

The reason for according opiates a stand-alone section is that the world's experience with them is so extensive. Their story throws light on every topic with which this book is concerned. They are drugs with which, in some periods and certain localities even today, people have lived, with an easy, non-criminalized coexistence. But in other times and situations they have given rise to hideously destructive drug epidemics. Understand opiates and much will have been understood.

It is not being argued that opiates are in some intrinsic sense more important than other substances. To avoid confusion, let us again emphasize that tobacco, wherever it is used, is likely to kill more people than heroin, even at that drug's most rampant. The opiates matter because their history is astonishingly rich and usefully perplexing.

The antiquity of opium

The Cueva de los Murcielagos (the Cave of the Bats), a Neolithic site at Albuñol, southern Spain, was first explored by archaeologists in the mid-nineteenth century. They found evidence of a people who placed poppy heads among their burial artefacts. When much later this material was carbon dated, its origin was put at 4200 BC. An anthropologist, Richard Rudgley, who has written extensively on drug use in early civilizations, believes that those people were probably using the plant for its intoxicant effects.

A cure for illness, a place in ritual, the drug probably spilling over to pleasure: all those modes and meanings are likely to have existed for millennia, often in overlapping form. As soon as any civilization reached a stage of development where an activity recognizable as the practice of medicine began to emerge (a profession often only uncertainly demarcated from that of the magician or priest), opium had a place as a panacea. All the great early medical authorities keenly advocated opium. Hippocrates, the Greek physician who is honoured as the founding father of medicine; Galen, the Roman physician whose theories on bodily humours guided medical thinking for centuries; Avicenna, a famous practitioner of the Arab school – they all sang the praises of opium.

The place of opium in European medicine was reinforced when the German alchemist and physician Paracelsus (1493–1541) showed that opium was soluble in alcohol so that a tincture could be prepared. The next few centuries saw the application of opium in therapeutics repeatedly advocated in European texts. A London physician, Dr John Jones, in his 1700 *Mysteries of Opium Reveal'd*, dared also to touch on the pleasures:

like a most delicious and extraordinary refreshment of the spirits upon very good news or any other great cause of joy – it has been compared (not without good cause) to a permanent gentle degree of that pleasure which modesty forbids the name of.

With modesty no longer in vogue, the 'rush' induced by an intravenous injection of heroin is frequently likened to an orgasm.

Many a medical doctor will remember the occasion when, as a student, he or she first saw the injection of an opiate relieve a patient's distress. It may have been the drug given to the person brought into the Accident and Emergency department with awful injuries, or agony taken instantly away from the patient suffering the crushing chest pain of a myocardial infarction. In 1680, the English doctor Thomas Sydenham (1624–89) wrote: 'Among the remedies which it has pleased Almighty God to give to man to relieve his sufferings, none is so universal and so efficacious as opium.' Today's medical students will be trained in the use of modern substitutes for Sydenham's efficacious remedy, but they are likely to be at one with him in their esteem for the derivatives or mimics of the poppy.

Opiates the drugs

Opium is derived from the milky exudate which leaks out when the ripe capsule of the white poppy, *Papaver somniferum*, is incised with a knife. Other species of poppy including the red garden variety may yield the drug in lesser quantity. The exudate is allowed to dry, scraped into a collecting pan, and then pressed into brownish or black blocks of commercial opium.

The crude resin is not very soluble in water and, from Paracelsus onwards, a medicinal product for oral administration was obtained by dissolving the opium in alcohol. This alcoholic tincture was called laudanum. Opium also came to be the constituent of a myriad patent medicines with evocative names such as Kendal Black Drop, Mrs Winslow's Soothing Syrup and Collis Brown's Chlorodyne. Cottagers might rest content with the bounty of their own gardens and boil up home-brewed poppy-head tea, which in some localities was called 'Sleepy Beer'.

Opium contains a number of active chemicals. The chief painkiller is morphine, which constitutes 10 per cent of the crude product. It was isolated in 1806 by the German chemist Friedrich Sertürner. He named the drug in honour of Morpheus, the Greek god of dreams. By the middle of the nineteenth century, and with the invention of the hypodermic needle and syringe, morphine sulphate, given by injection, was widely used in pain relief. Codeine is a constituent which found application as a cough suppressant, as well as a useful minor painkiller. In 1874, chemists working in London found that a little tampering with the morphine molecule would produce diacetylmorphine, which is more than twice as potent as morphine, weight for weight. The commercial exploitation of this semi-synthetic was taken up by the German firm Bayer in the 1890s, when it was given the trade name 'Heroin', deriving from the word *heroisch*, in witness to the drug's heroic power.

Besides the poppy-derived opiates, a number of synthetic drugs with similar central-nervous-system actions have entered the pharmacopoeia. Pethidine (Demerol) and methadone (Physeptone) provide examples. Although, strictly speaking, the word *opiate* indicates a plant substance and *opioid* a synthetic, the terms are often used interchangeably. In this book, *opiate* is used in the generic sense to cover all opium-like drugs, however derived or produced.

Opiates have an ability to attach to the opiate receptors which are present in certain areas of the brain and in the spinal cord. There are several subtypes of opiate receptors, each designated by a Greek letter. The mu receptors are the attachment sites particularly concerned with mediation of pain relief. The reinforcing potential of this class of drug derives from the release of dopamine within areas of the brain subserving the experience of pleasure. The body produces its own opiate-like substances (endorphins), which are part of the chemical messenger system and the brain is thus pre-tuned to receive the music of the poppy.

All opiates have a potential to instigate dependence, and injected heroin or morphine more so than drugs such as codeine. Tolerance, when it develops, can be of an extreme degree. For example, the standard medical dose for heroin is 10mg but a tolerant heroin addict may be taking a gram or more each day – a 30–60mg dose would kill a non-tolerant subject. Withdrawal symptoms from opiates can be extremely unpleasant, especially so if a patient is allowed to withdraw 'cold turkey' and without the cover of medication. But despite the distress, opiate withdrawal is rarely, if ever, fatal, and that contrasts with alcohol and other depressant drugs, where withdrawal can at the extreme result in physical collapse or a life-threatening run of fits.

Tolerance and withdrawal symptoms are the outward signs of opiate dependence. The inner and subjective experience of dependence on drugs of this type is an intense craving for their continuation, and life dominated by a need to ensure supplies. The person suffering from well-established heroin dependence is likely, from morning to night, to be leading a drug-centred existence. Hence the connection between heroin addiction and acquisitive crime, in circumstances where possession of the drug is illegal.

Opiates can be taken into the body by all the usual routes. Traditionally, opium for pleasure was smoked in China and the Far East. For medical purposes, it was in the past likely to be taken by mouth in tincture or in pill form. When morphine and the syringe became available, the injected route was opened, with the risk of dependence greatly enhanced. Although addicts today will usually inject their heroin, smoking of the drug or 'chasing the dragon' has also in certain periods and places enjoyed popularity. The story of opiate use is thus replete with variations in routes of use over time, between countries, and a to and fro within the individual's addiction career.

Opiates: intrinsically rather harmless drugs that easily kill

The medical complications associated with opiates include malnutrition due to dietary neglect, and chronic constipation. These drugs themselves do not, however, produce anything like the sum of serious adverse health consequences that can be caused by alcohol or by cigarette smoking. It is possible to encounter well-nourished adults who have been maintained for many years on a clinic prescription of heroin and who are seemingly in the pink of physical health, albeit rather dulled and inert.

But from the health angle, the worry about opiates is the ease with which fatal overdose occurs. This may be due to the drug itself depressing respiration, or the consequence of an interaction between the heroin and, say, alcohol or diazepam (Valium). The high degree of tolerance which an opiate user can acquire rapidly fades with abstinence. Heroin users who return to injecting after discharge from hospital or prison can therefore kill themselves if they go back abruptly to taking a dose with which their previously tolerant system could easily cope.

Although opiates per se are not tissue poisons, today they carry in many countries intense danger of AIDS or hepatitis transmission when injected. Addicts who regularly inject heroin will experience a death rate about fourteen times higher than people of the same age in the general population.

Mick tried a variety of illicit drugs while at art school and thought nothing of it. In his mid-twenties, while working in a gallery, he got in with a group who used heroin or cocaine at weekends. A few years later he was injecting heroin and heavily dependent on it, and was badly messed up by the drug. His parents paid for him to go for six weeks into a private treatment centre, where he came off heroin and seemed strongly committed to recovery. On the day of discharge, he went back in the evening to his gallery and was found next morning dead of a heroin overdose with the needle in his arm.

The paradox with heroin is that although it is so much less tissue toxic than society's favourite licit drugs and each year kills far fewer people, it has a capacity suddenly to kill, and its injected use can contribute to virus infections which may kill years after the injecting. Add to that its dependence potential and its association with crime, and it is unsurprising that it is a drug with a bad image.

But to view heroin as a unique evil is irrational and unhelpful. People can use heroin casually without ever becoming dependent on it. As already mentioned, it is possible for patients to continue on prescribed heroin for years, and remain healthy. The crime is caused not by the drug but by its prohibition. Heroin in the hands of doctors is an effective painkiller.

Opiates: what follows

This chapter has introduced the opiates. The following four chapters will explore the way these drugs have played out across very varied scenery. I will first describe the British nineteenth-century attempt to force opium on to China, with the idea of 'trade war' made literal by the mouth of the cannon. The British and American domestic responses to opiates will then be compared and contrasted over a run of two centuries. Next an account is given of the outbreak of heroin use which occurred among the American forces during the Vietnam War. The final chapter in this section offers a collage of close human experience with opiates through a range of cultures.

The opiates have much to tell.

8

Opium in China

China in the nineteenth century fell victim to a major national problem with opium. The country had had access to opium for centuries before the British arrived on the scene and the Chinese fed their national drug habit by substantial home production; the US and some European countries besides Britain at times had a hand in the opium trade. This was, however, an international episode where, for the sake of profit, Britain was the leading actor willing to force a drug epidemic on to a weaker nation, while defending its own conduct with cant and hypocrisy.

That is the outline of the matter, but go deeper and further complexities emerge. China at the beginning of the nineteenth century was still almost a closed country. The conflict which arose over attempts to impose opium imports was located in much wider issues relating to Western expectations of free access to the world's markets, with China determined to keep all foreign influence out. There was a conflict of beliefs and cultures, as well as of politics and economics. Contempt for a non-Western and non-Christian nation coloured British attitudes, and was repaid by Chinese disdain for the barbarian foreigners.

The prime focus of this chapter will be on what these happenings can tell us about an opiate ecology. It will examine the rates of use and the occurrence of problems in conditions of very accessible, cheap supply of the drug. Did all or most users become dependent, or did a good proportion stay as more casual and unproblematic users? Flood in opium and see what happens to drug use, that is what researchers are apt rather heartlessly to call a 'natural experiment'. But from such experiments much can be learnt.

India, opium and the imperative of profit

When opium first became available to the people of the Indian subcontinent is uncertain, but by the time of the Mogul emperors it was widely used. The Moguls for centuries shared with the Indian princes a monopoly in the production and sale of opium, as well as having a taste for it themselves.

Thus when, in the sixteenth century, British merchant adventurers began to trade with India, they found the use of opium already established. In 1660, the East India Company was given by Royal Charter the monopoly rights to trade with all countries beyond the Cape of Good Hope. Although the Company was originally constituted as a trading organization, in time it became a political, administrative and military presence. It succeeded in seeing off the Portuguese, Dutch and French, and eventually took over absolute control of large parts of India as the Mogul empire disintegrated. The battle of Plassey in 1757 helped complete this process, with Robert Clive the hero. The Company continued to ensure British power in India until 1857 when, subsequent to the Indian Mutiny, the British government assumed direct political control. On becoming the de facto rulers of India, the British took over the control of opium. Bengal was the principal area for cultivation of the poppy, but by threats and treaties the Company gained trading control over the so-called Malwi opium produced by the still-independent princely states.

The financial significance of opium as a tradable commodity went through two stages. In the early part of the eighteenth century, the servants of the Company were supplementing their notoriously low pay by a little do-it-yourself trading in opium, both within India and with an element of export. In the second phase, the Company later in that century put an end to this private enterprise, forcefully exerting its own monopoly rights. They then greatly encouraged opium production in India, with a huge acreage of good land devoted to the cultivation of the poppy. Opium shops were opened for sale of the drug to the indigenous population, but damage to the efficiency of the labour force became a cause for concern. With the adverse impact of the drug on the Indian population stirring opposition, the Company seems to have made the conscious commercial decision to go for the export market. As Warren Hastings, that most powerful servant of the East India Company, who had first gone out to Calcutta in 1750, put it in a passage which the anti-opium movement was later to stigmatize as the epitome of cynicism:

Opium is not a necessary of life, but a pernicious article of luxury, which ought not to be permitted but for the purpose of foreign commerce only, and which the wisdom of the Government should carefully restrain consumption.

That was interpreted by Hastings's critics as a declaration that poisoning foreigners was acceptable commercial practice.

The British, from then onwards, were caught on a treadmill. They were dependent on the export of opium to balance the books of the Company and to secure the tax to subsidize the Indian adventure. In 1832, a Select Committee of the House of Commons acknowledged the reality of this situation when it reported in the following terms:

In the present state of the revenue of India, it does not appear advisable to abandon so important a source of revenue, a duty upon opium being a tax which principally falls on the foreign consumer, and which appears, upon the whole, less liable to objection than any other that could be substituted.

That the profits of the enterprise were for British India substantial cannot be doubted, although precise actuarial analysis is not easy. Prices varied greatly over time, supply was sometimes hard put to meet demand, and in other periods there was a glut. The fact is that British India became, and for the major part of the nineteenth century remained, dependent on the opium trade for its economic survival.

Opium smoking

The opium imported from British India had been compressed to give blocks of prepared opium. Contemporary Chinese accounts spoke of three types of product: 'company' opium or 'black earth' came from Bengal, 'white skin' from Bombay and 'red skin' from Madras. For export, 140 pounds weight or approximately 52 kilos of opium cake were packed into a wooden chest; trade figures were usually quoted as numbers of chests.

In nineteenth-century China, the most common way for the opium to be taken was by smoking. Here is a picture of opium smoking as given by a medical missionary, Dr W. H. Medhurst, in 1855:

The person who is about to smoke reclines on a couch, resting his head on a pillow; with one hand he holds the pipe, taking the mouth-piece between his lips; with the other hand he takes up a small portion of the extract, and applies it to the little nozzle on the pipe's head, with a pointed steel wire or long needle, at the same time holding the nozzle directly over the flame of a lamp, making a deep inspiration, so that the fumes of the drug pass into the lungs. This is said to be unpleasant to those who first use the drug, but they soon get over it. The fumes being retained for a short time are allowed to pass away by the mouth and nostrils. Another application of the extract is then made as before, which is continued for a longer or shorter time, according to the effect wished to be produced.

And the effect produced by that inhalation, and the holding of the smoke in the lungs, was likely to be the rapid onset of morphine intoxication. Other than by use of a syringe, there is no way of getting morphine more quickly to the brain. But smoking opium is not a very efficient way of using the drug, in that about half the morphine is left behind in the charred residue or 'dross'.

The Chinese had known of the medical use of opium for many centuries, but such use had always been by mouth. The smoking route for opium meant its employment intentionally for pleasure. The custom was brought to China in the early eighteenth century from Formosa, where the Dutch had introduced the habit of smoking tobacco mixed with opium in the seventeenth century. Formosa had in turn learnt the habit from Java. As early as 1729, the Chinese Emperor issued an edict making it illegal to sell the drug or run an opium-smoking house anywhere within his territory.

In England in the late eighteenth and the nineteenth centuries, opium was predominantly taken by mouth as tincture of laudanum, or as various patented liquid preparations, or in pill form. Opium dens located in the East End of London put smoked opium on offer, but on the British scene they were never more than exotica. It is poignant that during this period when Britain was conniving, on a vast scale, with the running of smokable Indian opium into China, the British at home were becoming anxious about their own problem with oral opium. The Pharmacy Act of 1868, coming shortly after the Second Chinese Opium War, represented the first British attempt to regulate domestic opium supply. There were accounts circulating at this time of opium smoking in London's East End. Charles Dickens gave a melodramatic description of an opium den in his unfinished novel *The Mystery of Edwin Drood* (1870), but the smoking of opium was never more than rare in the UK.

The harm done

Among the Chinese who took to the opium habit, not all suffered adverse health and social consequences. But some were brought to ruin. Over many years, successive emperors repeatedly expressed anxiety about the damage being done, both to the people and the state, by the foreign poison stigmatized as 'black mud'.

Medical missionaries claimed that they could recognize an opium smoker by the haggard appearance. This is a picture given in a book by F. S. Turner, Secretary of the Anglo-Oriental Society for Suppression of the Opium Trade, published in 1876 (he quoted a missionary doctor as his source):

Opium smokers are easily recognised by their emaciated, consumptive appearance – stooped gait, raised and bent shoulders, dark yellow-greyish complexion and blue lips, caused by imperfectly arterialised blood, contour of mouth, projecting and pouting, caused by the large opium pipe . . . the small contracted pupil . . . and the dirty forefinger, caused by manipulating the drug over the lamp.

Elements in that description were probably exaggerated but one would be unwise to dismiss as mere propagandist horror this and similar accounts given by contemporary medical observers.

As regards the likelihood of physical harm resulting from opium use, the effects on the lungs of the smoked opium may have been deleterious, although modern evidence on the issue is scant. More probably, most harm would have resulted from nutritional problems due to wages spent on the drug rather than food. The claim that the opium user would, on average, experience a ten- or fifteen-year reduction in life expectancy was unsupported by hard evidence. The Revd A. S. Thelwall, in 1839, stated in his *The Iniquities of the Opium*

Trade with China that in the inveterate user 'the sudden deprivation of the accustomed indulgence produces certain death': opium withdrawal is in fact very rarely fatal and then probably only for the person who is already weakened by malnutrition and concurrent illness.

Claims made about the damage done to the individual's social well-being in terms of financial consequences, the forced involvement in petty crime, the impairment of work capacity and family hardships, do, however, have a considerable ring of authenticity. Here is C. M. Medhurst writing from Shanghai in 1855 and giving a description of such consequences:

Besides the cases of death arising from the excessive use of opium among the higher classes who can afford to gorge themselves with it until they die ... In the case of those who are in middling circumstances, and get inured to the habit, the enervating effects are such that they become after a time unable to attend to their ordinary avocation ... their business fails ... Gradually they part with their little property, furniture, clothes etc., until they come to the level of the labouring poor.

But it was the poorest people whom Medhurst saw as the most vulnerable.

Among the lower classes those who indulge in the use of opium are reduced to abject poverty sooner than the preceding. Having no property, furniture or clothes to dispose of ... as soon as they are unable by begging to obtain the half-burnt opium [pipe scrapings] on which their very life depends, they droop and die by the roadside and are buried at the expense of the charitable.

Many contemporary accounts show that opium's capacity to produce an intense dependence was well understood. Observers acknowledged that tolerance developed and that the dose would in the confirmed user have to be increased. Dr William Lockhart described tolerance in Turner's 1876 text:

When the pipe is first taken during the incipient stage, a few grains are sufficient to produce the full effect. This small quantity requires to be gradually increased to produce a given result; the times of use become more frequent, until the victim is soon compelled to use one drachm or sixty grains, in the course of twenty-four hours. This quantity per day will supply the smoker for some years, but it has at last to be augmented till two, three, four or even five drachms are daily consumed.

Lockhart also described how the opium smoker might in due time find himself using the drug not for the pleasure effect but for relief of withdrawal:

The smoker continues to use his pipe, thus accustomising himself more and more to dependence on his much-loved indulgence. By and by retribution comes: he cannot live comfortably without the stimulant; all the pleasure has gone, but he must obtain relief from the pain of body and dissipation of mind which follow the absence of the drug at any cost.

That description might well do for the plight of any modern-day heroin addict. And Lockhart accurately described the typical physical symptoms of opiate withdrawal.

Even allowing for the hyperbole which at times coloured the accounts given by contemporary observers, one cannot doubt that opium was quite commonly and severely damaging the health and welfare of the Chinese, rich or poor, who used this drug and might become dependent on it. That smoked opium use was not a harmless indulgence must in principle be conceded. But there is then the multiplication question. To assess the likely extensiveness of the damage to the population, one needs to form a view on the frequency with which opium was being used in a deleterious way as opposed to a casual manner.

That was a question to which nineteenth-century analysts, and particularly the anti-opium activists, gave repeated attention. Their approach was to take the total weight of opium exported from India (some may have gone to countries other than China), add something for the likely level of home-grown Chinese opium production, and divide the total presumed consumption by the supposed consumption level of the average confirmed opium user – that, analysts believed, should give the count of established users. Any present-day statistician would be likely to point out the inadequacy of this computational approach, with its assumption that every user is using at about the same level. But by the 1870s, an estimate of 3 million confirmed opium users was being quoted from text to text. China was at that time believed to have a population of about 300 million.

Geographically, the use of opium was unevenly spread. It was more prevalent along the coast than inland, more common in the cities than in the villages, heavier among the labouring poor than among the rich, although the intellectuals and the mandarin class, and even the Palace, had their opium smokers.

Perhaps at this distance it is best to regard nineteenth-century estimates as guesses made in difficult circumstances. They can provide no more than very approximate pointers to the true prevalence of use; they tell less still about the prevalence of opiate dependence at any period or in any particular city. What may, however, confidently be concluded is that the damage done to individuals by opium was in some localities common, obvious and appalling. The fact that such huge quantities of opium were available made that sort of outcome likely. Witnesses may have exaggerated, scares may have been got up, but the consistency of the eyewitness accounts, coupled with the import figures, support the conclusion that the British opium trade did significant harm to China. The problem was not just a fuss got up by missionaries and such-like troublemakers.

The Celestial Emperor protests

The question moves on now from harm done to individuals to the impact of the opium trade on the Chinese state. A remarkable document began to be circulated in 1839, claiming to be a letter written by the Emperor of China to Queen Victoria, whom he believed to be head of a subordinate nation – he as the Celestial Emperor ruled the world. The letter was extensively quoted by the anti-opium lobby, which did not question its authenticity. Here is a flavour of that minatory epistle:

Our Heavenly Court has for its family all that is within the four seas ... But there is a tribe of depraved and barbarous people, who ... manufactured opium for smoking ... daily do its baneful effects more deeply pervade the central source, its rich fruitful and flourishing people ... Hence it is that those who deal in opium, or who inhale its fumes, within this land, are all now to be subjected to severest punishment, and a perpetual interdict is to be placed on the practice so extensively prevailing ... We would now then consent with your honourable sovereignty a means to bring to a perpetual end this opium, so hurtful to mankind . . . As regards what has been already made, we would have your honourable nation issue mandates for the collection thereof, that the whole may be cast into the depths of the sea.

The letter ended with an admonishment which was in accord with the style favoured at that time by Imperial missives:

When your Majesty receives this document, let us have a speedy communication in reply, advising us of the measures you adopt for the entire cutting off of the opium in every seaport. Do not by any means by false embellishments evade or procrastinate. Earnestly reflect hereon. Earnestly observe these things.

Whether or not the document was genuine, its essential message was fully in line with the Chinese government's position on opium as reflected in many other statements and ordinances. Indeed, it might be read as an early warning of the risk of their extreme and condign response to the trade: in 1839, the Chinese seized all the British opium lying in warehouses in Canton, and provoked the Opium War of 1840–42; we will return to this conflict shortly.

If the Chinese regarded opium as a threat to their nation in general terms, they also had some more specific national concerns. Officials both petty and of higher rank were being flagrantly bribed. Opium smugglers trading along the coast would wait for a local official to come aboard and name their price for complicity, before clinching an agreement over a glass or two of brandy. There was concern about the drain on currency with much of the opium being paid for in silver. In the 1870s, it was calculated that the annual expenditure on this drug by the Chinese was running at about £8 million, a vast sum. There was concern about the impact of opium smoking on the efficiency of the imperial army, a worry strangely foreshadowing the much later American anxieties over heroin in Vietnam (see Chapter 10). Theodore Christlieb, a German theologian who wrote on the opium trade, stated that in 1832, 'out of 1000 men sent by the Governor of Canton against the rebels, the commanding officer had to send back as many as 200, whom opium had rendered quite unfit for active service'. Christlieb also asserted that the prevalence of opium smoking was 40 per cent among 'Manchu bannermen' and he reported one informant as telling him that 'Half of the eunuchs at the palace are opium smokers; they have each an opium room among their apartments'. That this Prussian Doctor of Divinity may have been more than a little credulous is, however, indicated by his willingness to quote a figure of 600,000 Chinese deaths annually due to opium.

Controlled use of smoked opium: myth or fact?

A frequent argument to be found in the case put forward by the proponents of the trade in opium was the contention that little harm resulted because in the Chinese population most smokers were able to limit their use to a moderate, social kind of level. An analogy with the drinking of alcohol in Western societies was often deployed: alcohol was not itself intrinsically a problem, they argued, but only its occasional misuse, and in their judgement exactly the same applied to opium in the East.

Here is that argument being expounded by Mr Winchester, formerly the British Consul in Shanghai, in a question-and-answer session conducted within a Parliamentary enquiry of the 1870s:

Mr R. Fowler: 'You have had experience of the effects of opium on the Chinese who take it, I presume?' – 'I have observed the effects. I have never smoked it myself.'

'But it would be your opinion that it has a very prejudicial effect on the health of the people?' – 'On the whole, I should say yes. But there are two conditions of opium-smoking; there is what you might call the moderate opium-smoking, and there is that stage which I would call *opiamismus*, as being equivalent to what may be called *alcoholismus*. I think you must view the two conditions as entirely separate in considering the effect of opium upon individuals.'

'Sir Rutherford Alcock expressed a doubt whether people ever remained moderate smokers. What would be your opinion on that point?' – 'My opinion is rather more in favour of the opinion that they do; and it is derived from my observations upon the general activity and energy of the Chinese, both in the neighbourhood of the ports, and in the Straits, and in California, from their being, on the whole, a useful people, and a laborious, diligent population.'

'Then it is your opinion that a man may continue to use opium as we use wine and the lower classes use beer in this country, without ever being inclined to use it to excess?' – 'Yes, I feel sure of it. I have known men who told me that they had smoked opium all their lives, and who were perfectly competent to do their duties.'

But the Revd Griffith John of the London Missionary Society in Hankow, as quoted by F. S. Turner in 1876, took the exactly opposite view on the controlled use question:

Tobacco, beer and wine may be taken in moderation and are generally believed to be harmless if so used, but even the moderate use of opium is baneful, and what is worse, it is impossible to take it in moderation. The smoker is never satisfied with less than the intoxicating effects of the drug . . . If time and means permit, he lies in a state of ecstatic trance or intoxication from which he desires never to be waked up. Opium-smoking cannot be compared with moderate drinking, but with drunkenness itself. This habit is more insidious in its approach than that of drinking, and holds its victim with a far more tenacious grasp.

Thus we have here two witnesses both with good opportunities to observe whether moderate use of opium was a common occurrence, but coming to very different conclusions. Further observers willing to give strong support to either of these views can easily be identified.

How is the conflict of evidence to be resolved? When opium is cheap and its smoking is epidemic, will most smokers slip quickly into dependence or is smoked opium commonly a personally controllable form of recreational drug use? Our witnesses did not disagree just at the margins, but radically. No one can return to the streets of nineteenth-century Canton with a clipboard and an exact epidemiological enquiry to resolve the dilemma, but there are a number of modern studies of opium use in countries which include Thailand, Laos and India, and which bear on the question. Smoked opium in those countries does not seem to lead inexorably to dependence, but the risk is greater with greater access to the drug and lower prices. Thus, heavier use carries enhanced risk; the percentage of users who develop dependence is not a fixed entity but will vary with the supply situation. It seems possible that at times, in China, opium use in most smokers did not lead to dependence, but it is a reasonable presumption that at least 10–20 per cent of users would have gone in that direction rather quickly.

Trading purple prose

Here is an example of the anti-opium rhetoric in full voice, as found in Thelwall's 1839 text. He was quoting a missionary doctor.

Upstairs I found one woman who had been an opium smoker for three years . . . I saw the woman pressing to her shrivelled sapless breasts, her weeping offspring, whose thin and yellowed face and withered limbs showed how little sustenance was to be obtained there. Its shrill cries and convulsive limbs, seemed now to excite the attention of the mother, who was all the time enjoying her pipe, when to my horror and astonishment, she conveyed from her lips to that of the child's, the fresh-drawn opiate vapour, which the babe inspired. This was repeated twice, when it fell back, a senseless mass into its mother's arms, and allowed her to finish her unholy repast. A poison brought [now] from 'Her Majesty Queen Victoria' whose servants prepare to the taste of that mother, and do their best to minister to a vice which has sunk her immeasurably below the brute!

In an era which had melodrama as a popular art form, it is unsurprising that both those attacking the opium trade, and the defendants, should have reached stratospheric rhetoric. Here is a passage exemplifying the pro-trade, anti-Chinese rhetoric of the time, taken from the *Illustrated London News* of 2 May 1857, when Parliament was debating Britain's involvement in the Second Opium War:

The most intense ignorance, the most insufferable conceit, and a brutal ferocity – compared with which, that of the Kaffirs or any other savages on the face of the earth is dignified and manly – are united in this extraordinary people [the Chinese] to a malignity and cunning for which no parallels can be found in the human race. It is unfortunate that Great Britain should be at war with such a nation; but it must be obvious by this time to the majority of Englishmen that, being at war, we must chastise them effectively; and that nothing but condign punishment will teach them to respect us. To have submitted to the insolence . . . would but have encouraged the bloody minded fanatic to insolence still greater.

This journal also insisted that opium was not all that harmful anyway, and the anti-opium lobby and the parliamentarians who supported their cause were dismissed as 'faddists'.

For the debate around drugs to excite a polarized taking of

positions, with truth the casualty, is perhaps always more the rule than the exception. Those nineteenth-century posturings certainly suggest that drugs invited melodrama long before the modern headlines.

China and the discussion over whether to legalize opium

It was not until 1773 that the East India Company made its first and very limited shipment of opium to China. The scale of activity escalated and by 1793 the Company had established depot ships first at Lark's Bay near Macao, and then further north at Whampao. Chinese anxieties were by then aroused; before long, the amount being shipped was clearly in excess of medical requirements. Reacting to this perceived threat, an imperial edict was issued in 1799, which decreed banishment or strangling as the penalty for the smoking of opium, and rendered all imports of opium illegal. From that moment onwards, stringent prohibition was at least titularly in place.

The East India Company accepted that, in these changed circumstances, for them to continue to use their own ships to send opium into China was too risky an undertaking. A row over opium might lead to retaliatory action by the Chinese and the closing down of all the other profitable trade which the Company was able to conduct through the single entry port provided by Canton. Apart from the permission to trade through Canton, within strict and invidious regulations, China was otherwise closed to foreign merchants. The diplomatic situation was extremely delicate.

However, the East India Company had in reality no intention at all of surrendering its profitable line in drug exporting. They soon had in place a well-contrived scheme to thwart the prohibitory Chinese intentions. The Company encouraged and subsidized the growing of opium in India, held the monopoly, and sold the opium at auction in Bombay and Calcutta to merchants who then smuggled it into China in their own ships, although some ships may have been provided for them by the Company. These merchants took all the risks and used small, high-speed rowing boats, so-called 'fast crabs' or 'scrambling dragons', to get the opium ashore, outpacing most Chinese enforcement attempts. Customs activities were progressively enfee-bled by the bribery of officials. An ineffective salvo might sometimes be fired for reasons of protocol, but not until the smugglers were seen to be on their way home and safely out of range.

In the face of this situation, debate began to develop in the 1830s among senior Chinese government officials as to whether prohibition should be replaced by a system of legalized import and control by taxation. The symmetry which this debate was to find in a later re-incarnation, as Western dilemmas over whether to prohibit or legalize dangerous drugs, is astonishing.

A contemporary source for those arguing for the lifting of pro-hibition is found in a document transmitted to the Emperor in 1835 by Heu Naetse, an official who held the title of 'Vice President of the sacrificial court'. Heu first identified himself in the manner prescribed by court etiquette as 'a servant of no value' and referred to the 'shame and remorse' engendered by his many failures. He presented his missive with 'inexpressible awe and trembling'. He then went on to argue his case with force and clarity:

the more severe the interdicts against it [opium] are made, the more widely do the evils arising there from spread . . . foreign money has been going out of the country while none comes into it . . . How is this occasioned but by the unnoticed oozing out of silver? . . . Moreover, the barbarian ships can repair to any island that may be selected as an entry port . . . it will not be possible to prevent the clandestine introduction of merchandise.

Heu then described the tentacles of corruption which had grown from prohibition.

The laws and enactments are the means which extortionate underlings and worthless vagrants employ to benefit themselves; and the more complete the laws are, the greater and more numerous are the bribes paid to the extortionate underlings, and the more subtle are the schemes of such worthless vagrants . . . All the custom-houses and military posts . . . are bribed . . . All these wide-spread evils have arisen since the interdicts against opium were published.

Having thus stigmatized prohibition as a total and costly failure with no hope of success, Heu proposed that the prohibition should be lifted, import of opium should be allowed as a category of medi-cine, and a tax on sales should be imposed to the Emperor's great profit. He suggested that this would result in the 'barbarians finding that the amount of duties to be paid on it, is less than what is now spent on bribes, [and] will also gladly comply therein'. The drain on silver reserves would be prevented by a regulation which would ensure that the opium was bartered for Chinese merchandise rather than paid for in silver. Legal prohibitions on use would be kept in place for bureaucrats, military officers and 'common soldiers', but with the penalty for all such persons brought down from banishment or death to dismissal from service. For the general population, all penalties on both the purchase and use of opium should, he suggested, be abolished.

Prohibition declared to be a failure, taxation to be substituted for prohibition with the state getting the profit rather than the black-marketeers, opium defined as a medicine, penalty levels reduced: it all has a very modern ring, other than the creative idea of different penalties for different social strata, a suggestion which has not as yet re-emerged.

The arguments that were at the same time being advanced by the prohibition lobby will be equally familiar to anyone who has listened to the present-day debate around drug legalization. An example of the pro-enforcement position is a Memorandum from Counsellor Choo Tsun sent to the Emperor in October 1836. Choo started by arguing that, if the prohibition policy was not working, the answer was to enforce this policy more strictly, not abandon it. He had great confidence that Chinese military might would, if properly deployed, far exceed the strength of the barbarian forces.

If the people aforesaid, will not obey these regulations, and will insist in opposition to the prohibitory enactments, the first step to be taken is, to impress earnestly upon them the plain commands of government, and to display before them alike both the favours and the terrors of the empire.

But if a dose of persuasion did not work, terror would indeed be the order of the day:

If, not withstanding, they dare to continue in violent and outrageous opposition . . . forbearance must then cease, and a thundering fire from our cannon must be opened upon them, to make them quake before the terror of our arms.

Next, Choo set about rubbishing Heu's idea that penalty levels could be differentiated by the social class of the smoker.

The great majority of those who at present smoke are the common people of the villages and hamlets ... if the people be at liberty to smoke opium, how shall the officers, the scholars, and the military be prevented?

The law, Choo continued to argue in a thoroughly modern mode, had a symbolic and educative effect, as well as acting as a deterrent, and by abolishing prohibition on the use of opium, a dangerous public message would be given.

And thus, though the laws be declared by some to be but waste paper, yet these their unseen effects will be of no trifling nature. If, on the other hand, the prohibitions be suddenly repealed, how shall the dull clown and the mean among the people know that the action is still in itself wrong?

Going through these documents in the musty basement of a London library, I must confess to have experienced a shock of déjà vu. Those Chinese mandarins foreshadowed all our modern arguments, point by point.

The clash between those who saw the answer to the opium problem in terms of legalization and others who wanted to see prohibition more rigorously enforced (if need be by the mouth of the cannon) was won by the latter party. The Emperor declared that opium had been a source of unspeakable evil to his country and ruled that prohibition should now be urgently and uncompromisingly enforced. In March 1839, he dispatched to Canton as his plenipotentiary a hard man, Commissioner Lin, who was bent on teaching the barbarians a lesson. He shut up the Europeans in their factories and humiliated the British by forcing them to surrender all the opium from the ships lying in harbour. The total haul was 20,283 chests of opium, to a value of well over a million pounds sterling. This sequestered material was then promptly washed away in the ocean. As a follow-through, the Emperor issued an edict in December 1839 that forbade all trade with Britain and expelled from China all employees of the East India Company.

Wars

The immediate result was the First Chinese Opium War, which in 1840 Gladstone denounced thus in the House of Commons:

> they had a right to drive you from their coasts, on account of your persisting in this infamous and atrocious traffic. A war more unjust in its origin, a war more calculated to cover this country with permanent disgrace, I do not know and have not read of.

The much-boasted prowess of the Chinese military was no match for the British guns. The Emperor was forced by the peace treaty of 1842 (the Treaty of Nanking) to pay compensation for the seized opium, to give Britain Hong Kong, and to open permanently five more ports to Western trade. The British tried to force into the treaty a clause that would have ended prohibition of opium imports, but the Chinese held their ground and for the time being escaped this imposition. Yet the opium smuggling continued, the profits went on substantially supporting the finances of British India, and the British government went on pretending to have no hand in the business. Between 1846 and 1854, the Indian export of opium to China doubled from 21,000 to 43,000 chests.

The next important development came in 1856 when the Chinese seized a merchant ship called the *Arrow*, which was engaged in opium smuggling. The ship claimed to be British (which in strict legal terms was probably not the case). This act was the pretext for the Second Opium War (1856–8). War again provided the British with a splendid victory and the satisfaction of wantonly burning down the Imperial Summer Palace in Peking. The Treaty of Tien-Tsin opened seven more ports, gave missionaries access to the interior of the country, and this time secured what was in Britain's terms the highly desirable outcome of abolishing the prohibition on opium imports. The roar of British cannon had finally triumphed in the prohibition debate.

The treaty allowed for a tax to be put on the imported opium. Contention developed as to the level at which the tax should be fixed: the Chinese protectively named a higher figure but the British insisted on a lower one. A compromise tax level was agreed in 1869, leaning more towards the British choice than the Chinese.

History does not reveal what occurred to corruption when prohibition ended. But as regards trade, the records show conclusively a climb in the imports of Indian opium. As mentioned earlier, imports were at about 43,000 chests annually in 1854, shortly before the Second Opium War started. By 1863, imports probably stood at about 71,000 chests annually, by 1867 they were at 81,000 chests and in 1879 they had climbed to an all-time high of 103,000 chests. The war had done its job. According to Peter Lowes, a Swiss historian of this period, over the years 1875–85 opium was the largest single item in Chinese imports. He suggests that, from the mid-eighties onwards, imports began to decline, at least in part, because by then China had become very active in producing its own opium. Home production at this stage was exceeding imports perhaps three- or fourfold. Some opium was also coming in from other countries, including Turkey and Persia, but India retained about 95 per cent of the import trade.

British imposition of opium on China was one of the prime factors which motivated the early moves towards international collaboration in control of drug trading and the Shanghai Opium Conference in 1909. By 1911, however, the glory days were well and truly over, and imports of Indian opium into China had fallen back to 31,000 chests. An agreement was signed between Britain and China to the effect that imports of Indian opium would thenceforward be reduced by 10 per cent per year. The remnants of the trade dragged on for a few more decades, but it had lost its importance for India.

Chinese opium: what engineered the epidemic

Taking the earlier part of the eighteenth century as the starting point, what appears to have applied in China at that time was a centuries-old and stable use of opium taken orally as medicine, with no one much worried, no great talk of harm, and no need for repressive control measures. In the early years of the nineteenth century, that coexistence was beginning to break down badly, and before long China was in the grip of a smoked-opium epidemic that was to last out the century. A more evident instance of stability in a drug ecology giving way over a short time to chaos is hard to find.

What are the factors that most probably contributed to this break-down? Among them should be included as powerfully determinant the emergence of smoking as the favoured route for opium use. The innovation was as simple as a bamboo tube, but it radically changed the relationship between a population and a drug, with opium still the same drug as previously but with the pipe a new pleasure and a new danger. Opium is not inevitably dependence inducing but by its chemical nature it carries that risk, and the risk will be greatly enhanced by smoking.

Another factor which contributed to the breakdown was opium suddenly becoming much more accessible to the population than ever before. And as is usually the case, the enhanced supply of the drug was not a random happening but something with its own set of causes. The dominant cause was British India's desire for profit, but that specific factor had as its context the wider changes that were going on in relationships between China and the Western nations. What one sees here is a case study showing how drug use can be caught up in economic and power relationships between developing and developed countries. Take alcohol or tobacco in the modern world: they show variations on that theme, even if international trade treaties rather than the cannon now force in the branded products.

If the introduction of opium smoking and the massively increased supply were important conjoint factors in bringing about the break-down in the ecological balance, those factors impacted on a vulner-able population. The bulk of the Chinese people were poor, engaged in labouring work, without access to consumer goods, and with no voice of their own or representation. The fact that Heu could envisage leaving this sector of the population to use opium to their heart's desire, while seeking to prevent use in the superior classes, speaks to the perceived social worth of these labourers. Where there is a large population which is poor and powerless, drug epidemics often seem to take root rather easily. In these circumstances, it is not surprising that opium became established in China despite its titular illegality. There was probably not much real attempt at enforcement of pro-hibition on use.

An invitingly simple interpretation of the story would be to see it as a persuasive case study in the folly of drug prohibition. An alter-native reading could, however, be made with a directly opposite conclusion: when prohibition on imports ended, consumption of the drug greatly increased and the case study becomes one of legalization as folly.

Chinese opium: the ethical questions linger on

There is then one final aspect of this history that is worth some thought. Seen with hindsight and standing back from reflex moral judgement, what are the ethical questions embedded in these events? Can the British actions be stigmatized as 'iniquitous' plain and simple, or can the free-trade ambition be seen as giving legitimacy to the drug trade and in the long run supporting economic development and being for the world's larger good? Should health or the macro-economic imperative be the proper and ultimate determinant of the response to drugs? That question points to the fundamental ideological battle line of the Chinese opium story. And that, with symmetry, is exactly the same moral dilemma that operates in the contemporary scene, as the developed world's multinationals (now armed by the force of tariff agreement rather than sending in their navies) run their branded cigarettes in to poor countries or set up local breweries to manufacture branded beers.

9

Opiates: a Tale of Two Nations

At the beginning of the nineteenth century, opium was ubiquitously available on both sides of the Atlantic and caused not a ripple of worry. In the twentieth century, Britain and America came to experience, with different timings and intensities, the ravages of mass heroin misuse. And heroin is of course a chemical derived from the once innocent opium, a child of lost innocence.

This chapter will trace the parallel US and UK shifts from uncontrolled availability of opium to heroin controlled by criminal sanctions, from opium as cause of no concern to the image of heroin as horror, the journey from total laissez-faire, with children sent to buy the quietening syrup from the grocer's shop, to prisons crowded with heroin addicts, the trail from the workmen taking opium pills on Saturday night to inner city communities devastated by injected heroin.

In Chapter 7, in the introduction to this section's discussion of opiates, I suggested that this class of drugs had much to tell. The two-nation comparison which now follows addresses the book's joint purposes of trying to help the understanding of drugs and their ebb and flow, at the same time throwing light on society's responses to drugs and the impact of control.

The nineteenth century: the opium tide runs high

Between 1830 and 1860, the average inhabitant of the British Isles consumed annually 127 standard therapeutic doses of opium. The nineteenth century, both in the US and the UK, saw opium reach an astonishing high-water mark. Here is Thomas De Quincey, in his

1821 *Confessions of an English Opium Eater*, describing what he saw as the escalating prevalence of the opium habit:

Three respectable London druggists in widely remote quarters of London, from whom I happened lately to be purchasing small quantities of opium, assured me, that the number of *amateur* opium-eaters (as I may term them) was, at this time, immense . . . some years ago, on passing through Manchester, I was informed by several cotton-manufacturers, that their work-people were rapidly getting into the practice of opium-eating; so much so, that on a Saturday after-noon the counters of the druggists were strewed with pills . . . in preparation for the known demand of the evening.

In times of economic recession, the price differential was likely to give opium an advantage over beer as the working man's recreational drug.

The open availability of the drug was also caught fifty years later in an account given in the *Medical Times and Gazette* by an anonymous doctor who visited a Fenland town, Wisbech, in 1871:

Went into a chemist's shop, laid a penny on the counter. The chemist said 'The best?' I nodded. He gave me a pill box and took up the penny, and so the purchase was completed, without my having uttered a syllable. You offer money, and get opium as a matter of course. This may show how familiar the custom is.

As for hard data on British opium-consumption trends over the nineteenth century, these are far from being complete or reliable. An estimate, based on five-year averages, for pounds of opium per thousand population has, however, been given by Professor Virginia Berridge, a historian of the British opium experience. Her graph shows consumption in 1825–30 (close in time to De Quincey's observation point) at about 1 pound weight per thousand persons annually. By 1870–75, and at a time when that doctor was laying his penny down on the Wisbech counter, the consumption index had risen to something over 7 pounds per thousand persons. Five years later, a continuing climb took the graph to the peak of 10 pounds per thousand persons annually, a tenfold increase over a fifty year period. Opium consumption in Britain, though down from its peak, had by 1900 still not faded out.

Regarding the parallel scene in the USA, in the 1860s there was concern that it could be getting out of control; but availability of opium remained free and easy although some state laws were enacted in the 1870s which restricted conditions of sale. Dr Charles Terry and Mildred Pellens, in 1928, gave an account of America's nineteenth-century experience with drugs and quoted Dr Fitzhugh Ludlow (1867) thus:

The habit is gaining fearful ground among our professional men, the operatives in our mills, our weary serving women, our fagged clerks, our former liquor drunkards, our very day laborers, who a generation ago took gin. All our classes from the highest to the lowest are yearly increasing their consumption of their drug.

Opium-containing patent medicines proliferated in America during the nineteenth century, as they did in Britain. Doctors were willing to prescribe opium with little heed for the dangers of dependence.

If the many aspects of the supply side – unrestricted availability of opium over the counter, its widespread presence in patent remedies, its open-handed prescribing by the medical profession – helped swell America's nineteenth-century consumption of the drug, there were also background social forces at work which were likely to contribute to the drug demand. This was, for America, a century of urbanization and industrialization, and of mass immigration. It has also been suggested that the disruptions of the Civil War contributed to an upsurge in opiate use, and morphine addiction was referred to as 'the soldier's disease'.

Two nations part company

In the first quarter of the twentieth century, the US experienced a problem with opiates intensely more worrying than the British situation at that time. The two countries favoured different types and intensities of official response because of the differing scale of their problems. The previous rather parallel tracks, which had run for the best part of the nineteenth century, began to diverge.

Prevalence estimates for the extent of the opiate problem, as it existed in either country over the early decades of the twentieth century, are likely to be trustworthy only at an order of magnitude level. An official estimate put the US prevalence at one million cases in 1918, but that was probably a severe case of talking up. According to Professor David Musto, a leading historian of America's drug problems, the peak US prevalence was reached in 1900 at about 250,000 cases nationally. That had fallen to perhaps 100,000 by 1914, and continued at about this level in the years immediately following World War One. But in 1935, when the British Home Office offered their first national estimate for combined opiate and cocaine addiction, the figure stood at a minuscule 700 cases nationally. With due allowance made for the likely inaccuracies in any of these projections, there can be no reasonable doubt that the US at that point in history was experiencing a vastly bigger drug problem than the UK.

If the available figures are taken at face value, the US had, post-1914, about twenty-five times the rate of addiction of the UK, with due correction made for population size. Beyond the bare and suspect statistics is evidence from actualities on the ground. When, in 1920, New York set up a free Narcotics Clinic, that centre was able to register during a short period a total of 7,500 patients, with the count of registered cases for that one city exceeding the likely UK national total by a factor greater than ten.

The opiates of choice in both countries varied over time and locality. In the Britain of the 1920s, the problem was largely metropolitan, and the opiate used was usually injected morphine, with heroin not much seen. A little opium smoking still continued in the Chinese quarter of London's East End. However, in America heroin soon gained dominance, and by 1924 over 90 per cent of East Coast addicts were heroin users. Not until 1954 did the British authorities think it worthwhile to give a separate entry for heroin in their tabulations, and in that year only a quarter of notified British addicts used heroin as their drug of choice. Very different overall national drug use prevalences thus contained within them very different choices of favoured drug.

In Britain, opiate users were over this period predominantly middle aged; the idea of drugs as the property of a youth culture was far from anyone's thought. Most of the users had been introduced to morphine by a doctor in the course of treatment for a chronic, painful condition. There were health professionals who had come to official notice because they were taking their own drugs. A few denizens of Soho – 'demi-mondiales' in the then current phrase – were using opiates by injection. But the majority of opiate dependents were citizens who had become involved with drugs through medical prescribing – not the deviant or the dispossessed.

In the US, the same kind of people who contributed to the UK addict population were represented, and many US addicts were men and women who would not have stood out as exceptional in any crowd. But in addition, there were reports of morphine misuse among 'skid row bums', and in 1917 there was concern that heroin was becoming a problem among urban youth. Opiates were not linked with any particular American ethnic group, other than for some residual opium smoking among the immigrant Chinese. America, in the opening decades of the twentieth century, had thus begun at least to taste the possibility of a link between heroin use and being young and socially deprived, half a century or more before such a connection was to become prominent in Britain.

Although during and after the 1914–18 war there had been concern about smuggled morphine, the great majority of British opiate addicts were getting their drugs on prescription from doctors. The drug peddler in London was a rarity, the black market thin and there were no foreign fields available illicitly to feed the British drug habit. At that juncture in the American drug history, in addition to medical prescribing, there was a grey market in prescription drugs that were sold on. Poppy growing in north-west Mexico contributed to a more flagrant black-market supply. The role of the 'evil drug peddlers' in spreading the habit may have been exaggerated, but there were at this time people in America selling opiates as street drugs.

Divergent drug problems provoked different styles of reaction

By 1920, with addicts queuing for enrolment at the New York clinic, America and Britain were two countries which, in terms of the nature and intensity of their opiate problems, were poles apart. At this point, the problem in America was a starkly nastier happening than anything that Britain had come near to experiencing.

The crucial differences in the response which then developed as a reaction to these different national situations have been characterized by David Musto as a contrast between the British stance of drug toleration and America's intolerance of its drug problem. That is an insightful encapsulation of the national style and temper of the two different governmental responses. The American prohibitionist attitude to drugs probably, in part, derived from the mental set engendered by the experiment, from 1920 to 1933, with prohibition of alcohol.

The first US attempt at Federal legislation against the opiate problem was an Act of 1909, banning the importation of opium for smoking. With the 1914 Harrison Act, a far more comprehensive piece of anti-drug legislation found its way onto the statute book. This Act was of historic significance. With it the world was being edged towards a new territory of assumptions, and into accepting the proposition that the criminal law was the prime and heroic modern medicine for a national response to drugs.

The Harrison Act was politically subtle. It aimed to constrain the behaviour of individual states and to gain acceptance at state level by dressing itself in the garb of a Federal tax measure: that seemed the best way to win the cooperation of state legislatures ever sensitive to the perceived dangers of overweening and expansionist Federal attempts to grab power. Physicians and pharmacists were required to register with the Inland Revenue for a derisory fee of $1 a year, and a doctor was then allowed to prescribe opiates or cocaine 'in the legitimate practice of his profession'. The Act implied that doctors and pharmacists were liable to prosecution if they prescribed or dispensed to their patients in ways the Treasury did not approve. Smugglers and peddlers were manifestly unlikely to apply for a licence, and so they were instantly criminalized.

Britain introduced emergency drug controls under the wartime Defence of the Realm Act (DORA 40 B), in 1916. Its main focus was on restricting the possession of cocaine to doctors, pharmacists and veterinary surgeons; opiates were not its central concern. As a signatory to the Versailles Peace Treaty of June 1919, the government was required to introduce domestic drug legislation to comply with the treaty's obligations. In 1920, six years after the Harrison Act, the UK brought in the Dangerous Drugs Act (DDA). That step was forced upon the country by the pressure of international obligations. It is doubtful whether, against the background of a relatively small and by no means burgeoning national drug problem, Britain left to its own devices would have reached for the criminal law as a remedy for its slight tally of addicts, with their largely non-deviant profile. The 1920 Act and its subordinate regulations sought to restrict possession of cocaine and opiates to professionals, although within terms similar to the American provisos a doctor would be allowed to prescribe 'as far as may be necessary for the practice of his profession or employment in such capacity'. In 1923 a further Act was passed which provided for heavier penalties for infringements.

In 1924, the US government banned the import and manufacture of heroin and debarred its prescribing totally from medical practice; in 1925, it tried to persuade other countries to support an international ban on the manufacture and distribution of the drug. That move was defeated, and heroin has to this day kept its place in the British pharmacopoeia. Doctors in Britain see heroin as a useful drug in treating, for instance, the pain of advanced cancer, and may prefer it over morphine, which is a drug slightly more prone to cause nausea as a side effect. There is no soundly based scientific case for viewing heroin as having a greater potential for abuse than morphine and to British eyes the Americans have seemed to be more influenced by heroin's image than actualities.

Drug laws differently interpreted

After much legal dispute along the way, the US Supreme Court in 1919 banned doctors from prescribing to addicts for maintenance of their addiction, and from thenceforward American doctors who prescribed opiates to their dependent patients were likely to find themselves prosecuted. Doctors and pharmacists became, for a time, the main targets of the Federal enforcement agency. Before long, the law was also going after the street dealers, and by 1925 the majority of people convicted under the Harrison Act were dealers rather than doctors. The ardour of Federal agents was soon causing prison overcrowding. As a partial solution to the overcrowding problem, two Federal 'Narcotic Farms' were commissioned in 1929, although they did not open until 1935. These were prisons under another name.

The US did, however, in 1919 and for a few subsequent years, experiment with prescribing clinics, which initially had the support of the Federal authorities. They varied in patient numbers but some were large-scale operations. Most of the enrollees were aged under twenty-five, with heroin their drug of choice. The clinic approach was underpinned by the claim that addiction was a disease, and giving heroin to addicts who were resistant to cure was viewed as a legitimate medical response to the disease. The treatment philosophy of the time did not centre on long-term maintenance, but there was an expectation that prescribing would put the black-market dealers out of business. However, no sooner had these clinics opened their doors, than they began to attract criticism. A large part of that assault was politically motivated; giving heroin to addicts looked too much like pandering to vice for some people's moral comfort. Dr S. Dana Hubbard of the New York Department of Health denounced the disease theory in these ringing tones:

There maybe those who say drug addiction is a mysterious disease; that it creates a disease mechanism; that it is not a matter for the authorities . . . Our opinion is that this habit is not a mysterious disease . . . In our opinion, drug addiction is simply a degrading, debasing habit and it is not necessary to consider this indulgence in any other light than an anti-social one.

It was also variously asserted that 'dope peddlers' were enrolling in the clinics and selling on their prescription drugs, that prescribing was usually much too generous, that addicts were still using street drugs while further feeding their appetite with the prescribed heroin, that undesirables were being attracted from far and wide to these centres, and that female addicts were flagrantly soliciting outside the clinics so as to get money to pay for their drugs.

These attacks, although exaggerated and at times vicious, did point to the kind of chaos likely to result from poorly organized and understaffed operations which attempted to maintain large numbers of dependent subjects on injectable heroin. There was little or nothing in place to prevent diversion, and no help given to patients other than the prescribing. In the face of political hostility, and the increasingly negative stance of the Federal authorities, the clinics had by 1925 shut down. Thus ended a bold, humane and muddled therapeutic experiment. For many years to come, application of the criminal law, rather than any sort of medical treatment, was to be America's prime response to its opiate problem.

When the Dangerous Drugs Act came into force in Britain in 1920, the Home Office sought to interpret the Act as a ban on doctors prescribing to addicts – Harrison and the DDA looked as if they were converging on the same track.

If British doctors were to be prosecuted under the DDA, an authoritative statement would be required to guide the courts on what should be deemed unacceptable medical practice. To address this lack, the Home Office asked the Ministry of Health to provide guidelines. To this end, a committee was set up under Ministry of Health auspices, with Sir Humphry Rolleston as chairman. Rolleston was a trusted establishment figure, who had been given a baronetcy as a former President of the Royal College of Physicians. Deliberations moved forward at a leisurely pace and the group met only on Saturday mornings. When, in 1926, their slim report was published, the Home Office found itself hoist by its own petard. Far from the document's being a set of guidelines on how to mount a prosecution case, it accepted that when an opiate addict could not easily be got off drugs, it was medically legitimate to continue with maintenance prescribing.

Sir Humphry and his colleagues were conceptually a million miles from Dr Hubbard. In a key passage they stated:

There was general agreement that in most well-established cases the condition must be regarded as a manifestation of disease and not as a mere form of vicious indulgence. In other words, the drug is taken in such cases not for the purpose of obtaining positive pleasure, but in order to relieve a morbid and overpowering craving.

With their conclusions rooted in an unambiguous acceptance of the contention that addiction was a disease, the Committee stated that maintenance was 'legitimate medical treatment' for patients who were being maintained on a drug because withdrawal could not be achieved.

In the wake of the Rolleston Report, Britain settled down for about forty years to a way of dealing with opiates which came to be known as 'the British System'. Individual private practitioners prescribed drugs to their addict patients without fear of prosecution. There were no special clinics set up; the size of the problem did not call for that kind of initiative. The number of prosecutions was remarkably few, with no contribution to prison overcrowding. In 1926 there were

fifty prosecutions related to opium and forty-five to so-called 'manufactured' drugs, a category which included heroin, morphine and
cocaine. Apart from a transient increase in opium cases during the
Second World War, not until 1964 did the tally for 'manufactured-
drug' convictions reach a total of 101. A little problem was being
managed sensibly and in a relaxed way.

Contrasting enforcement bureaucracies

Because the Harrison Act was promulgated in the guise of a tax
measure, the original location of the Federal enforcement agency was
in the Treasury. Responsibilities lay with a unit that was trying to
enforce the prohibition of alcohol. In 1930, a Federal Bureau of
Narcotics was set up in the Treasury, and it stayed there until 1968
when it was relocated to the Justice Department. What characterized
the Federal narcotic agency throughout its several incarnations was
a commitment to activism. By 1929, it employed 250 agents and
enjoyed a generous budget.

The bureaucracy created in Britain to support the implementa-
tion of the Dangerous Drugs Acts was, in contrast to the American
effort, vestigial, amateurish and passive in its style of operation. The
Home Office Drugs Branch was for many years staffed by only two
inspectors. It was their responsibility to chivvy local police forces to
inspect pharmacy records so as to identify any excessive prescribing.
Chief constables tended to be resistant, viewing these demands as
distracting officers from more proper duties. The senior Home Office
official responsible for overseeing Britain's drug policies was also
charged with responsibility for the protection of wild birds.

The activism of the intolerant American agencies gave a basis for
an early version of a war on drugs, long before that phrase was ever
publicly uttered. The corresponding British approach was supported
by a tolerant broom-cupboard kind of operation.

Opiate slang

Insight into the degree to which a drug has found its place in popular culture can be found in the vocabulary of drug slang. In Britain, 'dope' had become a generic term for illicit drugs by the 1920s and 'Dope fiend' had also arrived. But there was at that time no great blossoming of drug slang.

In contrast, American drug slang was developing at a pace in the 1920s, with some terms originating even earlier. According to Richard Lingeman's 1969 *Drugs from A to Z: a Dictionary*, 'Junk' was being used in the US as a synonym for heroin in the early 1900s; but 'Junky' was hardly heard at all in the UK until the 1960s. 'Kick the habit' and 'Cold turkey' were other early American inventions that did not enter British street jargon until much later.

A glossary of US drug slang appeared as an appendix to Anslinger and Tompkins's 1953 *The Traffic in Narcotics*. Here are some examples:

Banger A hypodermic needle; an addict who takes drugs by injection.
Bust the main line To take drugs intravenously.
Cook An attendant in an opium den.
Courage pills Heroin in tablet form.
Dream stick An opium pipe.
Dry grog Drugs.
G.O.M. God's Own Medicine, morphine.
Gong kicker An opium addict.
H, Harry, Hero, Horse, Noise, Number 8, Scag Synonyms for heroin.
Lean against the engine To smoke opium.
Miss Emma Morphine.
Mr Fish An addict who gave himself up to the law in order to break the habit.
Right croaker A doctor who sold narcotic drugs illegally.
Snow flower A girl addicted to morphine.
Narcotic bull, Uncle, Whiskers A Federal agent.
Wing-ding A feigned fit or spasm thrown by an addict in an attempt to obtain drugs.

On the evidence of that compilation, words about opium and opiates had gained diverse currency in the US by the 1950s, beyond anything seen or heard in the UK.

Divergent tracks – carts and horses

The basic facts are plain enough. America and Britain started the nineteenth century with the same type of easy, national coexistence with opium. But by the start of the twentieth century, America had outpaced Britain in the development of what was to become the all too familiar face of a modern opiate ecology. Two countries starting out from more or less the same base had moved or drifted into very different types and intensities of opiate experience.

To read this history as showing the American authorities getting things wrong and exacerbating their drug problem, while the clever maintenance-oriented British got things right and contained their problem, is to put the respective national horses before their national carts. The temper of the reactions was driven by the dimensions of the problems. Amazingly, that fact has been ignored by American and British commentators, who have seen in Rolleston the universally transferable golden key to rational, benign and effective heroin control.

Post World War Two: heroin goes badly out of control

After the Second World War, the American heroin situation went out of control at least ten years ahead of Britain's, a reflection in part of the greater American access at that time to illicit supply. The Mafia had become the suppliers. The Americans at first tended to react to this new threat with responses which built on the already established penal mode, while the British, when their crisis came, stuck to their own style and extended the prescribing of heroin.

The American heroin disaster
Disaster is not too extreme a word. The first hint that the relatively stable pattern of heroin use that had endured since the 1920s was

beginning to crack emerged towards the end of the 1940s. But it was in the early 1960s that the American problem really took off. Data culled from a variety of sources suggests that America had about 50,000 heroin addicts in 1960, and by 1967 over twice that number. In the 1970s, the estimate rose to 500,000, with the numbers then flattening out around this half million mark. From the 1980s onwards, cocaine and then crack cocaine mixed with the heroin picture, and eclipsed heroin as a cause for national anxiety. Some authorities now put the prevalence of heroin dependence at about one million, but none of these data should be taken as better than an approximation. They do not allow distinction between the number of people who are drug dependent and those who are using casually.

Within the escalating all-over prevalence lay the fact that heroin, from the 1960s onwards, became increasingly associated with ethnic-minority status and urban poverty. Fuelled by increased availability, the drug rooted itself, track by city track, in social deprivation. But that could not have happened without the ready availability of the drug: the major cause of America's post World War Two heroin epidemic was the flooding of the country, with an intensity never previously seen, with cheap black-market heroin.

Property crime on a scale never seen before became an integral part of the American heroin epidemic. The criminal justice system was clogged with drug offenders and the prisons overflowed with drug addicts. Huge resources were directed at blocking supply.

Here is Richard Nixon, speaking in 1973, when he was promoting a 'get tough' policy on heroin.

I am confident that the vast majority of Americans will support immediate passage of the Heroin Trafficking legislation I will propose to the Congress next week . . . It will require a minimum sentence of 5 years in prison for anyone convicted of selling heroin . . . For offenders with a prior conviction for a drug felony . . . it will require life imprisonment without parole.

It was as if the American government had become addicted to escalating punishment, as a drug to ease the social pain engendered by the drug problem. When one dose of punishment failed to relieve that pain, tolerance set in and the dose of punishment was increased; more people were put in prison and for longer. It is difficult to determine objectively and reliably whether draconian punishment achieved its intended effects, against background fluctuations in many other factors. Most analysts would, however, probably agree that upping the penalty levels made little difference to the dynamics of black-market operations. If anyone at any level of the supply chain was taken out of circulation, there would usually be someone to take their place, whether godfather or foot soldier. And even if the harsher laws succeeded a little in curbing supply, they could have no impact on demand.

Britain's slower slide into a heroin disaster

The Home Office, from the 1920s onwards, maintained an Index as a register of patients known to be dependent on any controlled drugs. The annual published tables provided a useful indication of trends in prevalence, although they underestimated the true figures (in 1997 the British government, in an economizing fit, abolished this imperfect but useful head-counting device). The number of addicts known to the Index in 1955 stood at 335, a laughable tally compared to the contemporary American count, and only about half the British total for 1935. In 1955 only 57 heroin addicts were on the Index.

Come the early 1960s, the annual totals were moving a little upwards, and by the end of that decade the situation had greatly deteriorated. During 1970 a total of 2,657 addicts (nearly all of them opiate addicts and most of them on heroin) became known to the Home Office. The 1970 estimate was thus swollen to more than forty times that of fifteen years previously. It was the exponential worsening, rather than the absolute numbers reached, that caused alarm.

The epidemic was fed, not by illicit imports, but by the spill from scandalously lax prescribing by a small number of London-based medical practitioners. The Rolleston system had seemingly collapsed while the broom cupboard drugs-control apparatus stood impotently by. One developing element of sameness with the US was, however, beginning to be seen, and the new heroin users no longer conformed to the profile of the Rolleston era addicts. They were younger and they were into the buying and selling of heroin. An injecting subculture was now to be found in London and in a few other locations, and addicts were to be heard ostentatiously referring to themselves as 'junkies'.

The lavishness of the wilder kind of prescribing that was going on at that time was exemplified by the behaviour of a doctor who was giving a patient repeat prescriptions for 1,200mg of heroin each day, and was making a charge for this service although the addict was supposedly an NHS patient who should have got his treatment free. The doctor was willing to let the patient write out a self-determined dose level and then he obligingly provided a signature. Although the Home Office inspectorate knew of this practitioner's behaviour, he was never prosecuted. That was Rolleston betrayed.

As for the British response to this deteriorating situation, another baronet from the medical establishment, Sir Russell Brain, was asked by the government to chair a committee. In 1961, he reported that there was little to be worried about, and no need for new policies. These findings were so at variance with the facts, and so extreme in their complacency, as to startle informed observers. With the situation continuing to deteriorate by the minute, the committee was reconvened and in 1965 produced a less sanguine report. The basic Rolleston principle was maintained that a doctor, acting in good faith, should be allowed to prescribe addictive drugs to an addict patient. But regulations were recommended, and shortly introduced, that restricted prescribing of heroin and cocaine for treatment of dependence to doctors specially licensed by the Home Office and practising from agreed premises. In 1967, NHS drug clinics were set up which mostly prescribed heroin and cocaine quite generously, and with some continuing diversion to the streets. The American prescribing clinics were thus reborn in Britain with exactly the same kind of good intention, with many of the same problems, a smaller scale of operation, and entire amnesia for the earlier experiment.

Over the next ten years or so, the clinics gave up prescribing cocaine, the prescribing of injectable heroin became much less common, and British clinics went in the American direction of relying on oral methadone as preferred heroin substitute. During the 1970s, notifications continued each year to increase, but the growth was no longer so steep or alarming. Lax prescribing and changed times had blown the British system off course, but with a bit of amendment it looked as if the situation had been brought back under control.

Tracks converged

In the present day, it is difficult to talk about 'heroin addicts' as a stand-alone category. Many heroin users will at the same time be taking other drugs, or over the longer term switching between drugs. Heroin, methadone, cocaine, amphetamine, benzodiazepines, cannabis, Ecstasy: they all mix in together, with cigarettes and alcohol pervasive elements in the mix. With definitions inevitably hazy, the UK currently has at least 200,000 people suffering from a serious problem with illicit drugs; heroin is often but not always the central thread in their drug use. Some authorities would put that estimate at least twice as high, but the more conservative figure accords with the research. America, with four times the population of Britain, has perhaps 500,000–750,000 people in the same kind of category, and with much shifting between heroin and cocaine. No researcher would want to swear on the exact numbers, but it is probably fair to conclude that, pro rata, the US does not at present have a greater drug problem than the UK. That convergence is radically at variance with any comparisons that could have been made over a period rather longer than the previous hundred years. The reason for the coming together is that, in the 1980s, the seemingly re-established stability of the British heroin scene was blown apart by the emergence of a new heroin epidemic. The number of addicts known to the Home Office (mostly heroin addicts), stood at 2,400 in 1979, was at about 18,000 in 1990, and had reached almost 45,000 by 1996. Remember that 700 figure for 1935, and talk of catastrophe seems unexaggerated.

Some voices are to be heard asserting that the prime reason for Britain, at that point, succumbing to heroin was the country's failure to stay with the principles of Rolleston. These people would have liked to see the clinics continue with generous prescribing of injectable heroin, so as supposedly to keep out the black market. The breakdown was rooted in a failure to keep faith with Rolleston, they would argue. The more probable explanation is that the situation was destabilized for exactly the same reason as had earlier been seen in America: the illicit supply had, in Britain too, now been greatly increased, with cheap heroin washing along the streets. The epidemic was once more supply led, and there was an expandable demand picking up that supply.

Within the convergence of numbers lies evidence of further strands in the national heroin experience coming together. For instance, with the arrival of the UK heroin epidemic of the 1980s, the drug began to concentrate in areas of poverty, and mimic the American experience. The highly important question of why drug use should at times show a linkage with social deprivation is a topic to which I will return in Chapter 20.

From the 1960s onwards, heroin use had made some contribution to acquisitive crime in the UK, but as use escalated and links with poverty and unemployment were made, the need for addicts to pay for their habits by stealing and mugging meant that addiction was making an increasing contribution to crime. At current costs, a British heroin addict, on average, will need £16,000 per year to pay for the habit. Crime in Britain is to a considerable extent driven by the drug epidemic. Curbing medical over-prescribing could in the late 1970s no longer be a sufficient remedy in the face of the heavily criminalized import and distribution system.

If the British had earlier been able to congratulate themselves on a response to drugs, which was benignly medical in its complexion as opposed to the American penal emphasis, that divergence was to become doubly eroded. Britain went more penal and America went more medical. In the 1970s, the Nixon administration, while making a show of being tough on drugs, simultaneously very considerably expanded the availability of treatment for heroin users. The history of that era has been told by Michael Massing in his 1998 *The Fix*. In 1971, Nixon appointed Dr Jerome Jaffe, a researcher and clinician in the drugs field, as America's first 'Drug Czar'. Jaffe increased the number of heroin addicts in federally funded treatment from about 20,000 in late 1971 to 60,000 a year later. From then on, it would have taken a very complacent British commentator to dare argue that Britain was ahead of America in the treatment game. It was the availability of oral methadone which allowed America to overcome its distaste for drug clinics, and move so radically towards the expansion of treatment services. Britain followed later and more slowly in its expansion of methadone treatment. Methadone is a synthetic opiate which, when prescribed in a single daily dose to a heroin-dependent subject, will relieve drug hunger, help the patient to stay away from injected heroin and allow that person to lead a much more stable life.

Opiate misuse and AIDS

The AIDS epidemic reached the US in the late 1970s, shortly before it took root in the UK. The fact that injected drug use could lead to transmission of the virus between addicts soon became apparent, and at the same time there was a worry that sexual transmission would take the infection from the addicts and out into the wider population. Both the US and the UK found themselves abruptly facing a new and worrying aspect of the heroin problem that stimulated attempts to get more patients into treatment.

The British dealt with the AIDS emergency by greatly expanding community projects which provided addicts with clean needles and syringes, gave out ampoules of sterile water, and taught safe injection practices. Teaching safe sex and providing condoms was also part of the approach. The American authorities have generally seen this harm minimization as looking too like connivance and a compact with the heroin devil.

Some divergence continues

It would be wrong to assume that Britain and America have after all these years ended up following identical opiate tracks.

British doctors continue to enjoy a greater degree of clinical discretion in their prescribing decisions for their heroin-dependent patients than is allowed in America. British doctors who hold a Home Office licence may, for instance, still prescribe injectable heroin to addicts if they believe this to be appropriate. Some doctors will prescribe injectable methadone or quantities of oral methadone in a way which would not be sanctioned in America. British GPs are more involved in treating heroin patients than their American counterparts. To this extent, the spirit of Rolleston lives on.

Divergence and convergence: what the tracks seem to tell

Back in the nineteenth century, every British or American citizen had unfettered access to opium, and every doctor totally unrestricted prescribing rights. That is the sameness from which the story told in this chapter starts out. What the evidence then shows is that the tracks for a time ran rather parallel, went on to diverge or even diverge dramatically, and then came again to run remarkably close. We are catching in that one summary word 'track' the number of users, the shifts in the demographics, the change in routes of use, and the sources of opiate supply. Add to that the trajectory of evolving, multiple policy responses, and 'track' becomes a summary word with a lot packed within it.

Imagine the lines drawn on a flip chart, one with the Stars and Stripes as an identifier, the other with a Union Jack. For two hundred years, those lines go this way and that, and seem even to wave goodbye to each other, but here they are today, astonishingly arrived at near points on the chart. With similarity now the dominant characteristic of the comparison, a pessimist might conclude that the shared point reached is the shared national defeat caused by the heroin problem. After all those years of legislation, the committee reports, speeches made, clinics opened and shut and opened again, rhetoric sounded, supposed variations and contradictions in national approaches, the two countries have remarkably similar, and equally distressing, levels of heroin dependence.

The optimist might, however, want to suggest that not everything along either track has been defeat. The record contains within it some stretches where the opiate problem was, for a period of years, more or less stabilized. It could also be argued that even if either country's opiate policies are far from having triumphed, they may have helped stop even worse developments. The sameness may be a mix of some failure, some success. But with the flagged lines there is still no sign at all of a happy ending for this tale and that is the most certain conclusion.

10

The Vietnam War

In April 1971, two US Congressmen, Robert Steele and Morgan Murphy, returned to Washington from a fact-finding visit to American forces in Vietnam. They alleged that 10–15 per cent of US personnel stationed in that region had become addicted to heroin. This was alarming news for a nation whose level of domestic drug use was causing national concern. There were at the time about 500,000 American servicemen in the war zone, with a thousand of them returning to the USA for demobilization every day. The fear was that tens of thousands of opiate-addicted ex-servicemen, hungry for heroin and with a taste for hand-guns, would be loosed by instalment across the length and breadth of America. An already unpopular and divisive conflict would be blamed for the mass introduction of heroin to a generation of young men. There was the potential here for a political debacle.

Heroin did not become widely available in Vietnam until 1969, but a couple of years later, in some fighting units, up to 25 per cent of private soldiers were using the drug. This episode can throw light on the possible causes of such extreme breakdown. Vietnam makes vividly real the idea of stability or instability in drug-use levels as an outcome determined by the play of the environmental influences. We have here a case study on what makes a drug epidemic flare. But it is also important that the follow-up of those soldiers on their return home defied the gloomy expectations.

The war in Vietnam: how it happened

Vietnam was for many centuries under Chinese rule. In the 1860s, with the European powers vying to expand their empires, it became as French Indo-China a colony of France. During the Second World War, the Japanese occupied the country. Afterwards, the previous French colonial regime was reinstated, and a communist-inspired guerrilla movement, under the leadership of Ho Chi Minh, sought to oust the French. The conflict lasted from 1946 to 1954, and ended with the defeat of the French at Dien Bien Phu. An international settlement brokered in Geneva then sought to divide the country into a communist North, and a supposedly democratic South Vietnam. The South was in fact a dictatorship which never held the promised free elections. Ho Chi Minh was unwilling to accept the partition, and his ambition was to establish a united Vietnam under communist hegemony. From the early 1960s onwards, the US sought to contain and counter that ambition by providing aid and large numbers of 'military advisers' in support of the South Vietnamese. In 1964, the US had escalated into aerial bombing of the North, and by 1968 an American ground force was committed in support of what was virtually a puppet state. The dates for the start and end of the Vietnam War are somewhat arbitrary but 1968–73 were the years of the major, open, US involvement.

After the Americans pulled out, the South Vietnamese government was left to fend for itself and faced imminent defeat. The capital of South Vietnam, Saigon, fell to the insurgents in 1975, with its name changed triumphally to Ho Chi Minh City. Underlying this conflict was a total contradiction between the two sides on the supposed justification for a war that caused appalling human loss. To the communists, the conflict was one of national liberation with the Americans another foreign power in line with the Chinese, Japanese and French. For America this was a war to defend democracy against communism, and to stop the dominoes falling across South-East Asia.

General Westmoreland, commander of the US ground forces in Vietnam, declared in his memoirs that 'Indeed, history may judge that American aid to Vietnam constituted one of man's more noble crusades'. But in resounding contrast, Martin Luther King called the Vietnam War 'a blasphemy against all America stands for'.

What it was like to be an American soldier in Vietnam

The dominant memory of the conflict, as reported by the Americans who returned home, was an image of terror: the dense and unfamiliar jungle and its steaming heat, booby traps and ambushes, comrades mutilated or blown to bits, an enemy who seemed able to kill at whim and move back among the trees, people in the city who smiled at you and might later be your assassins. America was to lose over 50,000 men killed in the war, with a larger toll of seriously wounded.

By 1971, and when those two Congressmen visited Vietnam, the 'noble crusade' had descended into nightmare. There was no prospect of winning the war, the American army was clearly on its way out, but still the fighting was going on, with escalating casualties. The state of the military's morale was shown by a desertion rate three times higher than anything experienced by American forces in the Korean War. Soldiers would, on occasion, try to escape the dangers of combat by killing their own officers with hand grenades, a practice that came to be known as 'fragging'. Confidence in the justice of the cause for which these young Americans were being invited to die had been greatly undermined. Far from the army's having the undivided support of people back home, although there had been earlier protests against the war, America was now affected by widespread anti-war sentiment, riots were taking place as demonstrators clashed with the police, and veterans were making their feelings felt by throwing their medals onto the White House lawns as they marched by in protest.

In 1971, Americans serving in different units and in combatant or non-combatant roles could have felt differently about what it was like to be in Vietnam. Any overall characterization of their experiences would therefore be simplistic, but there can be no doubt that by then morale had become very widely impaired. The fact of the army's demoralization is vital to understanding the extent and nature of the drug problem that occurred among the US forces. The Vietnam drug epidemic cannot be comprehended without an awareness of what it felt like to be an American caught up in that war.

The dimensions of the drug problem

Steele and Murphy had suggested a 10–15 per cent level of heroin use among the US forces, but later research showed that estimate to have been much below the true figure. To the great benefit of later understanding of this episode, in 1971 the US government funded, with remarkable promptness, a large-scale research study in which a representative sample of US soldiers who had been discharged in September 1971 were interviewed eight to twelve months after their demobilization and asked about their drug use in Vietnam. Medical records were checked and confirmatory urine tests performed, and the accuracy of the findings from this study were of a high order. Dr Jerome Jaffe, who has already featured in Chapter 9 as America's first Drug Czar, was the director of President Nixon's Special Action Office on Drug Abuse Prevention, and commissioned the project. An American epidemiologist, Dr Lee Robins, headed the research team. Getting that research quickly underway, and achieving the first report in 1973, was a considerable accomplishment. And it was research driven by national anxiety.

The study focused only on the army and the navy, with the air force excluded because of their relatively slight use of heroin. Furthermore, preliminary data had shown that in the army there was little drug use among officers, so research sampling was limited to non-commissioned personnel. A matched control group drawn from the US general population was interviewed.

The findings on levels of drug taking among soldiers, during what was usually a twelve-month stint of service in Vietnam, were in summary as follows. Heroin had been tried by 34 per cent and opium by 38 per cent; and 45 per cent had tried one or both of these drugs. The route of use for heroin and opium was in the great majority of instances by smoking roll-up cigarettes; only about 10 per cent had injected an opiate. Much of the opiate use was casual or at a low level, and had not progressed to dependence. However, about 20 per cent of these subjects said that they had been addicted to opiates in Vietnam, and most of these had suffered from opiate withdrawal symptoms. Almost 80 per cent had used cannabis, and illicit use levels both for amphetamine and barbiturates ran at a little over 20 per cent. Alcohol had been used by 90 per cent. The levels of illicit drug use reported by these servicemen were considerably in excess of those experienced by the control group.

These findings were, in sum, and by any reckoning, extraordinary. Lee Robins's research had caught a swirling drug epidemic in its lens.

Looking for explanations

No single factor was responsible for the astonishing levels of drug use among the soldiers of that army. Several different factors came together and interacted, so as to tip the ecology out of control.

- *Availability and cost* Drugs were extraordinarily available in Vietnam from 1969 onwards. Cheap, 95 per cent pure heroin was to be had at such low cost that a dependent user would only need $6 per day to support a habit; opium was also remarkably cheap. Myra MacPherson, in a book on Vietnam written in 1984, reported a GI whom she interviewed as saying, 'Heroin was plentiful, falling out of trees'. Where the opiates were coming from seems never to have been definitively determined, but Laos and Cambodia were probably the major sources. There were rumours of a dark and unverifiable sort that the CIA had stimulated poppy cultivation in those countries. Allegations were made that US airmen had a hand in the smuggling, but that may well have been no more than conspiracy theory.
- *Smoking* The second thing that contributed to the rapid spread of opiate use among soldiers was perhaps the fact that the drugs were available in smokable form. A GI did not have to make a big break and take up injecting when he started to use opiates: for the most part, opiate smoking, whether of opium or heroin, built on the previous experience with tobacco and cannabis. An opium-loaded cigarette was disarmingly known as an OJ (opium joint). Vietnam was never predominantly a needle culture.
- *Personal vulnerability* Lee Robins's research showed that pre-service drug use or delinquency were strong predictors of Vietnam drug use, with, for instance, only 27 per cent of men with no earlier history of drug use but 100 per cent of those who had

earlier used four or more drugs going on to opiate use in Vietnam. Similarly, 20 per cent of subjects scoring zero or low on a rating of pre-service delinquency, went on to use opiates in Vietnam, while among those scoring high on the delinquency scale the corresponding figure for opiate experience was over 70 per cent. One clear message from the research was, thus, that personal vulnerability is a factor that can significantly contribute to the likelihood of an individual misusing a drug. It was more common for the better educated to avoid call-up than it was for the less privileged sectors of the home population. But Robins's research did not suggest that the biasing of recruitment processes towards a vulnerable population segment was a substantial explanation for the high level of drug use in Vietnam.

- *Peer-group influences* Peer influences may have operated differently at different stages in the development of the Vietnam epidemic. When heroin first became available, there was no established peer group of opiate users for the novice to join, although the use of cannabis was already a behaviour approved by the majority of GIs. However, before long opiate use was so widespread as hardly to count as deviant, and there were peers to encourage and support such use. The use of drugs had become common among these young men and provided a shared social activity beyond anything likely to have been experienced in civilian life.

- *The adverse environment* Heroin use was as common among soldiers who operated in support roles behind the lines as in combat units. But in a guerrilla war safety is never guaranteed, even at the base camp, and demoralization in Vietnam did not stop at the front line. As already suggested, different soldiers were likely to have felt the personal impact of this war very differently, but many of them turned to opiates for psychological solace. Contemporary reports frequently make that causal connection. As MacPherson's witness, quoted earlier, put it, 'You see someone get blown away and, hey, you smoke some OJs and, hey, man, that's cool.' Heroin and opium are drugs well able to relieve the mixture of boredom, frustration and terror that coloured the Vietnam War.

- *Breakdown in deterrence* Another reason why use of heroin, opium and other drugs reached such high levels may have been that the authorities had become slack in their enforcement of military law against drug use. A rigorous enforcement would have wrought havoc with the army's manpower. And there was much else at the time to occupy the military mind. General Westmoreland was quaintly showing a deep personal concern for enforcement of regulations on length of haircuts: the general regarded long hair as a dire threat to good order and military discipline. He was to write later in his memoirs: 'One of my toughest decisions as Chief of Staff was on haircut policy . . . the anguish I underwent on this decision was almost farcical.'

- *Putting a lot of young men together* In this trawl for factors, each with some capacity to explain the Vietnam drug epidemic, there is one aspect of the story that is so obvious as to be rather easily overlooked. The war removed young men from the restraints of home and put them to live together in a predominantly male society. The average age on arrival in Vietnam was nineteen years. Whatever the country or study sample, it is an almost universal finding that young males are the population segment most prone to drug experimentation. Thus, when large numbers of young American men were put together in an environment in which heroin was easily available, a situation ripe for a heroin epidemic had been created. Add the mix of factors identified above and it is none too surprising that the epidemic flared.

No opiates or no ticket home

In May 1971, Dr Jerome Jaffe was asked to advise on how the American government should respond to the report by Congressmen Steele and Murphy on the alleged 10–15 per cent prevalence of heroin use among the US military in Vietnam. Jaffe's analysis of the Vietnam problem was that of a behavioural scientist. He argued that if all GIs were got off opiates before they embarked for home, home would be a place which for most of them had no association with drugs, and an environment which would therefore not trigger a craving for drugs. Deriving from that logic, a scheme was put in place to ensure that no one got on to the plane home until they were opiate-free, with detoxification accomplished in Vietnam and not after their return to America.

In terms of the behavioural paradigm, Vietnam might be loaded with environmental cues related to opiate taking or opiate withdrawal, but America was to be kept, as far as possible, an opiate-cue-free zone. Jaffe daringly predicted that if this scheme was put into operation, the US, across its breadth and length, would be welcoming home tens of thousands of ex-heroin addicts, rather than the country being flooded with drug-hungry and gun-happy addicts of the nightmare imaginings.

With considerable deftness, Jaffe begged and borrowed the then only existing early model of a urine drug-testing machine (Free Radical Assay Testing or FRAT machine), and had it flown to Vietnam. On 17 June 1971, a mass urine-testing scheme was in place. Every returning soldier of non-commissioned rank had, from that day forward, to submit to urine testing. If they tested positive, no disciplinary action was taken against them, but instead of getting on the plane, they would be directed to a detoxification centre to spend the next two weeks coming off opiates. Only with detoxification completed and a clear urine test reported, was the delayed flight home available. The moment of moving off down the runway was one for which every soldier keenly longed; having to stay for an extra two weeks in Vietnam would have been a keenly unwanted experience. Unsurprisingly, many drug-using soldiers got themselves free from opiates by their own efforts before facing a urine test. At the peak, only about 11 per cent of tested soldiers gave a positive test (as compared to Robins's 45 per cent estimate for opiate usage), and among these were probably a core of heavily dependent GIs who could not detoxify without professional help.

When the bloody war was over

The data gathered by Lee Robins and her colleagues, through interviews conducted at an early point after these soldiers returned home, was supplemented by repeat interviews conducted at points up to three years after demobilization. The researchers found that one year after return from Vietnam, 50 per cent of previously opiate-dependent veterans had at some time experimented with heroin back home. Some had never injected but stayed with smoked heroin, and many used heroin only occasionally. Only 6 per cent of men who had been dependent on opiates while in Vietnam became re-addicted to heroin during their first twelve months back in America. So although experimentation was common, re-addiction was uncommon. Those who became hooked on heroin after returning home were often also using barbiturates, amphetamines and cannabis, and heavy drinking was common among them.

It was that low 6 per cent relapse figure which surprised the drug experts. Researchers in the US had at that time become used to the idea that heroin dependence had an inevitably high rate of relapse. The usual expectation was that about two thirds of hospital treated heroin addicts would relapse within twelve months of discharge.

The explanation which Lee Robins gave for so small a proportion of previously dependent opiate users having become caught up again in dependence a year after their return to the US was ingenious. She argued that this finding was not at all out of step with what was usually likely to happen with heroin users. In her view, the explanation for the results going against predictions was that the commonly held gloomy expectation was based on an erroneous interpretation of the research base. She suggested that investigators had reached an exaggeratedly negative view of what was likely to happen to dependent heroin users over time, because their follow-up studies had focused on drug takers who had been treated in hospital. That kind of focus biased the picture, she argued, because people who go into hospital with a drug problem are an especially handicapped, extreme, and generally rather odd, sub-group. All the people who never went near a hospital, and who kicked the habit of their own volition, were left out of the reckoning when the conventional wisdom was being promulgated. In support of this position, she showed that Vietnam veterans who on return home had received hospital treatment for their dependence had indeed as poor an outcome as the conventionally gloomy prognostications predicted.

In the light of later research, it seems fair to conclude that those Vietnam veterans bucked the tide, but not extremely so. Here are some of the elements which may have contributed to the relatively good outcome. Heroin in Vietnam was cheap, widely available and of high quality, while in most parts of the US the drug was expensive, would have to be looked for rather than its falling from trees, and was at the time probably only about 10–20 per cent pure. It is doubtful whether most American heroin available in the 1970s would have been smokable. In Vietnam heroin use enjoyed wide peer-group support and was a social behaviour, but at home it was deviant. In Vietnam, civilian careers were on hold, while coming home meant careers and personal lives restarted. The explanation for the post-Vietnam recovery rate was in essence the obverse of the explanation for the Vietnam use rate.

A tale of two armies

Myra MacPherson, in her powerful book from which I have already quoted, reports one of the US veterans whom she interviewed as saying: 'Where did I get hooked? Nam. Why Nam? I'll give you one word: "despair" . . . I got hooked for jollies, to ward off the despair.' There is a void in the Western literature on what the parallel experience felt like for the Vietnamese who fought on the other side in that conflict. What happened to their drug use seems never to have excited much Western curiosity. Recently, by happy chance, I had contact with a Vietnamese researcher. A friendly exchange of letters followed and he kindly made some enquiries on my behalf. As far as he could ascertain, opiate use never became a significant problem among the Vietcong. That is only preliminary information and there is no proof.

But if the full evidence does in due course emerge, there will be a fascinating opportunity to compare the drug use of the two opposing armies, and the reasons why.

11

Opiates: the Wide Experience

The four preceding chapters have opened windows on to many aspects of the world's encounter with opiates. The story has been told all the way from poppies found in a stone-age burial site to contemporary epidemics of injected heroin. China has been visited by way of Bengal, and the way in which imperialism pushed opium into China has been recounted. British and US experiences have been compared along two hundred years of opiate tracks. Paradoxically, Vietnam gives a picture of a demoralized latter-day imperial army cut up by an opiate epidemic. Also seen across time and space have been different kinds of governmental reaction to opiates, with opium for a time ordinary and tolerated in the West, but with the Chinese so worried by opium smoking as to attempt draconian repression. There then comes injected opiate use, variously responded to as a criminal act or as illness to be met by the prescription of opiates.

These windows between them offer a broad view on to societies' experiences with a class of pharmaceuticals which contain good medicines; chemicals to be got into the body by multiple routes; drugs capable of inducing dependence and causing wreckage and death; substances which easily give rise to flaring epidemics and can become deeply rooted in the afflicted population, and which can provoke very varied responses. However, the view is of only a tiny section of the world's total encounter with opiates. There are few countries which have not got their own opiate story to tell.

In this chapter, no attempt will be made to paint the complete picture, but a few further images of different countries' encounter with opiates can add support to the assertion that the world has an extraordinarily rich store of experiences with these drugs.

Thailand

Dr Vichai Poshyachinda has given remarkable insights into the nature of opiate use among the hill tribes of the northern area of Thailand through research conducted in that region. These people have for long cultivated opium as a cash crop but the ready access has meant that many develop dependence on their own product. In 1995, he wrote as follows.

The experience of our research team in the hill tribe communities of northern Thailand actually yielded a dilemma concerning the community attitude towards opium use. Opium dependents openly smoked opium in their homes, nevertheless new users still tried their utmost to keep their smoking a secret. In ceremonies for marriages, funerals and others, opium was offered to guests in the same way as food and drink. Opium was given as presents to shamans, heads of households, and the elders. Yet, parents warned their young sons and daughters against consorting with opium users and frequently intervened with authority against marriage. Single opium smokers of both sexes faced great difficulty in finding spouses, as opium smokers were regarded in general as being economically unproductive.

Opium smokers, wrote Poshyachinda, with echoes of nineteenth-century China, 'traded all their property to purchase opium and eventually lived as itinerant labourers'. He described the tragic case of a young woman who killed herself when she discovered that her husband was an opium smoker.

The attitude of the hill tribes towards opium use is thus a mix of permissiveness and disapproval. In this part of northern Thailand there are no police to enforce drug laws. Control is instead exerted by the force of social disapproval, with sanctions on marriage a prime instrument. But there is also opium as a gift for people in the power elite and for guests at the wedding feast, a having it both ways, an uneasy ambiguity.

Opium in a desert area of India

Rajasthan is a state in the north-west frontier region of India; large areas are desert. The majority of the population is Hindu, with a small Muslim minority. In the rainy months a scant living is derived from farming, but in the hot months there is little to do but sit and wait for the rains to come.

Among the inhabitants of the arid western part of the state opium is established as a recreational drug. The opium poppies grow in the more fertile parts of the state and the drug is delivered to the desert villages by peddlers. This account of its use derives from a report by Dr K. K. Ganguly, who worked with the Desert Medicine Research Centre at Jodhpur. He found that opium circulated locally in two different forms. Nuggets of *amal* were dissolved in water and passed around at social gatherings as a drink. In contrast, *doda*, opium in powdered form, was mixed with cow or camel dung and then smoked in a pipe which the group would share. *Doda* is prone to adulteration and may at times be mixed with chopped-up rubber.

Ganguly reported that the users were exclusively male. They would gather under the shade of a tree or in someone's house. In the dry seasons these gatherings became particularly popular: 'The population faces hardship during dry seasons. At this time people deliberately take to opium for a reprieve (however temporary) from the worries and anxieties of drought.' As well as its employment in social settings, opium was used by both men and women as a folk remedy for many different types of ailment, and it was given to children. Much of the use was in a controlled, non-compulsive mode. But Ganguly estimated that about 10 per cent of the two hundred subjects whom he studied were hard-core users who did not perform any other activity: when they felt the craving for the drug, they desperately searched around the village for opium.

Ganguly concluded that the use of opium in these communities was 'certainly not benign in all respects'. He entered a strong plea, however, against heavy-handed application of the criminal law: 'It would be very unhelpful to start seeing the user of *amal* or *doda* as a criminal or a dope fiend.'

The Turkmenistan experience

In 1881, Turkmenistan was annexed by Russia. The new rulers of what was to be renamed by Russia the 'Trans-Caspian District', found the country populated by nomadic cattle breeders and some settled peasants. Living standards were poor and the people illiterate. As one contemporary observer put it, the 'entertainment and amusement of Turkmen are extremely plain'.

According to a historical account published in 2000 by Dr Nina Kerimi, a Turkmen psychiatrist, when the Russians arrived in Turkmenistan they discovered that opium use had for centuries been part of the way of life. The Persians supplied the drug in quantity and the Afghans also had a hand in the business.

Here is an extract which Kerimi gives from the dispatch sent by a local official to the provincial governor in 1890. It shows how the Turkmen themselves stigmatized the people who had become dependent on opium and excluded them from traditional social structures:

There is a moral retribution of opium smokers arising spontaneously . . . Those people are not allowed to participate in the community's assemblies, they do not have a right to vote, they are not eligible to be subpoenaed as witness in whatever case.

Soon after the arrival of the Russians, a petition was sent by the community to the government, requesting that opium smokers and dealers be susceptible to prosecution within the court system which the Russians had recently set up.

So here is a case of opium as a people's drug from time immemorial, but the law invited in when the newfangled courts arrived. To suppose that popular acceptance of this kind of opium use necessarily implies a scene of idyllic, trouble-free coexistence, with no kind of public unease at all, would be a clouded reading of the record.

Zurich's Needle Park

What will happen if a park in a modern Western city is set aside as an enclave where flagrant use of injected heroin is absolutely tolerated and declared to be as acceptable as any lunch on the grass? Christian Huber, in an article published in 1994, answered that question with a vivid description of Zurich's 'Needle Park'.

Before this park gained its soubriquet, it was plain Platzspitz, the park attached to a National Museum, and as well ordered as any other public space in a country renowned for its decorum. Come 1986, heroin takers moved in to, and virtually took over, the park. Their arrival was quickly followed by offers of assistance from a plethora of helping agencies. Huber gives the impression of a fairground: condoms handed out here, syringes being dispensed over there, soup kitchens, showers and toilets installed. Wandering over the grass were resuscitation teams with oxygen equipment. Trading in drugs within the park was open, as was their use. Soon the park was attracting visitors or squatters from other parts of Switzerland and even from other countries, with only a small minority of the people involved originating from Zurich.

What Needle Park had come to look like by the summer of 1991 is described by Huber:

Crime and violence increased to an extent which was publicly unbearable. Needle Park became a 'no-go' area without law; people were shot, stabbed and thrown into the river. Trade took place publicly and before the eyes of police officers; stolen goods were sold as if in a public market. The use of weapons became almost commonplace.

The local citizens were terrorized and made it clear that they could accept no more of this mayhem. The scandal became an issue of such proportion as to threaten the re-election of the city council. In February 1992, fences went up and Needle Park was closed to all comers. It took several years to achieve its reinstatement as a tranquil open space, dedicated to the quiet enjoyment of local citizens.

The conclusions fairly to be drawn? Platzspitz was an experiment in removing all controls on the use of heroin and other drugs, and then meeting the problem with varieties of sticking plaster. The intentions were good but the outcome appalling. Injected opiates let rip are likely to be immensely destructive. That surely is the message to be drawn from a benignly intended experiment which in the event created a scene ripe for Hieronymus Bosch.

Heroin addiction as status

Because of the stigma attached to the drug, using heroin can perversely confer status on the user caught up in a deprived subculture. No doubt this may also occur with other types of drug, but heroin becomes the status symbol at the top of the heap (crack cocaine today can be a rival). Being a heroin addict is an occupation, something that can be done well, a job to swank about. In the heroin-infested American ghettos of the 1960s, the heroin user was a 'cool cat'. Heroin dependence is a psychophysiological state, a 'brain disease' some would say. But for the addict the status of user can be experienced as a positive achievement, an accolade.

In the early 1970s, I had working with me a young German psychiatrist, Dr Rolf Wille. He obtained tape-recorded interviews with a series of heroin addicts recruited from among the new wave of British heroin users. One of his subjects was David. He had grown up in the poor East End of London, and had started on heroin at the age of fourteen. 'I liked to see myself as an addict, it was clever,' he told Wille. After five years of enjoying the addict role as the only status life seemed likely ever to give him, and having also achieved some success as a drug dealer, time was up. He was taken from hospital to a court, where he was lucky to escape a custodial sentence. But he knew that unless he gave up his drug career he would soon and inevitably have the jaws of the penal system close on him. He travelled by train back from the court to the hospital, escorted by a nurse. Mounting feelings of terror surged in on him at the prospect of surrendering his heroin-dominated way of life, and the drug scene which was the entire territory of his existence.

Where it all started was on the way back from the court to the hospital. I was sitting there in the train, thinking I knew that I'd been put in a situation where I had to get off drugs or kill myself. I just got so desperate, they're going to take something away from me, the only thing I know. And I said to the nurse, 'You might as well cut my right hand off . . . I don't want to stop.' And I jumped up to open the door of the train to jump out and he stopped me.

From that near-death experience came recovery. But what the story makes vivid is that recovery had to be, not only from the physical dependence on the drug, but also from the way in which heroin had come to define totally the meaning of life.

Telling it in their own words: a report from contemporary Scotland

A recent book, *Beating the Dragon: The Recovery from Dependent Drug Use*, derives from taped interviews with seventy Scottish former drug users who have managed successfully to break with drugs. The authors are two social scientists, Professor James McIntosh and Professor Neil McKeganey. The text conveys a sense of the front-line reality of what drug dependence means to individuals. From a section headed 'Becoming a regular user', here is Helen describing what her heroin habit gave her: 'You don't really get lonely on smack [heroin]. It's like having a lover . . . If you've got your habit, well for me anyway, I wasn't lonely.' Another section, called 'Recognising addiction', describes how various subjects came to realize that they had crossed the border from use to dependence. Here is Debbie talking:

I was waking up in the morning with stomach cramps, muscle pains and it's just a horrible feeling when you wake up in the morning and you really need to get a wee bit of kit, know what I mean, just horrible. That's when you know you're dependent on it, you need it.

Such micro-reports give the human dimension to the great play of the world's macro experience with opiates. Heroin as status and as lover are kinds of reality but so is the dependence and the horrible sickness in the morning.

Opiates experienced

The young woman in Thailand who killed herself rather than stay married to an opium user, opium in the dry season in Rajasthan, the opium user banned from the right to vote in Turkmenistan, a needle drug hell in a park, heroin use as the meaning of life for David as he contemplates his leap from the train, the young Scottish addicts talking: these are some diverse varieties of the opiate experience. It would be a singularly dull-minded observer who was not moved, troubled or amazed by these statements put together. All that and China, two-nations, Vietnam, one hardly needs to labour the point that opiates have a lot to tell.

The theme in this chapter? The reality of the dependence phenomena is one thread that comes through whatever the culture. Opiates are indeed drugs with a dangerous dependence potential, not take-it-or-leave-it candy, and that is true all the way from dependent user desperately searching around his village for opium, to Debbie waking to find she needed her 'wee bit of kit'. Another thread is that of ambiguity: opiates are good and valued but at the same time feared and destructive. Nowhere is ambiguity more vividly demonstrated than with opium as a gift to honoured persons, but with young people warned against consorting with opium users. There is the thread of the many reasons for use – opium as comfort while waiting for the rains to come, as a folk remedy, for Debbie a surrogate lover. And there is a thread relating to what to do about it. Leaving opium to informal cultural control may be feasible in Thailand and Rajasthan, but it is not a viable formula for heroin users in Zurich.

Although much of this book is necessarily about populations' experiences with drugs, the statistics, the quest for ways of understanding why epidemics run and balances break down, the large numbers, there are within these numbers a mass of uniquely individual people experiencing drugs in a myriad ways, who may find good things in drugs or be destroyed by them.

Part Three

Other Drugs Outside the Law

12

Cannabis

I am going to start this chapter by again calling on Louis Lewin. Here, from his inexhaustible fund of drug-related clippings, is an item acutely relevant to the present debate around what to do about cannabis.

It is recorded that in the year 1378 the Emir Soudon Sheikhouni tried to end the abuse of Indian hemp consumption among the poorer classes by having all plants of the description in Joneima destroyed and imprisoning all the hemp-eaters. He ordered, moreover, that all those who were convicted of eating the plant should have their teeth pulled out, and many were subjected to this punishment. But by 1393 the use of this substance in Arabian territory had increased.

After giving several further examples of failed attempts at deterrence spread across history, Lewin remarked: 'The passion for this substance defies all obstacles and extends throughout the immense territories of Asia Minor, Asia, and Africa, where it is indulged in by several hundred million people.' The passion for the substance still defies all obstacles. The only thing that has changed since Lewin's day is that its use has become much more geographically extended.

Cannabis is now often pictured as the prime example of the failure and stupidity of legal attempts to prohibit the use of a drug that the people view as benign, want to use, and by their millions engage in using. The Emir Sheikhouni deserves to be remembered as the Canute of drug history. After several hundred more years of metaphorical tooth pulling, or, in the case of the US at one period, the death penalty for the sale of cannabis to minors, why still stick with a failed prohibition, many people now ask?

Cannabis: what is it?

The hemp plant has been grown from time immemorial for rope making, and from similarly ancient times people have known that a mind-acting drug can be obtained from it. Herodotus, in 450 BC, described its use by the Scythians (I am relying on Paul Wilkinson's translation):

When the Scythians obtain the seed of this Kannabis, they throw it onto red-hot stones in the fire. It burns like incense, sending up more smoke than any Greek vapour bath. This they then inhale and begin to rave.

The Latin word *cannabis* derives from the Greek, while *hemp* is a word of Anglo-Saxon origin. In the sixteenth century, the vernacular names for the plant in Britain included 'barren hempe', and the sinister 'neckeweede' and 'galow-grasse'.

In 1753 Linnaeus, the father of botanical classification, gave the plant the name *Cannabis sativa*. There was debate as to whether a distinct subspecies of cannabis could be identified (Indian hemp or *Cannabis indica* seemed to be a candidate), but modern botany suggests that although more or less drug-rich varieties exist, hemp wherever it grows is essentially the same plant species – a lanky weed producing elegant multi-pointed leaves which have frequently served as emblem for pro-cannabis campaigners. The plant is hardy and has a worldwide distribution in temperate and subtropical climates.

The chopped leaves and flowering tops of hemp provide a smok-able material, often referred to as marijuana. The resin is known as hash (hashish). 'Hash oil' is a concentrated alcoholic extract. The word 'cannabis' in scientific circles tends to be employed generically to describe all the relevant hemp-derived drug products, but confusion is caused by 'marijuana' being favoured as the generic term in the US.

The enormous range of words for cannabis across different countries illustrates the wide dissemination of the drug. The Indian subcontinent has charas as the resin, ganja for the smoked leaves and bhang as an infusion of the leaves drunk like tea. Indentured Indian labourers brought the word 'ganja' to the Caribbean. In Southern Africa smoked cannabis is dagga and in North Africa it is kif. North America has been particularly inventive in the names which have been given to the drug: muggles, Mary Jane, Indian Hay, the weed, loco weed, tea, pot, are just a few. 'Reefer', 'zoot' and 'joint' have emerged on both sides of the Atlantic as the favourite name for a cannabis cigarette, although 'splif' and 'roach' have some currency.

Following scientific convention, this chapter will use cannabis as the generic designation for the drug-related products derived from Linnaeus's *Cannabis sativa*. The chemical contained in these products, which is responsible for the drug's effects, has been identified as delta-9-tetrahydrocannabinol, commonly abbreviated to THC. It is a substance that can exist in different concentrations in different parts of the plant, and in different botanical variants within the species. The chopped leaves contain between 0.5 and 5 per cent THC, but when hemp has been selectively bred it can yield up to 30 per cent THC. Such high-potency plant material is colloquially referred to as 'skunk'. On average, the resin contains about 10 per cent THC but can go much higher, while hash oil usually has a 40–50 per cent concentration.

The immediate impact of cannabis on the consumer

THC is taken into the body most commonly by smoking. It can be put into a cigarette by itself or rolled up with tobacco, or a pipe or water pipe may be employed. It can be baked in cookies or otherwise eaten, or, as with bhang, taken in an infusion. Occasionally it has been snuffed. A rapid and massive intake of THC can be achieved by putting hot knives on to a piece of resin placed at the bottom of a funnel (a rolled-up magazine will do). The vapour is then inhaled through the top of the funnel, a technique with echoes of the Scythian practice.

When cannabis is smoked, THC produces an initial impact on body systems very quickly, with a return to the baseline state within say six hours, but with disruption lasting up to twenty-four hours in complex functions such as motor vehicle driving or piloting an aeroplane. THC is soluble in fat, including the fatty sheaths that encase nerve fibres. With repeated high dosage it can accumulate in the body.

Traces of THC, or its breakdown products, can be found in the urine up to four weeks after last use.

When THC reaches the brain, it exerts its influence by attachment to a specific receptor site. In the early 1990s, the astonishing discovery was made that the body produces a THC-like brain-transmitter substance, anadamide. There is evidence for an anadamide chemical-messenger system operating as part of the brain's normal physiology, but with functions which are so far incompletely understood. Anadamide may interact with the serotonin, dopamine and other systems, perhaps more as a modulator than as a prime agent. Weight for weight, THC is several times more potent than the naturally occurring anadamide.

THC can have an impact on several different systems in the body, but the reason for people wanting to use the drug is its capacity to produce a pleasant mental experience. As ever, the wanted effects are partly learnt or culturally suggested, and in part innate to the drug. Whether the effect is pleasant or not is to an extent determined by the genetic constitution of the user. According to dose, the degree of tolerance that has been acquired and personal vulnerability, the impact may be unpleasant, a matter of only mild euphoria, or, at the extreme, the entry ticket to a world of thrilling mental scenery. The drug, as well as having sedative properties, has packaged within it a psychedelic potential.

Here is a French poet, Théophile Gautier, talking up an LSD-like cannabis experience of 1843 (the quotation comes from an English translation by Maurice Stang of Gautier's text):

A dose of a teaspoonful suffices for those unaccustomed to this true believer's feast ... Installed myself on the divan making myself as comfortable as possible among the Moroccan cushions, to await the ecstasy. Some minutes later I was pervaded by a general stupor. My body seemed to be dissolving and becoming transparent. I could see perfectly clearly within my breast the hashish I had consumed in the form of an emerald which was emitting millions of little sparks ... I could still see my comrades now and then but they were disfigured, half man, half plant, with the pensive air of ibises standing on one leg or ostriches flapping such extraordinary wings that I doubled up with laughter in my corner ...

That is a mental experience brought on by THC's attaching itself to the anadamide receptor sites in the brain of a romantic poet lolling on his brightly patterned cushions. The effect was by reason of personality, expectation and setting likely to be different for Gautier than the reaction to the drug of a kif-happy beggar in the streets of Marrakesh. That indigent would be likely to take the drug not as a passport to Gautier's world of hallucination, but as a soporific and comforter to dull the hardship of poverty. However, both poet and beggar are, in turn, seeking something different from the young cannabis smoker of the modern Western world, who is enjoying the drug for a mild 'high' and for enhanced social interaction, rather than hoping to turn friends into fantastic birds or to ease hardship. As already stated at a number of previous points in this book, drug experiences are never a simple reflex matter of drug meets receptor site, and cannabis cogently illustrates that general truth.

Cannabis goes West

Cannabis probably had a shamanistic use in Europe or at the edges of Europe, even in pre-historic cultures. From early times, it seems to have been used as a mind-acting drug in the Middle East, India and some other parts of Asia, and in parts of Africa. But for many centuries it never achieved popular use in Europe.

The first significant but still circumscribed stirrings of European interest in cannabis, other than as a herbal medicine, came with experimentation reported from Paris in the 1840s. In addition to Théophile Gautier's excited accounts of the drug's wondrous actions, Arthur Rimbaud wrote enthusiastically regarding his cannabis experiences. These romantics got their supplies from a respected French physician, Dr J. J. Moreau de Tours, who imported his material from Egypt.

In the nineteenth century, the British imperial authorities had awareness of cannabis thrust upon them when they encountered its use among the indigenous population in India. A commission on the topic was set up; in 1894 it issued a mighty seven-volume report. Having taken evidence from a wide range of witnesses, the commission concluded that there was no cause for anxiety:

the moderate use of these drugs is the rule, and the excessive use is comparatively exceptional. The moderate use practically produces no ill effects ... The injury done by excessive use is confined almost exclusively to the consumer himself: the effect on society is rarely appreciable. It has been the most striking feature in this enquiry to find how little the effects of hemp drugs have obtruded themselves on observation.

At the beginning of the twentieth century, the invisible cordon that kept cannabis out of the West was still largely in place. Given the presence of the drug in the pharmacopoeias, its ready potential for cultivation in Europe and the US, and the absence of any legal prohibition, its failure at that point in history to achieve any place for itself in the West, beyond experimental dabblings, is hard to understand. With alcohol much campaigned against by the Temperance movement and blamed for all kinds of social ills, with the Industrial Revolution providing exactly the sort of disruption to offer fertile soil for a drug epidemic, with the hemp plant easily grown in any field or garden and with no barriers to import, history might so easily have gone another way. If cannabis had exploited a window of opportunity and become established in the nineteenth century as an accepted Western pleasure drug, along with alcohol and nicotine, it is improbable that many governments would subsequently have wished or dared to enact cannabis prohibition.

The movement towards international control of cannabis was initiated in 1925 when, at a meeting held under the auspices of the League of Nations (the Second Geneva Conference), a convention was adopted which prohibited international trade in cannabis, other than for medicinal and scientific use. This measure was proposed, not because cannabis was perceived as posing a threat to Western countries, but because the Egyptian delegation was worried about the contribution the drug was allegedly making to mental hospital admissions in their home country.

Cannabis comes to the UK

The pace at which cannabis use was to spread and become a direct matter of concern in the West, during the twentieth century, varied between countries. In Britain, from the 1930s onwards, the press carried occasional sensational stories about young white women seduced into using cannabis by black men. It was not until the early 1960s, and with the development of a youth culture, the burgeoning of popular music and the emergence of pop stars who flaunted their cannabis use, that the drug achieved cult status among young people in the UK. The demand was then fed and encouraged by plentiful imports. Possession and supply of cannabis had first become illegal in the UK in 1928.

H. B. Spear, a former Chief Inspector at the British Home Office drugs branch, charted the development of cannabis use in Britain following the Second World War. In 1932, the annual report made by the Home Office to the League of Nations had stated that 'the illicit use of and traffic in the drug appears to be confined to Arab and Indian seamen'. The 1946 report asserted that the traffic in Indian hemp was 'practically confined to two Negro groups in London and those attempting to import the drug have generally been found to be coloured seamen'. In 1947, there was reference to use in 'clubs frequented by Negro theatrical performers and others in the West End of London'. According to Spear, by 1950 the drug was, however, beginning to achieve popularity among indigenous British users, as became evident when the police made a raid on a jazz club. On that occasion ten men were arrested and 'contrary to normal experience in the country in cases involving Hemp only one was a coloured man'.

The Home Office statistics for cannabis convictions can also be used to chart the trajectory of the drug's dissemination in Britain. In 1951 there were a mere fifty-one convictions under the Dangerous Drugs Act for offences involving cannabis, and not until 1960 did annual convictions first exceed two hundred. By 1971 that figure stood at 9,219, and at the end of the twentieth century cannabis-related convictions were running at an annual rate of 100,000. Something approaching 40 per cent of young people today in Britain are likely to have at least experimented with cannabis by the age of twenty-five. Join up the dots, and there is a graph of a drug epidemic climbing, at first slowly upwards, and then exploding.

As for the British social and governmental reaction to cannabis in the post-war period, unsurprisingly the arrival of a previously alien drug led, at first, to a rather confused response. In the 1960s, possession of a small quantity of the drug was quite likely to lead to imprisonment. Cannabis for a time became synonymous with long hair and disrespect for authority. On 24 July 1967, *The Times* of London

carried a full-page advertisement declaring that 'The law against marijuana is immoral in principle and unworkable in practice'. This advertisement had, at least in part, been funded by the Beatles. In 1968,
the Government's Advisory Committee on Drug Dependence produced
a report on cannabis under the chairmanship of Lady Wootton, a
social scientist famed for her critical acumen and fair-mindedness.
The group concluded that cannabis was not without dangers, but
suggested that the penalties were disproportionate to the threat. The
willingness to make the drug a symbol of subversion was subsequently
further reinforced by a statement made to Parliament in 1969 by
James Callaghan, the then Home Secretary, in response to Wootton's
modestly reformist proposals.

I think it came as a surprise, if not a shock, to most people, when that notorious
advertisement appeared in *The Times* in 1967 to find that there is a lobby in
favour of legalising cannabis ... It is another aspect of the so-called permissive
society, and I am glad if my decision has enabled the House to call a halt to the
advancing tide of permissiveness.

The Home Secretary forthwith rejected the recommendations of
Wootton's report absolutely.

Cannabis: the American trajectory

The parallel story in the US starts with some minor awareness of
cannabis use in the early decades of the nineteenth century, but with
no great social anxiety at that time. According to David Musto, the
American drug historian, there was mention in 1911 of cannabis use
in a Syrian community in New York, and in 1925 there was talk of
the drug's being used among 'Hindus' in San Francisco.

An interesting view of the extent to which cannabis had disseminated in the US by the 1930s is to be found in a paper published,
in 1934, by Dr Walter Bromberg, the then Senior Psychiatrist at the
Bellevue Hospital in New York. It seems that America was at that
time in advance of Britain in its encounter with the drug.

Within the past five years the spread of marihuana smoking has engaged the
attention of narcotic officers, and those interested in medico-legal problems. It

was observed first in seaports, then in the states bordering on Mexico and during the last eight years in the large metropoli in the United States.

Bromberg identified cannabis as a youth drug: 'The real drug addict . . . is rarely a user of cannabis. Youths between 16 and 25 years are frequently smokers and school-boys, in certain quarters, have taken up the habit.' Bromberg believed that in New York use was widespread but with a concentration among 'Porto Ricans, Mexicans and Negroes'. He quoted estimates that one in four residents in the southern states of the US was a smoker of cannabis.

Cannabis had not been included under the control provisions of America's founding anti-narcotic legislation, the 1914 Harrison Act (see Chapter 9). It was not until 1937 that the Marijuana Tax Act, a curious legal device modelled on the Migratory Birds Act, gave the drug illicit status. This was a government decision, not based on the considered assessment of the harm being done to the public health by cannabis, but the result of arcane political manoeuvring between different power groups in Washington. As with the Harrison Act, this was a piece of Federal legislation framed so as to be acceptable to individual states, and, despite its curious title, its simple intention was to secure the criminalization of supply and possession of cannabis.

Following the enactment of the Marijuana Tax Act, the Federal Bureau of Narcotics (FBN) began energetically to talk up the dangers of the drug with scant or no regard for the science. The emphasis was on the hideous dangers of crime, and the unleashing of sexuality, likely to result from intoxication with what was now deemed to be a highly addictive drug. Furthermore, cannabis use would lead on very probably to heroin addiction. Here is the head of the FBN, Commissioner Harry Anslinger, who had at the start not been at all keen on the Tax Act, giving his assessment of the drug in 1953:

Marijuana is only and always a scourge which undermines its victims and degrades them mentally, morally and physically . . . a small dose taken by one subject may bring about intense intoxication, raving fits, criminal assaults . . . the moral barricades are broken down and often debauchery and sexuality result. Where mental instability is inherent the behaviour is generally violent . . . The drug has a corroding effect on the body and mind, weakening the entire system and often leading to insanity after prolonged use.

In 1944, La Guardia, the Mayor of New York, had issued a carefully evidenced report on cannabis with findings much more in line with the Indian Hemp Commission's than with Anslinger's fantastic denunciations. And yet by 1957, under the Uniform State Narcotic Act, the penalty for a first possession of marijuana was two to ten years or a $5,000 fine, while for a first sale of the drug the mandatory sentence was ten years in prison.

Cannabis was already popular among certain groups in the 1940s and 1950s, perhaps with a concentration in black communities. By the 1960s, cannabis had crossed all ethnic barriers in the US. And it was available on college campuses and in high schools. Over a few decades, a drug, which had been rather exotic, became a pervasive and widely accepted part of the American way of life. There are still about 350,000 arrests in the US each year for cannabis possession, but simple possession is unlikely to lead to a prison sentence.

So much for a look at the UK and the US as case examples illustrating how over quite a short period a foreign drug may become naturalized in previously largely immune societies. In both instances it was a matter of a slow trickle, some ethnic affiliation, and then the epidemic floodgates open, with America at first somewhat in the lead. But cannabis has become over a mere fifty years a common Westernized commodity spread far beyond those two countries. Although still officially illegal in most Western countries, it has come to be tolerated and societies live with it. The invisible cordon has been blown comprehensively.

1961: strengthening international controls

In 1961, the UN Commission on Narcotic Drugs promulgated the Single Convention, a comprehensive international drugs-control treaty which, among other things, sought for the first time to criminalize cannabis and prohibit its use throughout the world. This was a step considerably beyond the League of Nations Agreement of 1925, which had aimed only to control the trade in hemp products, while leaving what happened within national borders to the discretion of individual governments. Now cannabis was to be controlled within the same framework as heroin and cocaine. Symbolically, but also importantly in legal terms, this was the company with which cannabis would henceforth be expected to keep. The Single Convention can be seen as an attempt to globalize the Marijuana Tax Act, and America at the time exerted heavy international pressure to achieve that end.

So what were, in 1961, the perceived threats that led to an international attempt, at a high official level, to outlaw a weed with which the East had coexisted for millennia, and for which the West was developing a little fondness without evident resulting death and destruction? A background process of expert consultation – the drafting of position papers and convening of committees – had gone on for several years before the Single Convention emerged, and it is possible to trace the build-up over that period of a consensus view that cannabis was a dangerous drug. Cannabis, said the experts in their statements circulated around the conference tables, was an addictive drug, a route into heroin and likely to cause violent crime and madness. Beyond these particular charges, there was the belief that cannabis was, in a general sense, evil.

That this dire view prevailed was not just a result of lobbying by Anslinger. Important input to help construct this appraisal came from WHO (the World Health Organization), as the body with the responsibility to advise the Commission on scientific facts. In 1952, a WHO Expert Committee had stated that cannabis had no legitimate place as a medicine, so that defence was got out of the way: cannabis was medically obsolete. A position paper prepared by the WHO secretariat in 1955 concluded:

It is important to realise that not only is marijuana smoking *per se* a danger but that its use eventually leads the smoker to turn to intravenous heroin injections . . . cannabis constitutes a dangerous drug from every point of view whether physical, mental, social or criminal.

So there was the familiar extreme view surfacing again with Anslinger-speak become Geneva-speak. The 1961 appraisal of cannabis as requiring regulation within the same treaty as the opiates was driven by politics, not by science. Cannabis was metaphorically tried and found guilty at an international court on expert evidence of such dubious quality, and with the expert witnesses so lacking in independence of mind, as to make the trial a farce.

Phases of response

The acceptance or non-acceptance of cannabis in the West has evolved differently from country to country. The mapping of four distinct phases can, however, give shape to the story.

- *Phase 1: The pre-history of the Western encounter with cannabis* The drug over many centuries had an entry in the pharmacopoeias, it was known to travellers and to colonial authorities, but it achieved only a trivial penetration of Western society. That was the situation in the US up to the 1920s and in Britain until as late as the 1950s.
- *Phase 2: Prohibition* This phase was precipitated by a growing and anxious awareness of cannabis use among ethnic minorities and marginal or disapproved groups in the US, and among rather similar sections of society in the UK, with some spread to the music and entertainment world and to an emerging youth culture in both countries. Prohibition was enforced with the scant available science subverted to bolster the repressive position. In the US, this phase began in the 1930s, in Britain not until the 1950s or 1960s.
- *Phase 3: The de facto easing of prohibition* This is the present phase of evolution. Cannabis use has spread so that it is now a commonplace, absorbed into ordinary lifestyles. Penalty levels on both sides of the Atlantic have been reduced. In 2004, the British government downgraded cannabis from Class B to Class C with a consequent reduction in penalties for possession to nil, in most instances, but without the drug's being formally legalized. Calls for legalization or decriminalization are underpinned by appeals to research, interpreted as suggesting that cannabis, if not actually harmless, is not very harmful. Phase 3 had its stirrings in the US as early as the 1940s, with the publication of the La Guardia Report, while in Britain the 1968 Wootton Report was a similar marker of transition.
- *Phase 4: Unknown territory* This is tomorrow's phase with a script yet to be written, and at present one can only speculate on how the story will unfold. What we must hope to see become a

feature in this part of the story, is the influence of extensive and high-quality research to inform decisions. Cannabis science is today pouring from the scientific presses.

That a new wave of research has emerged over the last decade which supports neither extreme position, but which gives serious cause for public health concern, seems, however, not yet to have entered the media's awareness. The public debate on cannabis all too often still proceeds in a kind of science-free zone, with the research findings excluded lest unwelcome truths should undermine fixed positions.

In moving towards the type of debate one may hope to see characterize Phase 4, there are two linked questions which need to be addressed. First, what does science say about cannabis and the risk of dependence? Second, what does it reveal about the risk of cannabis-related harm? The paragraphs which follow will provide a synopsis of the science base bearing on the answers to those two questions.

Cannabis and the risk of dependence

Evidence that cannabis can produce a clinically significant type of drug dependence comes from several directions. One line of evidence is provided by surveys which show that, among frequent users of the drug, symptoms suggestive of withdrawal experience are reported by as many as 15–25 per cent of interviewed subjects. That is a higher dependence rate than is found among users of alcohol. A study of cannabis users who were attending an American outpatient clinic for treatment of cannabis dependence, reported a range of withdrawal symptoms including mood disturbance, strange dreams, headaches, nausea, shakiness and sweating. Over 90 per cent of these patients reported craving on withdrawal from cannabis. Studies on human volunteers who had been admitted to a research ward, and dosed with oral THC, showed that when the drug was withdrawn marked withdrawal distress developed, and these symptoms were relieved when subjects were put back on the drug. Confirmation of the evidence from human research has come from laboratory work which produced cannabis dependence and cannabis withdrawal symptoms in several animal species.

There can, therefore, today be reasonable confidence that cannabis is a drug with dependence potential. That does not mean that everyone who uses it is bound to become addicted. But something approaching 20 per cent of regular users will find it difficult to give up the habit when they want, will feel unwell on withdrawal, will crave for the drug if they stop using it, will feel better again on resuming its use, and will be prone to relapse.

The significance of the emerging evidence on cannabis dependence is that if the drug does harm (a separate question), then the dependence will mean that some users are trapped in a long-term and harmful behaviour.

Cannabis and risks of harm

The evidence today bearing on questions of harm is of vastly higher quality and extensiveness than at the time of the Indian Hemp Commission, Anslinger, La Guardia or Wootton. This account will focus only on topics where the research base is substantial.

Cannabis as a cause of mental illness

Cannabis users often report minor and short-lived adverse mental health consequences of their drug use – panic for instance, paranoid feelings, or bizarre experiences such as 'an arm floating off'. No great harm results, and such occurrences seldom deter a young person from further use. The expectation of pleasure rates higher than a few rather trivial bad happenings.

For many years there have, however, been reports that cannabis can sometimes cause more major kinds of mental disturbance. Here is a doctor (he signs himself as 'W. W.') describing his encounter with cannabis, in a paper published in the *Lancet* in 1890. This was an era when there was no likelihood of the disturbance having been caused by LSD or some other street drug, and the claim that this was a cannabis reaction is therefore convincing.

Sirs ... Not long ago while suffering severely from neuralgia, I was induced by a medical man, to whom I was then acting as an assistant, to take forty drops of the tincture of *Cannabis indica*, which I did ... with relief from neuralgia and no unpleasant symptoms following. The neuralgia was soon forgotten, and in about an hour's time I began to feel giddy, full in the head, and very faint and soon experienced a sensation of heaviness and numbness in the feet and legs ... During this time there was great anxiety and fear of death through cardiac paralysis that seemed almost imminent. On return of sensation to the extremities, I was possessed with an almost irresistible desire to commit suicide, by rushing into the adjoining canal or cutting my throat ... I was seized by alternative fits of laughter and crying, without any apparent cause ... The following morning I awoke after a very sound sleep and a good night's rest, determined never again to take *Cannabis indica*, and to be most careful of prescribing it to others.

Other accounts were published at around the time of this *Lancet* article, from Indian and Egyptian mental hospitals, suggesting that in countries where cannabis was widely available it had become a common cause of mental illness of sufficient severity to demand hospital admission. Over the following years, the idea that cannabis could cause mental illness was widely accepted; the possibility that the seeming connection between cannabis use and mental illness could have been coincidental was completely overlooked. However, by 1970, laboratory work was appearing which showed that when THC is given to human volunteers it can cause severe mental disturbance of short duration.

The sum of the present evidence suggests that cannabis can cause severe, acute mental disturbance lasting a day or a few days, and then clearing completely. That THC has this propensity constitutes a somewhat random but quite unpleasant risk. Against this should be weighed the fact that severe reactions are uncommon and hospitals are not flooded by them.

Cannabis can precipitate relapse in otherwise successfully treated schizophrenics. Schizophrenia is a condition which affects 0.5–1 per cent of the general population. In a country where cannabis use is widespread, its impact on schizophrenia is likely to be a matter of concern for mental health services.

There are also a number of reports indicating that cannabis use in adolescence increases, and perhaps even doubles, the risk of schizophrenia developing in early adulthood. Such reports have appeared only recently and it is still too early to form a conclusive view on their significance. But if their validity is confirmed, the implications will have to be taken very seriously.

Cannabis and the possibility of subtle damage to the brain

There is no evidence that cannabis can cause brain damage of a gross kind, even with heavy and prolonged use. However, recent work by researchers who have used advanced techniques, capable of picking up subtle brain damage of a type and degree which would have been missed on older kinds of testing, has suggested that cannabis can impair so-called 'executive' brain function. Executive function comprises a cluster of mental abilities relevant to successful performance of intellectually demanding work. Such impairment can occur on exposure to the drug at what would be regarded by users as a 'social' level of smoking. The deficits may then persist for at least some years after cessation of use, and perhaps even permanently. A likely underlying mechanism to explain this kind of impairment is the damage caused at microscopic level to nerve connections in the frontal lobes of the brain.

Dr Nadia Solowij, an Australian researcher who published a book on this topic in 1998, concludes:

If the use of cannabis is prolonged for more than three years for example . . . the ability to focus attention and ignore irrelevant information may be progressively impaired. Some users may become aware of this impairment, primarily in the form of memory problems, difficulties in concentration, or distractibility, others may be unaware of any such impairment. Nevertheless it is likely that their general level of performance will be below that of their optimum level of functioning.

If it were to be confirmed that cannabis, although not a drug to cause dementia, can none the less impair subtle aspects of information processing, what would be the implications? Would the consequence be that a small percentage of clever people would be so marginally impaired that in reality no one would notice, or would a significant proportion of cannabis users have disadvantaged themselves?

The answers to these questions are at present not at all certain. It would be unwise to inflate the significance of the research and to start speculating about the likelihood of cannabis intellectually crippling its users on a large scale. But it would be equally incautious to dismiss these findings as 'only subtle', and therefore irrelevant to real life.

Cannabis and educational attainment

No one is suggesting that for most students cannabis-induced impairment of the sort discussed under the 'subtle damage' heading is likely at that stage in their lives to be of significance. The concern is whether repeated experience with a drug that has a transient capacity to blur short-term memory and other aspects of mental functioning is likely to impair their ability to learn.

That there is a statistical relationship between early cannabis use on the one hand and truancy, poor grades and early school leaving on the other, has been confirmed in several countries. The question remains as to whether these outcomes reflect a primary effect of THC on the brain, or are a consequence of personal attitudes and peer-group involvement, with the cannabis use a secondary phenomenon.

Cannabis and respiratory disease other than cancer

What the science here has begun to show is that continued and heavy smoking of cannabis can cause bronchitis and possibly also obstruction of the airways, with later risk of emphysema. Cannabis and tobacco add together to produce impairment when people are smokers of both substances.

Cough and shortness of breath are a less dramatic outcome than Anslinger's alleged cannabis-induced mayhem on the streets. But cannabis-related lung disease, while catching no headlines, is probably real and likely to affect a lot of people, adding up in the long term to a substantial health burden for the population.

Cannabis and cancer risks

Cannabis smoke is about 50 per cent more laden with cancer-producing chemicals (carcinogens) than is tobacco smoke. There are at present relatively few chronic cannabis smokers in the fifty-plus age group to form a basis for the kind of study that Doll and Hill contributed on cigarette smoking (see Chapter 2). One has, therefore, for the present, to rely on relatively small case studies. These suggest that a connection can be detected between cannabis smoking and cancer of the mouth, tongue and throat. Other research has shown changes in the lining of the airways of cannabis smokers that appear to be pre-cancerous.

Given the time it took for scientists to establish that cigarette smoking causes lung cancer, it would, on the evidence of these still early findings, be unwise to rule out the possibility that some years down the research road, cannabis will be found to carry the same type if not the same level of risk as tobacco.

Cannabis use and motor vehicle accidents

Research suggests that cannabis can to some degree impair driving ability, especially so if it is combined with alcohol. The significance for what happens out on the road is uncertain, and it is possible that someone who has smoked cannabis and has not taken alcohol may be able to avoid danger by monitoring and correcting their driving behaviour. That contrasts with the drunk driver who will not be able to correct for their alcohol-induced impairment of reaction time.

Cannabis as a gateway to other and more dangerous drugs

Despite the assertions of an earlier decade that cannabis will, as night follows day, lead on to heroin, that claim is manifestly untrue. The great majority of cannabis users will never go near heroin. An American researcher, Denise Kandel, has, however, suggested that cannabis acts as a 'gateway' to heroin. The basic fact of a strong statistical association between cannabis use and escalation to other drugs has been demonstrated beyond reasonable doubt. But most researchers would probably not accept that the statistical connection implies existence of a true causal link.

Cannabis as medicine

Physicians in ancient Greece used cannabis medically. Later it had a place in European herbals. Leonhard Fuchs had this to say about it in his *Great Herbal* of 1542.

Since it is clear from what has been said that *Cannabis* excites the mind and so injures it, those [physicians] who unwisely, follow a common error, administer potions made of this seed to those with mental ailments, especially the serious ones, do so with great risk to the patients.

A boost was given to therapeutic interest in cannabis when, in 1842, Dr William O'Shaugnessy, a surgeon who had had extensive professional experience in India, published a favourable report on the drug's medical usefulness. He recommended it for a variety of conditions, including rabies. Less exotically and more in accord with today's interests, he gave it a place in the treatment of pain and muscle spasm. Incidentally, O'Shaugnessy also had a hand in setting up the electric telegraph system in India.

In Britain in the nineteenth century, experiments were made with domestic cultivation of cannabis for therapeutic use, thus obviating the problem that imported material was likely to lose its potency in transit. The 1890 *Lancet* report bears witness to the therapeutic interest in this drug that O'Shaugnessy's writings had provoked. However, cannabis never attained anything like so important a place in the physician's available choice of drugs as did opium. When, in the 1940s, cannabis was taken out of the US pharmacopoeia, with a similar move in Britain in the 1970s, there was hardly a whisper of medical complaint. The reason for cannabis never gaining wider therapeutic popularity than it did, lay partly in the difficulty of obtaining a standardized product, partly also with the side effects, but probably, most importantly, with the fact that the majority of doctors did not find it of much use in their clinical practice. For a long time, questions around cannabis as medicine dropped from sight. But in due time the questions came back. Cannabis is effective in the treatment of the nausea that can occur with the chemotherapy of cancers. It may act as an appetite stimulant in wasting diseases. Whether it is an effective painkiller is less certain. There are suggestions that it can relieve the spasticity that is often an unpleasant complication of multiple sclerosis (MS). Raised pressure inside the eye (glaucoma) may, if not treated, lead to blindness, and it seems likely that cannabis can lower the pressure. It may be useful in the treatment of asthma.

National agencies charged with responsibility for the control of medicines have strict criteria for determining whether a drug should be made available for therapeutic use. Before licensing any cannabis preparation, these authorities will want to determine, by rigorous testing, whether the drug is likely to be both safe and of significant benefit to patients. No external pressures should ever make licensing authorities cut corners. Tension arises because some patient groups (MS sufferers for instance) feel certain from personal experience that cannabis can relieve their suffering. For them and their families, procrastination by licensing authorities appears cruel. Increasingly, juries are reluctant to convict people who claim that the lump of resin seized by the police is their self-prescribed medicine.

The science of therapeutics has, however, moved a long way beyond the days when enthusiasm and a doctor's advocacy were sufficient to secure for a drug an established place in the pharmacopoeia. Rabies was never curable by cannabis despite O'Shaugnessy's suggestion that it could cure the disease. That should be a caution for today's debates around the medical value of cannabis: at present the enthusiasm runs ahead of the evidence. Probably it will be synthetic cannabinoids or cannabinoid derivatives that ultimately provide useful medicines, rather than the direct products of the plant. It may be possible to produce medically useful synthetics that are free from abuse potential. Cannabis-like synthetics are already available on licence in America as Dronabinol and in Britain as Nabilone.

Meanwhile, the medical value of cannabis does need to be uncoupled from the debate around its recreational use.

The Cannabis Road

The Scythians, that sense of a long journey with the lank weed ever growing beside the road; travellers all go by variously chanting their denunciations or plucking the leaf as a badge of pilgrimage; science in blossom now, exaggerated talk of fantastic dangers, sanguine dismissal of all dangers: all are equally untenable along the road ahead. The spectre walking towards us is not one of raving fits and moral barricades broken down, but a range of less dramatic consequences. We do not entirely know what to make of it, yet the shadowy and frightening resemblance is with the dangers in tobacco, with a little bit of psychosis, some brain impairment, and a few further complications thrown in. And here we are walking forwards, meanwhile confronted by that question posed at the start of this chapter: why stick with a manifestly failed prohibition? Why keep pulling teeth? Why not accept that the cordon sanitaire long since came down? Good questions and I will return to them in Chapter 20.

13

Cocaine

Cocaine tells a story about the multiple metamorphosis of a drug's image and mode of use; of how epidemics come and go and come again; of society's capacity to forget the dangers of a drug; and cocaine's present triumph over control.

Let us start with one moment in its long history and hear cocaine celebrated in a 1920's lyric, 'Dope Head Blues'; it is a woman singing:

> Just give me one more sniffle
> Another sniffle of that dope
> I'll catch a cow like a cowboy
> And throw a bull without a rope
> Just give me one more sniffle
> Another sniffle of that dope.

The song captures with the precision of a flash bulb the image of cocaine as a nightclub drug, 1928. The woman makes her insouciant plea for the magic powder to transform her into a rodeo performer with her companions made her cattle. Her voice breathes above the saxaphone.

According to legend, cocaine started out as a gift from the Sun God to the Inca royal family, but, by the 1980s, it had progressed to become, as crack cocaine, a commodity traded in the inner cities of the US, thanks to a gift from the Colombian cartels. A few years later it was fuelling gangland gun-battles in Britain. That nightclub scene marked just one of many transitions in the sequence of cocaine's shifty personae.

Cocaine, the drug

Whatever the setting – crack house or penthouse or Andean potato field – in which cocaine is being consumed, the drug is likely to originate from the leaves of the South American coca bush. *Erythroxylum* grows with great ease as forest undercover or in plantations; its preferred habitat is a hillside at, say, 1,000–2,000 metres elevation. The major producer countries are Colombia, Peru, Ecuador, Bolivia and Brazil.

Cocaine is a powerful stimulant. Indigenous users employed it to give them energy and endurance for hard agricultural work at high altitudes, or to fortify themselves in the arduous labour of the silver mines. Europeans were impressed by travellers' tales of messengers who could trek for days across the high Andes with nothing but the drug to sustain them. Cocaine also has the capacity to produce euphoria and an intense rush of pleasure.

The drug was first pulled out of the leaves (as cocaine hydrochloride) by a German chemist, Albert Niemann, in 1860. Within a couple of years its chemical structure had been identified. The drug's action on the brain began to be understood in the early 1990s when Dr Michael Kuhar, an American researcher, suggested that cocaine might interfere with the body's dopamine transport system.

What Kuhar proposed, and the work from his laboratory and other centres seems to confirm, is as follows. Dopamine is the chemical which helps carry messages along the nerve tracts in the brain so as to mediate pleasure. For a message to pass from one nerve cell along to the next in the chain, a little gap must be leapt between the end of one cell and the beginning of the next. This leaping is achieved by the release of dopamine as a chemical messenger which flows across the gap. There is then a scavenging system with transporters to pick up the dopamine and terminate the message. Circulating cocaine can move in, attach itself to and immobilize the transporters, dopamine accumulates, and the pleasure-giving message stays for a little while longer switched on. Take a lot of cocaine and the switch-on is more sustained.

Cocaine as a drug of dependence

If heroin were taken as the template, cocaine would not immediately look like a drug of dependence. With cocaine there are none of the evident and agonizing physical withdrawal symptoms that are the hallmark of heroin dependence, but only tiredness and depression as the euphoria induced by the cocaine wears off. It is therefore all too easy to dismiss cocaine as 'not physically addictive', and by implication not *really* addictive. Animal experiments, however, show cocaine to have an immense capacity to stimulate drug-seeking behaviour. A primate will press a lever many times to obtain one shot of cocaine, and keep pressing the lever until the animal has convulsions and is rendered senseless by the drug. If dependence is viewed as the capacity for a drug to build up a drug-seeking habit, then experiments suggest that cocaine has a frightening ability to instigate dependence. That dependence is for the most part driven by the drug reward (the effect on the dopamine system), rather than by the need to relieve withdrawal.

The paradox with human beings is that many people will use cocaine in an intermittent way, which does not look monkey-like. And they are not all on the inevitable slippery slope. There are persuasive accounts of people who have used cocaine in a controlled way and without marked escalation over many years. But there are also those who do slip down the slope, quickly or after a longer period, and who then go on to an appallingly compulsive pattern of use closely resembling that seen with the experimental animal. A binge of several days' duration will only be interrupted when that person collapses into a twenty-four-hour sleep. The truth is somewhere in the middle ground: cocaine is a dangerous drug but harm does not always or necessarily follow its use.

And the cocaine user who has become dependent is notoriously prone to relapse. Here, too, an understanding of the impact of cocaine on the brain may help explain what happens. It seems possible that repeated high-dose cocaine exposure will impair the workings of the dopamine system, so that on withdrawal the capacity to experience ordinary pleasures is dimmed. Life for weeks or months after withdrawal may feel chronically grey – the sun is behind the clouds. The

Greek word *anhedonia*, indicating the absence of joy rather than the frank experience of depression, aptly describes this state. Another dose of cocaine and the *anhedonia* is temporarily banished, and that is what invites relapse so often.

An important further finding from primate experiments is that if animals are given only limited access to cocaine they will not develop dependence, but if they are given unlimited access, dependence will quickly follow. That observation, at least in part, explains the human paradox: when cocaine is scarce and expensive, its use will more often be low-dosage and controlled than when it is cheap and offered promiscuously across the table. And it is again a drug where route of use will greatly bear on the dependence risk.

A cocaine addict presented at a clinic with this picture.

He was forty, a big shambling man who had made a fortune earlier in life through commodity trading. Now he lived on his investments. He admitted that although cocaine had previously been for him 'a toy, safe, no problem', for the last couple of years he had been bingeing compulsively – 'Forget about the date on the calendar, it's binge, don't open the curtains, crash out, more crack and round again, literally it's brought me to my knees.'

This story sounds sadly like the caged animal in the experiment. The patient went into treatment, came off the cocaine, and when last heard of was living soberly in an ashram. 'I need to be absolutely away from it,' he wrote.

Psychological and physical problems resulting from cocaine

Continued high-dose cocaine can result in anxiety, agitation and gross disruption in behaviour. A person who is profoundly intoxicated with the drug will not be in a state to conduct their business. If high-dose intoxication continues, there is risk of a short-term, drug-induced psychotic state, with mental confusion and paranoid misperceptions. A bizarre symptom of cocaine psychosis is the feeling of bugs crawling under the skin, and this can lead to severe excoriation as the user attempts to scratch out the hallucinatory insects.

The psychological symptoms can be unpleasant but, apart from the *anhedonia*, they will disappear with abstinence. Of far greater health concern is the array of possible adverse physical consequences. A single high dose of cocaine can on occasions lead to instant death due to a disorder induced in the heart's rhythm. The surge which cocaine induces in blood pressure can cause a stroke in a young person, who at their age would never have expected such a mishap. High doses or overdose can lead to fits or collapse, and a sudden steep rise in body temperature. Cocaine carries the risk of myocardial infarction (heart attack), and can occasionally lead to kidney or liver failure. When cocaine is used intravenously, there is a risk that the drug will result in overdose, or in a virus infection (the AIDS virus or hepatitis): the chaos and confusion associated with cocaine use exacerbates the risk of unsterile injecting or unsafe sex.

Most users will take cocaine without any bad effect on their health, and recreational users may therefore be inclined to dismiss what has been said here as scare-mongering. The fact is that cocaine not infrequently cripples or kills: the heavier and more frequent the usage the greater those risks. But it can also randomly strike down the casual or first-time user. Halfway between the blasé dismissal and the exaggerated alarm lies the truth that cocaine is not a safe drug.

Traditional coca use in South America

Centuries before the scientists came along to explain what cocaine does to the dopamine system, the Incas developed a simple technique for getting the chemical out of the leaf and to the brain. Their method is still used today by millions of people in the Andes region of South America. The Western world refers to the practice as coca chewing but that is a misnomer. A wad of coca leaves is tucked between the gums and the cheek, and to aid absorption the pH is adjusted by the addition of alkaline ash. The wad is left in place for two to three hours while it is gently and intermittently squeezed and sucked. Chewing on the leaves would not give the desired slow release. The verb for this sucking is *acullicar*, the people who use cocaine in this way are *acullicadores*, and an *aculli* is the short work-break which labourers take as they pause for a replacement of fresh leaves.

The ancient technique is a sophisticated way of obtaining, and maintaining, a relatively low but constant cocaine blood-level. There will be no great troughs of withdrawal or peaks of mind-blowing intoxication, but a steady impact which will energize, suppress hunger and provide a mild sense of euphoria and well-being all day long. It has for long been believed that cocaine is especially valued because of its capacity to bolster physical activity at high altitudes, but the drug is equally popular in the Andes among the valley people.

The cocaine wad is a pharmacological device, simply but brilliantly developed so that the *acullicadores* can get cocaine from the leaf to the brain in a slow-release, maintenance kind of way, rather similar to that achieved for nicotine by tobacco chewing or impregnated gum. The practice has over time acquired powerful, symbolic meanings. In the Andes, to be an *acullicador* is to be a comrade, a trustworthy member of the community, a virtuous person who honours the ancient culture. On the Altiplano, being a person and being an *acullicador* are almost synonymous states. Any attempt to debar such a society from its traditional use of coca is likely to be resisted as an attack bordering on genocide.

Thus, for centuries, the South American people continued to use a powerful stimulant rather harmlessly. The reason why the balance held good no doubt lies partly with the manner and route of use, which made intoxication or dependence unlikely. The isolation of the communities, their lack of spare cash and the absence of advertising, pushing or commercial exploitation of the product, must have helped keep use down. But it was also the cultural embeddedness of the practice which constrained the level and mode of use. The leaves released a drug: tied to the forehead they would relieve illness by magic; they could be used for divination; a wad in the mouth and the peasant farmer could feel assured that the snakes would not bite. The culture did not, however, propose or sanction intoxication with the drug.

The Spanish conquerors never took up the coca habit but despised it as primitive and un-Christian. They made money out of its cultivation and paid with coca leaves for labour. During the colonial period, the coca habit did not spread to the rest of the Americas, or more widely. Protracted ecological stability is in favourable circumstances entirely possible, even with a potentially very addictive substance.

Doctors become interested

Coca received some slight medical attention in Europe from the 1600s onwards, but this interest was limited by the fact that the leaves were apt to lose their potency on the long journey from the Andes. In 1859, an Italian, Paolo Mantegazza, published a book on coca, which stirred professional interest. After consuming a generous dose of an infusion of coca leaves, he experienced 'an unthinkable beatitude'. He declared, 'I prefer a life of ten years with coca, to a life of a million centuries without coca.' He recommended the use of this preparation for the treatment of various physical disorders and for neurasthenia (the then current name for nervous exhaustion). Mantegazza had practised medicine in Peru, where he had had no difficulty in accessing high-potency leaf for personal and therapeutic experimentation.

With the availability, from 1860 onwards, of cocaine hydrochloride in pure form, medical exploration of the drug's properties began in earnest. Cocaine had by the late 1870s won a place both in the US and British pharmacopoeias. Scientific experiments were conducted to test ancient claims for the drug's ability to enhance strength and endurance. Edward Payson Weston, who was billed as 'the world's greatest pedestrian', attempted in 1876 to complete 500 miles in six days around the Royal Agricultural Hall in London, and he chewed coca all the way. Writing anonymously in the *Lancet* that same year, a doctor described beneficial effects on another kind of sporting prowess – 'Filling my flask with the coca tincture instead of with brandy . . . down went the birds right and left'. An army doctor reported favourably in 1883 on the use of cocaine by Bavarian troops engaged in autumn manoeuvres.

Ernest Jones related in his biography of Sigmund Freud how, in 1884, the then relatively unknown young Viennese doctor came to develop an intense interest in cocaine. Born in 1856, Freud was at the age of twenty-eight desperate to establish sufficient private practice to let him marry his fiancée, Martha Bernays. He obtained a supply of powdered cocaine from the German pharmaceutical firm Merck, at what seemed to him an extortionate price. Immediately swallowing a little of the drug, he found that it cheered his mood and made him feel as if he had dined well. Before long he was taking 'very small doses of it regularly against depression and against indigestion with the most brilliant success'. He posted presents of cocaine to his beloved Martha 'to make her strong and give her cheeks a red colouring', and he also gave it to his sisters.

Freud called cocaine a 'magic drug'. Disastrously, he championed its deployment as a cure for morphine dependence, and did appalling harm to a fellow doctor, Ernst von Fleischl-Marxow, who had become addicted to morphine during treatment for a chronic painful disorder. The cocaine injections that Freud supplied to Fleischl led to escalating use, gross intoxication with the drug and a state far worse than the original 'morphinism'.

In July 1884, Freud published a monograph on cocaine. To his chagrin, it was not, however, his own career which was launched into the stratosphere by the drug, but that of a young contemporary. Working in Vienna, Carl Koller held a junior appointment in ophthalmology. He had noticed that when he swallowed cocaine, his mouth became numb. Experiments on animals followed, and then some experiments on Koller's own eyes and those of a colleague. In September 1884, a lecture was given at a medical congress in Heidelberg on these investigations, together with a practical demonstration of the drug's utility as a surface anaesthetic for the eye. By demonstrating cocaine's powerful local anaesthetic properties, Koller had opened up opportunities for eye surgery and surgery for the ear, nose and throat (ENT surgery), which previously did not exist. Such surgical procedures had been too painful for most patients to endure, and a general anaesthetic with ether was often technically impossible for surgery at these sites. Koller's discovery was, therefore, of considerable practical importance and created immense professional excitement. As for Freud's reaction, he ungraciously blamed the distraction brought about by his engagement to Martha as cause for his having lost in the race for an epic discovery.

The news of Koller's work spread rapidly around the international medical network, and his ideas were taken up in America. Inspired by Koller's report, the first application of cocaine in cataract surgery took place in the US as early as October 1884. Towards the end of that same year, American surgeons were reporting the revolution brought about in ENT surgery by the availability of a safe and effective local anaesthetic, employed as a spray or by injection into the tissues.

Cocaine escapes to the streets

Internationally, it was the US that led the way in to the first epidemic encounter with cocaine. The story at the end of the nineteenth century might happily have stopped with cocaine taken from the Andes to become a medical blessing for mankind. One might have hoped to see a quick professional evolution towards awareness that the drug's true worth was limited to its role as a local anaesthetic, with faddish use for indigestion, neurasthenia, or other minor ailments deemed impermissible, and with cocaine as a cure for morphine dependence a folly to be condemned and rejected. It is not that warnings regarding the dangers of cocaine were a long time in coming: as early as the 1890s, medical reports were being published in America, warning that cocaine by injection could cause an extremely destructive dependence.

Unfortunately the warnings were ignored and rank indiscretion triumphed. Cocaine leaked out; the careless medical use of the drug helped provide a bridge for misuse. Many doctors prescribed it for trivial and inappropriate reasons. The medical profession was not the sole instigator of the developments that put America as lead victim in a cocaine epidemic which, over the next forty or fifty years, affected many other countries also, but doctors must take a share of the blame.

The underlying cause of the American epidemic was undoubtedly the sudden overwhelming availability of cocaine in pure form. Imports rocketed as purified cocaine and coca leaves were brought into the US for local processing. It is impossible to tot up the diverse sources and to chart the overall US national consumption. Dr Joseph Spillane, in his excellent 2000 book *Cocaine*, has estimated that importation of coca leaves into New York was at rather under 25,000 pounds weight in 1884, but by 1885, as the boom took off, the imports had climbed to something approaching seven times the previous level. By 1905 the figure was a little above 1,277,000 pounds, more than fifty times the 1884 import level. Spillane also states that 10kg of manufactured cocaine were imported into the US in 1881 and 440kg in

1886, years which closely mirror the take-off in professional enthusiasm. In 1890, imports stood at a peak of 890kg, and thereafter, for many years, fluctuated but remained close to this peak.

A proportion of the drug was used in legitimate medical practice, but much of it was sold directly by pharmacists to their customers, with few questions asked. As any economist might have predicted, rising consumer demand and competition between suppliers steeply drove down the price of cocaine in the US. Spillane states that the price dropped from $1 a grain (30mg) in 1884–5 to as little as 2 cents in 1887.

From the moment in 1860 when Niemann extracted cocaine from the coca leaf, the danger of an epidemic outbreak existed. Cocaine can be a pleasure-giving drug for the individual user; its use can be pleasurable in group activity; it can lead rather easily to intense dependence: all this profiles a promising candidate for epidemic spread. Yet while it had to be taken by injection (swallowing is not a cost-effective mode of use), there would be limits to its popular acceptance. That was an era before the days of widespread heroin misuse and a street needle culture.

The discovery that cocaine could be rapidly absorbed and provide an excellent high if sniffed up the nose was a remarkably simple innovation that greatly facilitated individual use and ratcheted up the likelihood of an epidemic. It was a folk-innovation without a named hero, but tobacco used as snuff must have hinted at the possibility. Contemporary reports suggested that cocaine sniffing in America began to make its appearance around the start of the twentieth century. Some commentators suggested that the habit had originated among the poor, black population of the southern states, but any ethnic boundaries were soon gone. Blaming the cocaine problem on black people was a strong and repeated feature of American talk about cocaine.

What the advertising industry refers to as 'endorsement' is always helpful in building a climate favourable to a drug's epidemic spread. In turn-of-the-century America, the endorsement of cocaine came sometimes from famous individuals, but also through the widespread marketing of the drug as a constituent of soft drinks, tonics and over-the-counter remedies of many sorts. Cocaine was made acceptable and familiar, and advertisements showed children relieved of toothache through its beneficence.

Coca-Cola originated in 1886 as the brainchild of John Pemberton, a pharmacist from Atlanta, Georgia. The presence of cocaine in the drink was trumpeted in the advertising, and Coca-Cola easily saw off such pallid rivals as Celery Cola. Thus was coca linked by name to one of the supreme American marketing successes, and to a brand that became a symbol of Americanism. The all-time prize for the famous-person kind of endorsement must go to the manufacturers of an alcoholic coca wine called Vin Mariani, which had originated in France but went on to achieve great popularity in the US. Angelo Mariani was a chemist whose incredible coup was to persuade Pope Leo XIII to endorse this wine and award the inventor a gold medal for his contribution to the good health of humanity. The American Hay Fever Association officially adopted cocaine as its favourite cure, and cocaine was advocated as a sea-sickness remedy. One way and another, cocaine contrived for itself a degree of endorsement which would make any modern public-relations agency green with envy.

The cocaine epidemic took off in a vacuum of legal restraint. There were no legal controls in place at state, Federal or international level. There were no curbs on import or wholesaling or on the zeal of the pharmaceutical houses, no control on medical prescribing, none on pharmaceutical retailing, with some evidently venal pharmacists peddling the drug, and no legislation bearing on use, possession or supply of the drug. It was today's often heard call for the legalization of a dangerous drug made florid reality.

The image that comes to mind is of a flood with no flood defences. The sudden, easy availability, coupled with rave reviews and a total lack of regulatory control, allowed cocaine to flood out in to the population. Agitation began to emerge calling for action against what came soon to be seen as a dire social threat. The first state law aimed at the cocaine problem was passed by Illinois in 1899. Legislative responses of many kinds followed, often as part of broader measures aimed also at opiates. Dispensing began to be prescription-only, and doctors in some states were not allowed to prescribe cocaine to addicts. In 1914, Federal legislation in the shape of the Harrison Act provided, for the first time, a comprehensive framework for control of cocaine and opiates (see Chapter 9).

In 1910, a US government report described cocaine as the worst drug problem that America had ever encountered. The national mood was by then coloured by panic got up by the press, and panic was certainly more rife than hard facts on the problem's extensiveness. The image of the 'dope fiend' first gained currency as an epithet for the cocaine user. Cocaine was in popular reports linked to criminality, and as one commentator put it, 'the Chicago gangsters are not seldom cocaine maniacs'. There were lurid stories of schoolchildren falling victim to the drug. And as mentioned earlier, there were repeated suggestions that black people were especially prone to cocaine abuse, with the consequent wild unleashing of lust and violence.

There were reports of cocaine misuse from many different states, and from rural areas as well as the cities. The sniffing habit had spread across America, although the better off might still inject the drug. Cocaine had acquired a negative image – as the drug of prostitutes, gamblers, itinerant labourers, the poor, and the black minority. That was an image utterly different from cocaine as medical miracle.

Dr Koller's launch of cocaine as a revolutionary anaesthetic agent had taken place in Heidelberg. He later emigrated to set up practice in New York. There he must have witnessed with horror the spread of his drug in to the New World, which had so recently welcomed him and his discovery. But cocaine, over those same decades, became a cause for concern in many other countries besides the US. The story is of an international drug epidemic sparked by a European medical discovery, led by and concentrated in America, but with wider dissemination.

The British experience

From the late 1880s up to the beginning of the 1914–18 war, doctors in the UK were seeing occasional cases of cocaine misuse. Usually the drug was being taken along with morphine, rather than constituting a problem in its own right. Injection was the preferred mode of use.

Concern was expressed in Britain about the proliferation of coca wines; this paralleled similar American anxieties. Vin Mariani was marketed in the UK. In a pamphlet entitled 'Drink in Disguise', Dr Elizabeth Beatty narrated a story of cocaine-induced decline and fall (quoted in a 1912 article by Dr Mary Sturge):

A lady who was an ardent temperance worker, said: 'I would not allow wine or spirits into my house, but when I see the girls tired and dull I send to the chemist for some coca wine and give them a glass and it does them good'...She thought, as many persons do, that coca is just the same as the ordinary cocoa we use for food. It contains this poison which forms a habit which ruins soul and body, wrecks the nerves, and sends the victim to the asylum.

And inevitably the temperance worker's youngest daughter 'ended her days in the asylum'.

At the outbreak of the Great War cocaine sniffing came over from Paris to London, and little wraps of cocaine were sold in Soho at the price of half a crown (12½p in present-day UK currency or 20 US cents). The sniffable drug became available to troops on leave from the Western Front and the War Office was perturbed. In May 1916, an order under the wartime Defence of the Realm Act (DORA) made it a criminal offence to sell morphia, cocaine and certain other drugs to members of the armed forces. This was the first drug-control regulation of its kind ever to be seen in the UK.

There was concern in Britain about the hazards posed by lax prescribing and the over-the-counter cocaine-containing remedies. Dr W. E. Dixon, a pharmacologist, in 1925 expressed this view:

Most of us have seen patients or friends who have, after advice, used the cocaine spray for the relief of hay fever or asthma, and so the habit was formed until the spray was carried everywhere and resorted to as soon as symptoms of depression, lassitude, irritability, or restlessness, manifested themselves ... The habit was, however, rare in this country.

Dixon described how, with cocaine, 'the flagging nerve cells are whipped into activity' – not a bad metaphor for what happens when the dopamine re-uptake is blocked.

During the war years, cocaine achieved notoriety in London as a nightclub drug, and the death from a cocaine overdose in 1918 of Billie Carleton, an actress who was a heavy user, caused scandal and generated many column inches in the newspapers. Noël Coward, in 1924, put on to the West End stage *The Vortex*, a play about a man destroyed by cocaine.

Despite the alarms, cocaine in Britain never gave rise to an extensive epidemic over those years. After the passing of the Dangerous

Drugs Act of 1920, which put cocaine and the opiates under strict control, the drug gradually faded from sight.

Cocaine across the rest of the world

Between the 1890s and 1930s, parallel to the years that saw cocaine as a problem in the US, it was misused to a varying extent in many other countries. Outside America, the spread was never more than on a relatively small scale. The supply came from a mix of lax prescribing, pharmacists selling direct to their customers, petty black-market dealing and sometimes more organized dealing and smuggling.

Dr Oriana Kalant's translation of Hans Maier's 1926 German classic on cocaine addiction, *Der Kokainismus*, gives a picture of the international experience with cocaine in the early decades of the twentieth century. Maier described, for instance, a report on the ingenious practices employed in the 1920s by cocaine dealers in Geneva:

the case of an amputee whose artificial leg was full of cocaine-containing boxes which could be reached directly through the pocket of his trousers. Another trafficker concealed cocaine in a jar over which there was always a sleeping cat. A street musician had devised a method to carry 1 kg of cocaine in his mandolin.

Maier feared that unless preventive measures were taken, cocaine would spread 'like an oil slick' across every canton of Switzerland.

According to Maier, cocaine was available in Paris and in the 1920s its use was said to be prevalent in Montmartre and the Latin Quarter, and in 'some fashionable clandestine places near the Champs-Elysées'. Cocaine misuse was reported from Belgium, Italy, Austria and Spain, and there was talk of its use in the Tsarist army. Maier quoted a 1927 report from post-revolutionary Russia, which described the drug as prevalent 'among patients from the venereal disease section of a Moscow prison hospital and among the inmates of two concentration camps and a correctional institute for minors'.

As for use outside Europe, for reasons that are obscure, India became a focus of concern. The source may in part have been the smuggled Japanese pharmaceutical product, and it was rumoured that the Japanese navy played a part in protecting the transportation. Maier quoted an Indian physician, Kailas Chunder Bose, writing thus about cocaine:

Its consumption as a drug for intoxication is so great in Calcutta that unless measures be adopted to control its sale . . . its demoralizing effects will soon spread among the juvenile members of respectable families . . . at no distant date special asylums will be required for the safety and treatment of cocaine inebriates.

Bose describes the case of a learned Hindu priest who was required by his religion to fast three days each week. A 'pundit' recommended cocaine to him as a way of suppressing hunger. He soon escalated the dose with disastrous results – 'He has given up his priestly duties, mixes freely with low-class persons'. Cocaine, declared Bose, had 'tenacity and ruinous power'. Cocaine misuse was also said to be rife among the upper classes in Egypt.

The demands that were generated by the international spread in the medical and recreational use of cocaine led to a matching expansion in the world supply. Rivalry occurred between entrepreneurial pharmaceutical companies of different national origins as they sought to swamp their rivals. Coca cultivation was expanded far beyond the traditional areas in Latin America, with commercial plantations established in the former Ceylon, Java, the Malay States, Formosa and Iwo Jima.

The epidemic fades

As the habit spread and the pharmaceutical companies achieved previously unimaginable productivity, each country touched by the world epidemic was introducing its own attempts at legal control. There was no doubt in the minds of most national authorities that the core response had to be the strengthened control of prescribing and pharmacy dispensing, and penal measures directed at the black market. In the 1920s, France introduced 10–15 years banishment as the penalty for anyone who promoted or encouraged the use of narcotics; the term 'narcotic' included cocaine. And there was a demand across Europe and America for conjoint action against the international trade in cocaine.

In 1939, and with the lights again going out over Europe, there may still have been an occasional corner of Soho or Montmartre, or in some other city, where the drug was being sniffed. But cocaine had become yesterday's news. Its use faded out in Calcutta, although at one time chewing cocaine with betel nut and a little alkaline powder had got as near to the Andean technology as was ever to happen outside the Altiplano.

Cocaine strikes back

When the comeback came, it was in America. Data from the US Federal Narcotic Hospitals (Lexington Hospital in Virginia and Fort Worth in Texas) showed that a total of 3,301 addict patients were discharged from these institutions in the year 1962. Among them, not one had cocaine as their primary drug. The earlier cocaine epidemic had vanished completely.

By the latter part of the 1960s, a small amount of cocaine was circulating in the US, as a negligible contribution to the drug ecology. That ecology featured heroin as the most dangerous constituent, with its use concentrated among the urban poor and ethnic minorities, and with smoked cannabis as the increasingly available 'recreational' drug for all comers.

And so we come to the 1970s, when cocaine rather abruptly established for itself a market niche as the drug of rich Americans. Michael Massing, in his 1998 book *The Fix*, identified several milestones in the comeback story, in terms of quoted magazine coverage. Thus, in 1974, the *New York Times* magazine described cocaine as 'the champagne of drugs' and stated that in moneyed circles 'an after-dinner sniff of the fine white powder . . . is as common as a snifter of brandy'. By 1981, *Time Magazine* was adulating cocaine as 'the all-American drug' and 'the drug of choice for perhaps solid, conventional, and often upwardly mobile citizens'.

In the 1970s, the new image of cocaine was untainted by any hint of the 'drug fiend' image. The dangers were shrugged off or forgotten. And the songs were back, with J. J. Cale offering a new endorsement for the wonder drug:

If you've got bad news, you want to kick them blues, cocaine
When your day is done and you want to ride on, cocaine
She don't lie, she don't lie, she don't lie, cocaine

The words may have changed since 1928, but the message was the same – cocaine was again promising magical personal transformation.

Such echoes of the past, but the scale of use was now far greater. Cocaine penetrated all social classes. In 1974, it was estimated that 5 million US adults had used cocaine at least once in the previous year, and by 1985 that figure had swollen to an astonishing 25 million. Much of that use was casual, but by the late 1970s there were probably about 3 million Americans who were cocaine dependent.

The return of cocaine was thus not just a matter of a little innocent hedonism with a reprise of the nightclub songs of yesterday. Despite the popular belief that cocaine was a habit which most users could control without risk of escalation, people were developing dependence in large numbers, harm was done, and deaths were being reported. When in May 1983 'Cocaine 800' was established in America as a national helpline, in the first eighteen months of its operation 450,000 calls were taken.

The new wave of cocaine misuse had started off with sniffing still the preferred route. The idea of a 'line' of cocaine, neatly segmented with the edge of a razor blade, had become a familiar and much photographed image, with the line sniffed through a rolled dollar bill, preferably of high denomination. The onset of the desired euphoria took about ninety seconds.

Freebase and crack cocaine

In the late 1970s, a cocaine technology emerged which was a considerable advance on anything that had been available to users during the earlier American cocaine experience. Someone had the idea of boiling up powdered cocaine hydrochloride with an alkali such as sodium bicarbonate, with the cocaine base thus split off from the chloride. The procedure could be dangerous for the amateur chemist because the end product had to be extracted with ether, and that could lead to an explosion. But this simple procedure offered 'freebase' cocaine in a smokable form. Within ten to fifteen seconds of smoking there would be an overwhelming euphoria of a type which users claimed went beyond anything ever previously dreamed. It was the same drug that the people of the Altiplano had extracted for centuries from their wads of coca leaves, but here was a vastly accelerated means for getting a hit to the brain cells.

In 1984, an even more improved technology became available with the arrival of 'crack' cocaine, the name allegedly deriving from the crackling sound made as the product was cooked up in a test tube. The process did not involve ether extraction and a 50mg 'rock' of smokable material could be sold for $5. A euphoric one-off dose of cocaine was being made available at pocket-money price – it was not that crack cocaine was in any real sense cheaper than cocaine hydrochloride, but the $5 rock was a brilliant marketing strategy. It was equivalent to 'liquor by the drink', in the American phrase. Crack rapidly changed the course of the new American cocaine epidemic. The drug was now available in a form to appeal to the inner cities.

With the advent of freebase and crack, the image of cocaine as 'the champagne of drugs' was, over just a few years, replaced by that of cocaine as a drug of the urban poor, with its use linked to violent criminality. Cocaine-related deaths became a news story, and for a time such deaths in the US exceeded those due to heroin. The epidemic plateaued around 1990, the numbers of casual users declined, but the hard-core problem of heavy use and dependence remains to the present a feature of urban poverty across America. Some heavy use continues in all sectors of American society, and cocaine alone or mixed with other drugs or alcohol is a familiar road to the self-destruction of the rich and famous.

The cocaine to feed the giant demands of this second American cocaine epidemic came entirely from the criminal entrepreneurs who had gained ascendancy in South America, rather than from diverted pharmaceutical supplies.

The pharmaceutical trade that fed the first epidemic had been relatively easy to curb compared to the activities of the lawless, immensely wealthy and murderous modern drug barons. What characterized the US government's strategy to control the second wave of epidemic was a massive attempt to stop cocaine being smuggled into America and to suppress coca production in the producer countries. These efforts at control were probably an almost total failure, with the street price of cocaine falling in America and the purity levels increasing. Enhanced police activity at community level within the US may have somewhat cut back the local trade, with a consequent reduction in the more casual type of use.

Why was the US so badly hit by cocaine's resurgence?

Cocaine also made a comeback in countries other than the US from the 1970s onwards. In Britain, crack became a significant problem a decade or more after the American epidemic took off but it is now widespread. Crack dealing became frighteningly associated with violence; the people killed are predominantly young, black males. The cocaine now coming in to Britain originates from Latin America, with the Caribbean providing staging posts. Other European countries have also experienced an upsurge in cocaine use over recent years. But Europe has not as yet caught the full anarchic American epidemic.

So why should America have been so assaulted by the return of cocaine, while the rest of the world was not so badly hit? In the earliest phase of the US comeback, sniffed cocaine established itself in a wealthy stratum that had been ripe for the plucking. It is difficult to believe that media hype did not at that juncture have something to do with the acceptance of the drug. But essential for the further development of the epidemic was the progressive cheapening of the drug as the market expanded. The American consumer market was outstandingly attractive for the criminal entrepreneurs in producer countries. The trade routes were relatively short and these criminals showed an almost limitless capacity to expand supply in response to the growing demand. The willingness of ethnic-minority groups to take on the sale and distribution within America was also important. Without the urban poor, who were seeking a better hourly wage than could be had at a filling station, there would have been no sales force to staff the community distribution system. A further factor contributing to the epidemic was the sheer happenstance of freebase and crack cocaine coming on to the market at just the right time for the marketeers. As for why America rather than Europe took the brunt of the epidemic, one would probably have to look no further

for an answer than the business plans of the Latin American operators, and the relative lengths of the trade routes to the US and to
Europe.

A final factor that seems to have made the America of the 1970s
and 1980s vulnerable to the recrudescent problem was the almost
wilful amnesia of the US for the previous painful happenings with
cocaine. The dangers in a drug which can so easily tip towards a
compulsion were ignored. The doctors had dense amnesia, as
witnessed by this entry for cocaine in the 1985 edition of the American
Comprehensive Textbook of Psychiatry: 'High price still restricts
consumption for all but the very rich, and those involved in trafficking . . . If used moderately and occasionally cocaine creates no
problems.' Dr Herbert Kleber, a leading American authority on that
country's drug problem, notes that this text arrived in the bookshops
almost exactly as crack hit the American streets.

Cocaine: a tale of two epidemics

Cocaine has a capacity to act on the brain cells in a way which causes
pleasurable sensations, or as Mantegazza opined, it offers the user
an experience of 'unspeakable beatitude'. A drug that can give a short
cut to beatitude is likely to be the stuff of frail ecological balances.
That the indigenous people of South America managed to maintain
a balance for so long is remarkable, but they only had the leaves
available to them and not Niemann's powder.

The alkaloid extracted in 1860, Koller's experiments of 1884, the
medical launch-pad, the pharmaceutical supply . . . so to Epidemic
One. Given the drug's innate properties, the discovery of sniffing, the
initial total lack of controls and the pharmaceutical industry's willingness to pour in the drug, it is no surprise that cocaine got out
onto the streets of America and ran widely.

Yet the first cocaine epidemic in due time largely faded out.
Populations are unlikely to tire easily of an attractive drug and give
it up as yesterday's fashion. People do not readily become satiated
on beatitude. The inference must be that it was the control measures
that by the 1930s had succeeded in more or less eliminating the cocaine
epidemic, both in America and more widely. The pharmaceutical supply

had been brought under control and there was at that time no other large-scale, primary source. Cut off the supply in conditions where no alternative supplier is waiting around at the global street corner, and the epidemic will wither away. A new ecological stability meant that cocaine was back in the medicine chest, as far as Europe and North America were concerned, while the old patterns continued in the South American countries which produced the coca for their own consumption.

But cocaine came back, and Epidemic Two was a matter of 'give me one more sniffle', only writ larger. Multiple factors acted together again to tilt the ecology out of balance. But this time the tap could not be so readily turned off. The media flirted and flattered, doctors had forgotten the dangers, crack offered new packaging; at every level this was an economically driven destabilization. Without the economic plight of debt-ridden South America and the poverty of the street dealers in the US, Epidemic Two would never have happened. The cocaine epidemic had to a large extent the same kind of socio-economic dynamics as the contemporary Western problems with heroin, but it happened to involve a different and cheaply packaged drug.

Opium is a powerful drug even if available only in the resin of the poppy, and the opium pipe was effective technology before alkaloids could be extracted from the resin. But with cocaine, it was extraction of the alkaloid from the Andean leaves which was needed before anyone could have a sniffle and an epidemic could spread. That event was the opening of a dangerous box.

14

Amphetamines etc.

Amphetamine is a synthetic stimulant which produces effects on the user almost identical to those of cocaine. It has never attained cocaine's adulated image, nor has it stirred such fright and condemnation. Year after year in Britain, and to a lesser extent in America, misuse of amphetamine has rumbled along as a low-key contribution to the total national drug problem. It would be easy to dismiss amphetamine and other synthetics as a pale postscript to the big-time story of cocaine.

Such dismissiveness would, however, be a grievous error. The fact that an amateur chemist can produce drugs with the same damaging and dependence-inducing properties as cocaine must be seen as intrinsically threatening. The history of the last fifty years shows that the threat has been realized in several epidemic outbreaks around the globe. Very recent developments in Thailand and some other Asian countries suggest that a previously rather underestimated species of drug misuse may be breaking into an epidemic of appalling disruptiveness.

Synthetic stimulants: the drugs and their medical uses

Amphetamine is a drug with a chemical structure closely resembling adrenalin. Amphetamine base, or amphetamine sulphate as commonly manufactured, contains two forms of the molecule with mirror-image structures (stereo-isomers). Dextro or d-amphetamine is more potent than the laevo or l-variety and is marketed as Dexedrine, the proto-typical 'pep pill'. Because the available products are often a mixture of the two isomers, it is technically correct to talk of 'the amphet-amines' rather than 'amphetamine', but for most purposes amphet-amine will do.

Amphetamine was originally marketed as an over-the-counter nasal decongestant. It also enjoyed a brief vogue in the treatment of depres-sion but was likely only to turn a depressed patient into someone who was depressed and also anxious.

Before long, it was two other pharmaceutical properties of amphet-amine that attracted attention. It can energize its users and help keep them awake, and it can suppress appetite and act as a slimming aid.

The energizing and sleep-postponing properties were welcomed by several groups of people. Students could use the drug to assist midnight studies. Truck drivers could plunge through the night without fear of falling asleep over the steering wheel. Dance bands could play on inexhaustibly until dawn. And when the Second World War came, amphetamine was dubbed the stirrup cup of the Panzers. The eighty-year-old classics scholar I cited in the introduction to this book had a habit that was a relic of that same kind of wartime amphetamine use. Recently, there have been press reports suggesting that US commanders have required their aircrews to take amphetamine before flying long-distance combat missions.

Amphetamine and artificial energy, it is the story of the Inca messen-gers and their chewed cocaine all over again. Unfortunately, along with the drug-induced ability to keep going and stay awake, will be the impairment of concentration and judgement. The consequences of such a side effect will be horrendous if a pilot mistakenly launches a rocket attack on his own ground forces.

As for the use of amphetamine as an appetite suppressant, the drug enjoyed wide popularity in that role over many years. Patients will, in the short-term, lose weight on the medication, but there is unlikely to be long-term benefit. A number of amphetamine-like drugs, including phenmetrazine (Preludin) and diethylpropion (Tenuate Dospan), have been marketed by pharmaceutical companies, with the claim that they were less addictive than amphetamine. But patients can easily become dependent on any of these synthetic stimulants. Today, the prescription of stimulants for weight reduction is not considered good practice.

Amphetamine does have a legitimate role in the treatment of

narcolepsy, an unusual medical condition in which the patient may suddenly crash asleep for a few seconds at any time of the day, in mid sentence.

Ritalin (Methylphenidate) is used in the treatment of children suffering from Attention Deficit Disorder (ADD), with or without accompanying hyperactivity (ADHD). In America up to 20 per cent of pupils in some school classes will have been put on Ritalin. A percentage of children appear to be genuinely helped by such treatment. Critics have, however, questioned whether it is wise to expose children on a large scale to long-term dosing with this drug. The fear is that many of these prescriptions represent the medicalization and drugging of children with adjustment difficulties, which could be better dealt with by a skilled class teacher, without recourse to a stimulant drug.

Amphetamine and other synthetic stimulants are generally taken by mouth, although amphetamine sulphate is sometimes smoked as a street drug or dissolved in water and injected. Methamphetamine has an amphetamine nucleus, modified by the substitution of one methyl (CH_3) radical for a hydrogen atom. That modification adds significant abuse potential because it results in a product which is more easily dissolved for injection, and is also very easily smoked. Ampoules of methamphetamine in solution (Methedrine) were previously used in anaesthetics to restore blood pressure. Like the parent substance, the methyl derivative can easily be manufactured by a black-market operator.

Long and troubled experience with the medical deployment of synthetic stimulants leads to the conclusion that their use is limited to just a few conditions, and their risk of misuse such as to demand great caution in prescribing. In the UK and the US, amphetamine was brought within the dangerous drugs regulations and became a prescription-only drug in the 1960s.

In the drug argot, 'speed' is the name given to amphetamine or methamphetamine, while 'ice' is a term specific for methamphetamine.

Synthetic stimulants: what sporadic misuse looks like

The picture of a rumbling, low-key kind of problem with amphet-amine and other stimulants, has for the most part been a matter of the respectable citizen becoming distressed when their new doctor cuts off the long-standing and steady-dose prescription for Dexedrine; the client at the slimming clinic becoming agitated and sleepless as a side effect of an appetite suppressant; a member of a rock group becoming heavily dependent on amphetamine, consuming the drug in large quantities.

From that undramatic background, now and then a case of florid, short-term amphetamine-induced mental illness (amphetamine psychosis) will emerge. Here is a description of such an occurrence taken from a case series reported by Dr Philip Connell in 1958:

He felt depressed and bought an amphetamine inhaler, ingesting the contents over six hours. Some people began to look at him in a peculiar way. He began walking the streets and spent the night in the park. The next day he spent looking for gold in the park. Stones seemed to be gold. That evening he heard people talking about him and was sure they were going to kill him. Cars and people followed him and there were numerous special 'signs'. Finally he climbed on to the roof of a building and began throwing tiles at the gang in the street below.

That sort of frightening and dangerous drug-induced disturbance will be well known to psychiatric services wherever amphetamine is avail-able on the streets.

Summer of 1968: a picture of epidemic stimulant misuse

In June 1968, I could not walk more than a short distance down the road outside the hospital where I worked without encountering a young man or woman swaying around the pavement, grossly agitated, gesticulating, muttering or shouting accusations at me or other passers by. That was the summer of the Meth Heads – a methamphetamine epidemic gone suddenly wild on our doorstep.

When, in April 1968, the new Drug Dependence Units (DDUs) were opened, the previous uncontrolled hand-out of heroin by private GPs ceased. By law, only doctors working in the clinics and possessing a Home Office licence could now prescribe heroin to addicts (see Chapter 9). There was a heroin drought.

And hey presto, the Meth Heads appeared. Some of those over-prescribing GPs switched nimbly to giving their heroin-dependent patients prescriptions for ampoules of Methedrine. These ampoules soon flooded London. Prescriptions of the drug did not require a Home Office licence and the prescribing doctors had outflanked the Dangerous Drugs Act. When a prescription for Methedrine was issued to a patient who had previously developed an injecting heroin habit, the doctor was giving the patient an overt invitation to substitute an injectable amphetamine for the no longer prescribable injected heroin. The instructions might as well have been written on the ampoule.

The scale of this prescribing is revealed by records which show, for instance, that in one month of 1968 a practitioner gave a total of 24,000 ampoules of methamphetamine to 110 addict patients who fed on his largesse. That worked out at about 46 ampoules per patient per day. At least 40 out of each 46 ampoules would probably have been sold on by the recipient, further spreading the epidemic.

This was a drug epidemic of venal medical making. If anyone requires evidence of the never ending capacity of doctors in every age to turn the addict's plight to personal profit, look no further than the summer of 1968.

And so to Camberwell and a rather glorious and distant summer. The great majority of these young men and women had turned to methamphetamine following previous heroin misuse. Here is a typical description of the inner world one mumbling young woman described.

Suppose I would usually be shooting up 5 amps a day, try to space them. Buy from my friends or sometimes I get a script. Won't sleep for days, hyperactive like hell and then I'll crash out for a day or two. Sometimes I'll go out of my mind – funny smell of fruit, bugs under my skin, hear voices. I'd think everyone is a cop after me, I can go raving paranoid, and then terror really.

Methedrine was producing short-term epidemic madness.

Throughout the summer of 1968, the epidemic became more evident on the streets and the misprescribing – which was its origin

– an ever more evident scandal. Here is a transcription of a note which I made on 27 June 1968 after visiting the offices of a prescribing doctor:

His office is in an elegant Georgian town house left over in a poor quarter of town. Fifty yards down the road, ill-looking youths leaning against the wall. Cars stop, put their passengers down, skid off quickly. I go into the building, walk in through the open door. Go upstairs and find ruin, an angry father of a drug user yesterday laid about the room with an iron bar, someone tells me. Open another door and there are a group of people sleeves rolled up, Fixing Room, every face seems distorted. Man called Digger bursts in brandishing a car radio, he offers to sell it to any bidder cheap. Bernie is declaiming gratuitously on the pleasures of sadistic sex but no one listens to him. I go into the doctor's office. He greets me effusively, offers me a job, is suave and well suited, might be a male model. Digger charges into the room, wants to give the radio to the doctor in exchange for a script. Cigarette ends, dropped syringes and other miscellaneous filth litter the floor. The doctor has a new brass plate waiting to go up which declaims his numerous professional qualifications.

It was a circle of hell.

Then, in October 1968, the manufacturers of the drug agreed on a voluntary basis to withdraw all supplies from retail pharmacies. From that point onwards the ampoules would only be available in the more secure and controlled setting of hospital pharmacies. A few weeks were needed for black-market stocks to run dry, but the epidemic was by a simple regulatory device brought to an end. Come Christmas of 1968, the Meth Heads had gone from the streets.

The inferences? The first conclusion must be that when controls are able to get a handle on the misuse of any particular drug which has had over-prescribing as its source, and where there is no ready alternative black-market supply, control measures can close down the drug-specific epidemic. There are echoes of the first American cocaine epidemic, and, in a more minor key, of ether drinking in Ulster. Control can in favourable circumstances close an epidemic at a stroke. Control works: that would seem to be the first inference fairly to be drawn from the Meth Heads experience.

But the second inference to be taken from the methamphetamine epidemic gives not nearly such a favourable rating to the likely benefit of control. The public health gains will probably be ephemeral when there is an alternative drug easily brought on to the market. If, as is often the situation, there is an established drug culture, with a well-primed appetite for drugs and eager to take up the new offer, the gains are likely to be highly transient.

Thus, by the summer following withdrawal of methamphetamine, there were young people on those same pavements who were now drunk with injected barbiturates deriving from lax prescribing. Sleeping pills were ground up, dissolved in water and drawn into a syringe. When concerted medical action brought the barbiturate epidemic more or less to an end in the early 1970s, addicts went back to any heroin they could get, and soon black-market supplies of heroin came in to supplement the spillage of heroin from prescribing. Chasing after one drug can give worthwhile temporary benefit, but it is unlikely, by itself, to give more than a small respite if there is a drug-hungry population eagerly waiting to be fed. In the real world, control does not necessarily work, and that is the second and equally fair conclusion to be drawn from the summer of 68.

Earlier stimulant epidemics

In the annals of synthetic stimulant epidemics, the first to achieve notoriety was the amphetamine outbreak which occurred in Japan following the end of the Second World War. During the war, amphetamine and methamphetamine had been used in large quantities by the Japanese military. When the war was over, the drug seems to have been virtually dumped, but it found its way on to the black market, and its use spread quickly through a demoralized civilian population. In the early 1950s, the authorities estimated that Japan had a total of about one million amphetamine addicts. Over the ensuing years, the figure declined, but a second epidemic took off in the 1970s when criminal gangs began to enhance their income by manufacturing and trading in stimulants.

In the 1950s, Sweden experienced a Preludin epidemic. Why this particular slimming drug should have acquired popularity is unclear, but illicit imports fed a lively demand for the substance. The government at first favoured a permissive reaction, with open-handed prescribing encouraged but with a later swing towards strict control, motivated by a general change in political attitudes towards drugs in Sweden. What happened to the level of use will have been influenced by many factors besides revised legislation and it is difficult to tell whether Sweden's strict response achieved its intended ends.

Perhaps because cocaine has been so generally available in the US, synthetic stimulants have never been a major problem there. Geographical distribution has remained remarkably patchy, with San Diego, California, having a reputation as 'ice' capital of the US. Joel Dimsdale, professor of psychiatry in San Diego, reported in 1998 on what he had seen of stimulant misuse in his city:

> I have no patience for anything value-free when it comes to amphetamines. In San Diego patients driven mad by the drug gouge their eyes out, hack their penises off and murder bystanders ... They steal weapons from the United States Army and storm the highways in a frenzy. They blow up themselves and their neighbours in the process of synthesising the drug.

The extent to which the drug was directly responsible for all the reported Californian mayhem, as opposed to its being just one element in the endemic American mix of guns and violence, is open to question. But amphetamines and methamphetamine continue to pose problems in circumscribed regions of the US.

Methamphetamine: today's crisis

In the 1990s, smoked methamphetamine began to be a drug of epidemic misuse across a large part of the Asia-Pacific region. Sometimes the drug was injected, but mostly it was smoked. Countries caught up in the outbreak include China, Indonesia, Japan, Malaysia, Myanmar (Burma), the Philippines, Singapore, Thailand and Australia. It is as if a dangerous sleeping giant had woken and strode out to create lamentable havoc.

Thailand provides an example of this recent explosive spread. By 1993, the Thai government was suggesting that the country had a count of methamphetamine-dependent subjects which had already climbed to the 200,000 mark, but by 1997 the figure had been revised upwards to 850,000. Villages which had historically been opium territory turned to the stimulant. The mental health services were overrun by drug-induced psychosis. Tablets of methamphetamine are colloquially known as 'Ya ba' or 'Mad medicine', and 83 million tablets were seized in 2002. Various private armies have a hand in the trade.

Smokable methamphetamine has now let synthetic stimulants well and truly out of the box. With the drug easily manufactured from apparatus carried on the back of a truck, there is every prospect of a stimulant epidemic that will run and run, and spread ever more widely. The pale copy of a cocaine image is replaced by that of the malignant, crazy giant.

15

Psychedelics

Drugs exist that can offer to the user visionary encounters. Cannabis can provoke something of the kind (see Chapter 12), but over the centuries the effects sought from Indian hemp have mostly been mellowness and reverie rather than visions. Cocaine can cause hallucinations when taken in high dose, as can synthetic stimulants, but no one has suggested that these sorts of chaotic misperceptions are mind-expanding. The adolescent who sniffs model aeroplane glue may see visions. Withdrawal from alcohol can result in the horrible snakes of delirium tremens. But these sorts of distortions only crudely resemble the experiences caused by psychedelics.

Psychedelics, psychomimetics, hallucinogens – the terms are interchangeable. These substances are chemical tickets to worlds of enhanced sensation and hallucination. Profound and revelatory experience of self, and of the self's relationship with the universe, can be the mental scenery on a journey that many people will identify as mystical.

In his classic text of 1931, the German pharmacologist Louis Lewin designated this group of drugs as the 'Phantastica'. The summary description he gave of what they can do to the mind cannot be bettered:

their properties of evoking sense-illusions in a great variety of forms, of giving rise in the human soul as if by magic to apparitions whose brilliant, seductive, perpetually changing aspects produce a rapture which is incessantly renewed and in comparison with which the perceptions of consciousness are but pale shadows. Harmonious vibrations of sounds beyond all human belief are heard, phantasms appear before men's eyes as if they were real ... offered to them as a gift from almighty God.

Such chemicals were for a long time known to the Western world mostly through travellers' tales, or the occasional titillating descriptions furnished by scientists or aethetes who had played with the magic. And so it would have remained had not LSD come on to the scene as a synthetic hallucinogen offering mass access to a world beyond pale reality. LSD, briefly and gloriously, became the jewel of a counter-culture. Why a drug which does not cause dependence should have spread so quickly and so widely sets a puzzle to which we will return later.

What are the hallucinogens?

They are drugs which in a one-off and rather small dose (micrograms in the case of LSD) can cause an astonishing range of mental effects. The actions on the brain's biological systems vary from drug to drug. But they probably share a common mechanism, the ability to act on the brain's receptor sites that exist for a naturally occurring chemical transmitter, 5-hydroxytryptamine (5HT). Very high degrees of tolerance to hallucinogens can rapidly build up. Someone who takes, say, three doses of LSD over a few days will get only a disappointingly slight reaction with the third experience. There are no withdrawal symptoms.

Plants yielding these substances have a wide geographical distribution. Atropine is found in deadly nightshade and LSD is present in the seeds of morning glory. In Siberia and other remote northern regions, the fly agaric mushroom, *Amanita muscaria*, has been used for its hallucinogenic effects. The major sources for such plant-derived drugs are, however, to be found in Central America, where the button-like peyote cactus yields mescaline, and the *Psilocybe* mushroom provides psilocybin. Besides LSD, a number of recent synthetic products have hallucinogenic potential, including MDMA or 'Ecstasy'. It can be difficult to draw the boundary between drugs which should truly rate as hallucinogens and those many plant-derived substances, such as nutmeg and catnip, or synthetic chemicals, such as nitrous oxide or laughing gas, from which someone at sometime has obtained something mind-bending.

All drug reactions are of course shaped by environment and

expectation, as well as being provoked by the drug. That is especially true of the hallucinogens. If the user is primed to believe that he or she will have a mystical experience and takes mescaline within the ritual of a Native American church, divine visions may well ensue. If in a modern-day, Western social setting the novice LSD user is primed and prompted by friends to believe that the experience will be positive, and is helped and comforted when transiently the experience becomes disturbing, the 'trip' will probably be an interesting and pleasurable journey.

But 'probably' is the necessary qualifier. Every individual's response to a hallucinogen is to a certain extent unpredictable. Someone who has previously had many good experiences, may on a subsequent occasion have a nasty reaction. And an intriguing and enjoyable session may on the instant turn into something intensely threatening, with dreams becoming nightmares. The first-time experimenter will be at greater risk than the experienced user. Some people will be more vulnerable than others by reason of personality. The bigger the dose, the greater will be the potential risk of an adverse reaction. If someone takes one of these drugs unknowingly (their beer perhaps spiked with LSD), a catastrophic reaction is probable.

What needs to be emphasized is that no hallucinogenic experience can ever be given a guarantee of safety. The negative mental impacts, when they occur, may be of several degrees and kinds. A so-called 'bad trip' can involve no more than mild and short-lived panic or can be a devastating storm of disoriented terror, with hideous visions crowding in and hell let loose. In that state of temporary insanity, a person may harm themselves or attack someone else.

Usually a bad trip will last only for a few hours, and an experienced user may be able to 'talk down' their friend and bring them again into touch with reality. Sometimes, however, the mental disturbance will last for a few days and will be of an intensity to require hospital admission. It is difficult to put a figure on the extreme kind of occurrence. In any city where high-dosage LSD is common among young people, LSD psychosis will be a familiar emergency room presentation to mental health services.

Hallucinogens can produce mild physiological reactions such as nausea, palpitations and sweating. Death by overdose is extraordinarily unlikely. When death occurs, it will probably be due to an accident as the intoxicated person engages in bizarre behaviour, such as jumping out of a window in the belief they can fly. That LSD or other hallucinogens have ever directly caused a single death is impossible to prove. But few who have had close experience with people who take these drugs would doubt the proposition.

Plant-derived hallucinogen use in history

Here is a brief botanical tour, profiling just a few of the many plant chemicals that have been used by mankind as doorways to strange perceptions.

Belladonna

Belladonna's place in history is due to the atropine found in deadly nightshade. Dropped into the eyes of a woman, it could enlarge her pupils and make her a *bella donna*, a beautiful lady. Although a poison, atropine has its use in medicine. When used in a carefully adjusted sublethal dose, it can produce delusional states. Belladonna was employed by sorcerers to induce trance in themselves and their clients. Witches might rub themselves with belladonna ointment and take imaginary flight over the church spires.

John Baptista Porta wrote a book in 1658 called *Natural Magik*, in which he recommended drugging people with belladonna and similar plant products as a practical joke:

Bella Donna, a Drachm of the Root of which . . . will make Men mad without any Hurt so that it is a most pleasant thing to behold such mad Whimsies and Visions . . . I had a Friend, who as oft as he pleased knew how to make a Man believe he was changed into a Bird or a Beast, and cause Madness at his pleasure . . . I remember when I was a young Man, I tried these things on my Chamber-Fellows.

Porta was not someone with whom it would have been comfortable to share lodgings.

Various other references to plant-induced intoxication can be found across Europe, and at times there was a fear that these drugs might be used to facilitate rape. But belladonna and other plant hallucinogens, in Western Europe, remained drugs only of sporadic, whispered use, and they never became integrated in religious cult or popular culture.

Fly agaric in Siberia

Fly agaric has a deep history in Siberia as a recreational drug. People in that hard climate prized the mushroom which would put them into a trance state, and paid a good price to obtain their supplies. This drug taking was a convivial social activity, with no quest for mystical revelation.

What surprised Western observers, in the nineteenth century, when their merchants travelled into Siberia and became acquainted with the fly agaric habit, was the curious practice of conserving supplies by drinking the urine of the person who had recently partaken. Passage through one user was standard practice and that individual might drink his own urine or pass some of it on to a friend. A further recycling meant the drug would lose its potency. A tin can was a necessary adjunct to the fly agaric party.

The peyote cult in Mexico

In the sixteenth century, the Spanish conquerors arrived in Mexico and found that the indigenous people were using the peyote cactus for magical and religious purposes. The Spaniards took against this practice as ungodly, much as elsewhere in their conquered territories they tried to suppress the use of the coca leaf. Catholic priests were instructed routinely to enquire in the confessional as to whether people had engaged in the heathen habit.

Efforts at suppression only partially succeeded. With a nice capacity to merge religions, a mission station emerged with the name El Santo Nombre Jesus Peyotes (The Saint of the name Jesus Peyotes). When in the nineteenth and twentieth centuries anthropologists started to look at folk use of peyote in Mexico, they found that the practice was alive and well and had outlived the conquistadors.

In this culture, rather than the hallucinogen's being a witches' oint-ment, a rape drug or a way of getting out of one's mind as in Siberia, its use was constrained by ritual. The party that went to find the cactus in the desert was on a mission to obtain the flesh of the gods, and would fast and abstain from sex to purify themselves for the venture. When, later, the cactus was brought back to be eaten in the village, the men would be sitting in a circle in the evening, the shaman would hand each participant their portion, drums would beat and together everyone would enter the world of the spirits. Novice takers would be guided by the priest as to what spiritual doors the drug would open for them. To have gone casually to the desert and eaten one's own cactus for private kicks would have been unthinkable.

Mescaline as artificial paradise

In the late 1890s, two reports appeared which helped bring mescaline to scientific and popular attention. Silas Weir Mitchell, an American neurologist, published a paper on the drug in 1896. The focus here will be on a more complex and detailed account given two years later by Mitchell's British contemporary, Havelock Ellis. He conducted experiments both on himself and on several aesthetically gifted friends.

Ellis trained at St Thomas's Hospital in London, and achieved fame with the appearance, between 1897 and 1928, of his seven-volume *Studies in the Psychology of Sex*. Written in a spirit of objective enquiry and free from moral judgement, this remarkable work pre-dated Kinsey's 1948 *Sexual Behaviour in the Human Male* by a good few years. For a time it was banned from public sale in Britain.

With a bow to Charles Baudelaire, Havelock Ellis published in 1902 an essay on mescaline, entitled 'Mescal: a New Artificial Paradise'. That report predated by fifty-two years another contribution to the genre of psychedelic adventure, Aldous Huxley's famous 1954 *The Doors of Perception*.

Ellis conducted his experiments at his apartment in the Temple, an enclave in London largely given over to barristers' chambers. He chose a Good Friday for the first experiment and drank an extract made from three peyote 'buttons'. How he came by his supply is not revealed. He described the ensuing paradisiacal experience thus:

a vast field of golden jewels, studded with red and green stones, ever changing . . . at the same time the air around me seemed to be flushed with vague perfume . . . I would see thick, glorious fields of jewels . . . Then they would spring up into flower-like shapes beneath my gaze, and then seem to turn into gorgeous butterfly forms or endless folds of glistening, iridescent, fibrous wings of wonderful insects . . .

He stated that 'a large part of its charm lies in the halo of beauty which it casts around the simplest and commonest things'. And with that comment Ellis directly foreshadowed what Huxley was to write many years later about mescaline taking in a Californian garden.

Intrigued by the potential of the drug to enhance aesthetic awareness, Ellis persuaded an artist to visit the Temple apartment and swallow peyote. On the first occasion nothing happened and Ellis suspected that he had made a bad job of the extraction process. He then tried again and to 'make sure of success the experiment was repeated with four buttons'. The result was perhaps the first hallucinogen-induced bad trip to be described in the literature. The victim wrote of the experience:

I saw an intensely vivid blue light begin to play around every object . . . Such a silent and sudden illumination of all things around . . . seemed like a kind of madness beginning from outside me, and its strangeness affected me more than its beauty. A desire to escape from it led me to the door. But a sudden difficulty in breathing and a sensation of numbness at the heart brought me back to the armchair from which I had arisen. From this moment I had a series of attacks or paroxysms which I can only describe by saying that I felt as though I were dying . . . My speedy dissolution, I half imagined, was about to take place, and the power of making any resistance to the violent sensations that were arising within was going, I felt, with every second.

The terrified subject experienced 'a sensation of a nauseous and suffocating gas mounting up into my head'.

Not daunted, Ellis then recruited two poets to his experiments. One of them did not like the mescaline at all and declared that he much preferred 'haschisch'. The other achieved a state of beatitude, and while playing the piano with closed eyes 'saw one or two appearances which might have been shields or breastplates'.

What is interesting about these Victorian goings-on is again the evidence that different people can respond very differently to the same drug. Sweet perfumes or poisonous gas, panic or beatitude, with hallucinogens the customer pays the piper but does not necessarily choose the tune.

Beyond the surface content of the report lies the intriguing question of what place a freethinking Victorian sexologist was likely to give to mescaline in his scheme of things. The reason why Ellis or

Baudelaire played with drugs was no doubt in part a nose for a good story, psychological voyeurism and the wish to be at the leading edge. They were playing with exotic pleasures, but rather than perceiving their drug taking as flirting with the devil, their drugs were not at that time illicit, evil or seen as dangerous. Mitchell and Ellis came to mescaline through scientific interest. Yet within Ellis's overall reactions, there was a foretaste of the belief that hallucinogens could open the doors of perception – 'It may at least be claimed that for a healthy person to be once or twice admitted to the rites of mescal is not only an unforgettable delight but an educational influence of no mean value.'

After Ellis, Western interest in vision-giving drugs lay dormant for many years. The first half of the twentieth century did not provide the right climate, and the world, perhaps, had too many waking nightmares.

Enter LSD

Ergot is derived from *Claviceps purpurea*, a fungus which grows on rye and other grasses. In the Middle Ages, contamination of flour by ergot led to mass epidemics of a poisoning known as St Anthony's Fire, because of the burning sensation experienced by the victims.

In due time, ergot found its place in medicine as a drug used by midwives to hasten delivery. In 1917, the Sandoz pharmaceutical company started a research programme on ergot, and identified the active constituent of the fungus as a substance to which the name ergotamine was given. Ergotamine became a widely used drug in the treatment of post-puerperal bleeding, through its power to contract the uterus. Out of the poison had come benefit.

In the early 1930s, a young Sandoz research chemist, Dr Albert Hoffman, started to work on the synthesis of ergotamine and of derivatives which might hopefully have further pharmaceutical potential. One of these substances, the twenty-fifth in a series, was named lysergic acid diethylamide, or LSD 25. It had interesting properties but lacked sufficient promise for research on it to be taken further.

In April 1943, Hoffman returned to the investigation of LSD, and synthesized a new batch. As given at a symposium held fifty years later, here is Hoffman's account of what happened that day:

I was very surprised when in the afternoon of 16 April, 1943, after I had repeated the synthesis of LSD, I entered suddenly into a kind of dream-world. The surroundings had changed in a strange way, and had become luminous, more expressive. I felt uneasy and went home, where I wanted to rest. Lying on the couch with closed eyes, because I experienced daylight as unpleasantly glaring, I perceived an uninterrupted stream of fantastic pictures, with an intense kaleidoscopic play of colours. After some hours this strange but not unpleasant condition faded away.

Hoffman at first thought that he might have been reacting to a solvent he had used in the preparation of the LSD, but further self-experimentation proved this not to be the case. With considerable courage, on 19 April, he went back to his laboratory and took a small dose of LSD by mouth to see whether the drug itself was the dream-world agent. The experience this time was less pleasant than on the first occasion:

I asked my laboratory assistant to escort me home. Having no car, we went by bicycle. On the way home my condition began to assume threatening forms. Everything in my field of vision wavered and was distorted as if seen in a curved mirror ... familiar objects and the furniture seemed grotesque ... The substance with which I had wanted to experiment had become a demon ... I was seized by the dreadful fear of becoming insane ... My body seemed to be without sensation, lifeless, strange. Was I dying? Was this the transition?

The reaction on 16 April had been to a minute dose of LSD accidentally absorbed through the skin. Three days later Hoffman had administered to himself what he at the time thought to be an extremely cautious dose, but it had been enough to turn the LSD experience into a hideous bad trip. Thus did Hoffman discover the unprecedented potency of the first ever synthetic hallucinogen.

Subsequent to 1943, the story of what happened to LSD has several strands. LSD became a drug used, or misused, with great enthusiasm in the treatment of mental illness. It was taken up with zeal by prophets who claimed that its visionary properties could change the world. And it became a recreational substance, a toy, the symbol of the beat generation.

What characterized each of those responses was the proselytizing exuberance of the drug's champions. LSD turned on the psychiatrists, the gurus, the cult figures, and turned on the streets. The wild exaggeration of the benefits and joys was accompanied by wilful disregard for the dangers.

LSD and psychotherapy

In the 1950s, the legacy of Freud's suggestion that bringing buried memories into consciousness could be psychologically healing, led to psychiatrists experimenting with LSD as a tool to aid exploration of the subconscious. Psychoanalysis met up with a drug to give birth to psychedelic psychotherapy. LSD was first employed to this end in America, but by the mid-1950s such practice had spread to Europe. The patient would be talked through what might be expected of the forthcoming session by the therapist. The scene would be carefully set, music played perhaps, and a dose of LSD repeatedly administered in sessions held over weeks or months. The psychotherapist acted as guide and interpreter.

Therapists were not too conservative in their claims as to the range of conditions which would yield to LSD-assisted treatment; this is demonstrated in a 1970 catalogue given out by two American practitioners of this approach, Robert Masters and Jean Houston:

Types of conditions repeatedly stated to respond favourably to treatment with psychedelics include chronic alcoholism, criminal psychopathy, sexual deviations and neuroses, depressive states . . . phobias, anxiety neuroses, compulsive syndromes, and puberty neurosis. In addition, psychedelics have been used with autistic children . . . with terminal cancer patients . . . and with adult schizophrenics.

Not content with a listing of target conditions which embraced most of the chapter headings to be found in any standard psychiatric textbook, Masters and Houston went on to discuss the use of LSD in circumstances which might terrify less bold practitioners:

The risks frequently have been considered too great for . . . those with a history of suicide attempts or who may be currently suicidal. However, as we have previously suggested . . . psychedelic psychotherapy may be indicated in cases where suicide seems probable and imminent. By his being enabled to die symbolically and then be reborn, the patient's need to die may be subsequently eliminated.

Or not.

When looking at the therapeutic enthusiasms of thirty years ago, one does well to judge the protagonists within the then prevailing climate of ideas. Psychotherapy was speculative, and the scientific investigation of psychotherapeutic efficacy was at that time poorly developed. When a wonder drug arrived on the scene, it was easy for it to meet up with that unquenchable element in the medical mindset: the quest for omnipotence. The willingness of some doctors to use LSD as a psychological cure-all was breathtaking. The side effect was that a dangerous drug was helped towards public legitimacy. Once more, medical endorsement coloured a drug's popular image.

Recruiting sergeants

The drum beat in the message on LSD and other hallucinogens was that they could revolutionize human consciousness, remake society and reshape religion. To illustrate the intoxicated sweep of the ambition, here are some representative quotes spanning the years 1957 to 1970, starting with Dr Humphrey Osmond, the Canadian psychiatrist who coined the term 'psychedelic' and who introduced Aldous Huxley to mescaline (1957):

These agents have a part to play in our survival as a species . . . Surely we must seize the chance.

Aldous Huxley (1960; reproduced in Huxley 1980): These new mind changers will tend in the long run to deepen the spiritual life of the communities in which they are available . . . biochemical discoveries that . . . will make it possible for large numbers of men and women to achieve a radical self-transcendence and a deeper understanding of the nature of things and this revival of religion will be at the same time a revolution.

Dr Robert S. Davidson, clinical psychologist practising in New York (1961): The inability to love is now being recognized as the root of the major tragic sicknesses of our day . . . The wonder of LSD is that it can bring within the capabilities of ordinary people the experience of universal love.

Dr Ira Einhorn, an American writer (1970): I feel that those on the moving edge of new culture will eventually use these tools in a way that will utterly transform the nature of human consciousness.

These are just a few examples of the grand assertions, untouched by any tinge of doubt, that were made by people who declared that LSD had the capacity to effect universal human betterment. There was a vying to be messianic.

The chief of all propagandists for the psychedelic revolution was Timothy Leary, a psychologist who, in the early 1950s, held a chair at Harvard, and who had Aldous Huxley, Allen Ginsberg, William Burroughs and Arthur Koestler among the volunteers for his drug-taking experiments. It was Havelock Ellis's Temple flat born again. Leary started out with psilocybin but his interests were soon centring on LSD. In 1963, he administered LSD to ten theological students in a Boston university chapel and this produced a startling spectacle. With echoes of John Baptista Porta dosing his fellow lodgers, one student believed himself transmuted into a fish. Over a few years, hundreds of Harvard students were given LSD in the name of scientific investigation, and Leary launched the International Federation for Internal Freedom as a front organization for the LSD cause. He set up an LSD-taking commune in Mexico, lost his job at Harvard, fell foul of the Mexican authorities, was expelled from that country, and later found himself convicted on drug charges in the US. In passing, he had claimed that LSD was the best ever aphrodisiac.

In the 1960s and 1970s many of the leading figures of the literary and music world made LSD part of their advertised lifestyle. Not only those people as individuals but an entire cultural movement acted as advocate for the drug. There is uncertainty as to whether the Beatles intended 'Lucy in the Sky with Diamonds' to convey through acronym a subliminal statement, but that is the way in which many audiences interpreted the song.

Leary may, today, be looked back on fondly as an eccentric who teased the establishment. The hippy enthusiasm for dropping acid can be viewed nostalgically as the indulgence of a lost age when adolescence was infinitely extended. Put that together with all those portentous statements made by writers and academics, and an overall picture of a do-it-yourself publicity machine, unequalled in the annals of drug history, emerges. What surely remains surprising is the way in which a facile analysis of the human predicament was used to derive the astonishing conclusion that the world could be put to right by a little taste of artificial paradise.

LSD as anyone's trip

To have described LSD in the mid-60s as having 'got out into the street' would have been too down-market a metaphor. At the beginning, the drug got into the sitting rooms with piled cushions. In those early days, LSD was used largely by the young and psychologically aspiring. Dropping acid at pop music festivals was de rigueur, and there would be an informal first-aid tent for talking down bad trips. What was wanted from the drug was a badge of youth revolution, fully paid-up membership of the Beat generation, the Doors of Perception thrown wide open, all that and everything else that the easy preachers promised.

Even at that early stage of pleasure trips for everyone, the scene was not as idyllic as the propaganda would have had it. There clearly were some terrifying, immediate experiences, and sometimes very unpleasant flashbacks could also result. Here is an account given by a patient.

Doesn't happen all the time but several times a day suddenly I get this feeling that every line in the room is bending, tables bending, contortions where the ceiling meets the walls, carpet twisting on the floor. Then panic that I might be the next thing to bend.

There was disjunction between the promises of the gurus and what users were themselves discovering. LSD was beginning to get a bad name.

The authorities made moves. The British controlled LSD, psilocybin and mescaline for the first time in the Drugs (Prevention of Misuse) Act of 1964. In 1965, Federal US Law criminalized manufacture but not possession of LSD. In 1966, California brought in legislation to outlaw the manufacture, supply and possession of the drug; comprehensive Federal legislation followed in 1968.

New variants of hallucinogens began to appear as so-called 'designer drugs'. Government then started to control the supply of chemicals employed in the illicit manufacture of LSD and similar substances. The medical use of LSD was virtually shut down. A long way from the propagation of universal love, the CIA in America became interested in the use of LSD for nefarious purposes.

The image of LSD was, by the 1980s, tarnished, but its use continued albeit in different patterns. It was now more often used for a cheap thrill than for mystical insight, and anyone who took LSD was probably a user of other illicit drugs too. By this time, LSD was well and truly out on the street, and the microdots were often contaminated with other synthetics. Over the years, LSD moved in and out of fashion in a fluctuating, unpredictable way. At times it seemed to flood the market and yet a year later supplies would be scant.

In the mid-80s, the illicit manufacturers of LSD had an innovative idea that was good for the user's health, and also favourable for profit margins. Traditionally, LSD had been sold in doses of around 100–150 micrograms. That kind of dose was likely to bring about other-worldly experiences, and it was prone to provoke a bad trip. When the kitchen chemists decided to halve the marketed dose, LSD as circulating on the street effectively ceased to be a hallucinogen. It was now more the instrument for a non-specific high, with no attached symbolism or promise of revelation. Take acid and dance the night through.

LSD's reputation is today exactly that – a dance drug. There must still be some people who swallow a double dose, listen to the Beatles, lie back on the scatter cushions and go questing for the psychedelic dreams of yesterday. But much more commonly, LSD finds its place in the modern teenage clubber's world, among an array of chemicals such as Ecstasy, amphetamine, ketamine and cannabis, which together comprise the spectrum of dance drugs (see Chapter 16).

Hallucinogens: what they tell about drug taking

In 1956, Humphrey Osmond sent a note to his friend Aldous Huxley, which contained this couplet:

> To fathom Hell or soar angelic,
> Just take a pinch of psychedelic.

Heaven and Hell may have been supplanted today by the chill-out room, and probably there will be further twists before the psychedelic story is done. But at this juncture let's try to form a view on what insights hallucinogens may offer towards understanding of why people take drugs.

Earlier in this chapter it was suggested that what is curious about the spread of hallucinogens is that they are not dependence inducing. They offer a controlled experiment on the epidemic spread of drug use, with the dependence element washed out. What seems amply confirmed is that drugs do not need the capacity to set up dependence for an epidemic to run. To understand how LSD spread, we should be looking as much at skateboards or yo-yos, as at drugs.

What the hallucinogen story also so powerfully tells is that the spread of drugs is often carried by the chance coming together of multiple factors. With LSD, there was first the sheer accident of Hoffman's discovery that when he went back to look again at the twenty-fifth modification in his ergotamine series, strange things happened to him. There had been the long history of society's previous use of hallucinogens: witches flying on their broomsticks; Central American religion and the flesh of the gods, fly agaric and tin cans in Siberia, Havelock Ellis brewing up his cactus in London. But, suddenly, the spin-off of Hoffman's enthusiasm for ergotamine gave us a cheap and easily manufactured synthetic.

The psychotherapists played with Hoffman's drug and gave it their so-helpful imprimatur, and LSD was out into an America which was eager both for salvation and fun. Contemporary America was a society with which LSD fitted a societal receptor site, as it soon did too in Britain and other European countries. As for what it was in society and the contemporary mindset which made LSD so appealing: that is a question as difficult to answer as what made *The Naked Lunch* become a cult text, and what influenced the development of contemporary music or the fashion for long hair. There are explanations in terms of the youth revolution, the Vietnam War, plenty of money around and quite a lot of young people in the wealthy West living only for the pleasures of the day: all these influences may have contributed. Popular culture at that time embraced LSD, cheered on by the new cult priests.

What is, in retrospect, also remarkable is the way in which appraisal of the drug changed over a relatively short time. LSD lost its glamour, not because of health education or Acts of Parliament, but because awareness of its dangers got out on to the streets. The clubbers today are a different generation, expecting different things from themselves, of society and from their drugs than did an earlier generation in California. Fashions changed, and drug taking is partly about fashion.

16

Dance to the Music of Drugs

Dionysus was a Greek god who came down from the mountains of Thrace to praise, practise and disseminate voluptuous drunkenness. There was something inherently ambiguous about his position, as he stood both for life and destruction. He was portrayed with vine leaves in his hair and an outstretched arm would characteristically be clutching a goblet. Wine dripped from his patulous lips. His cult expanded in content over the centuries, and, in addition to the grape, came to embrace the more general patronage of things orgiastic. Dancing, ecstatic states, sex, were all mixed in with the drink when he presided. In his retinue, he had a rat-pack of nymphs, satyrs, centaurs and the infamous Pan. His festivals became occasions for exuberant goings on throughout Greece. In the final phase of his incarnation he gave up orgiastic delirium and was born again.

Dionysus may have reformed in his later years but people have never stopped dancing. Men and women have throughout the ages danced on secular and religious occasions, in the Dance of Death, for military display, to make the rain come, to cure the bite of the tarantula or because they felt like dancing.

One of the strangest episodes in dance history occurred in Europe during the Middle Ages, with the outbreak of a dancing mania as a mass event, with features remarkably similar to the modern rave. Here is an account of one such outbreak, as given by Frances Rust in her 1969 *Dance in Society*:

There are ... numerous reports that in July 1374 thousands of men and women, who had come to Aachen from various parts of Germany to celebrate the midsummer festival of St John, suddenly began to leap and scream in the streets. Losing all control they danced for hours until overcome by exhaustion. Some saw visions ...

Contemporary accounts talked about peasants leaving their ploughs, mechanics their workshops, housewives their domestic duties. In the streets and market squares they danced as if possessed. It has been suggested that rye contaminated by a fungus produced ergot poisoning (see Chapter 15), with people then dancing to relieve the burning sensations in their limbs. This poisoning may perhaps have contributed to outbreaks of the 'wild, leaping dance' which reoccurred sporadically, even up to the eighteenth century. But the mania can be more persuasively interpreted as evidence that dance itself can intoxicate and have its own epidemic spread – dancing mania, the old-fashioned waltz, the tango, Rock around the Clock – dance has always been infectious.

Over the centuries and across many countries, drink often played a role as facilitator of public or private celebrations where dancing and music were happening. The drink and the dancing blended; no fiddler in any era would ever have wanted to play at a wedding without the drink flowing. Alcohol can claim precedence as the prototypical 'dance drug'. But it has always had disadvantages in that its effects on coordination and balance are more likely to result in bumping, tripping and falling than enhanced performance on the dance floor. Alcohol is pharmacologically far from being an energizing pep pill to keep dancers active all night long. Its value lies not in a stimulant effect but in its ability to loosen inhibitions, create a merging of self, partner and dance, and help make a moment.

From past centuries there are a few accounts of drugs other than alcohol being used as accompaniments to dance. When cocaine in the 1920s began to mix with the jazz age, that was probably the first time in history that alcohol was seriously challenged on the dance floor. The story here is the flow of drug use shaped by popular culture.

Settled times

In the 1950s, post-war and still austerity laden Britain had in the Palais de Danse a folk institution of considerable importance. It is easily forgotten that long before the birth of the rave, three million people in the UK each week paid their entrance fee of 1s. 6d.–2s. 6d. (7½p–12½p) for an evening at the local Palais. Foxtrot, quickstep and the waltz would have been the staple, with an occasional tango for the more daring. The band wore dinner jackets. The Hammersmith Palais was down the road from the hospital where I was working, and in our evenings off we young doctors could sample the delights of the dance hall.

The Palais as an institution of popular culture is vividly sketched in Seebohm Rowntree and G. R. Lavers' 1951 *English Life and Leisure*, previously referred to in Chapter 2. The public dance halls were respectable places, and an unreformed Dionysus would have been turned away at the door. No drink was served and proceedings stopped sharp at 11pm; pubs closed at the same time so the dancers were likely to go soberly to bed. The manager of one of these halls is quoted as saying, 'We supply clean entertainment to people who want it. To get a bad name would ruin us.'

The dancers were mostly aged under twenty-five, and predominantly working class. 'I love dancing. I'd go every night if I could, but Daddy only lets me go twice a week,' said a sixteen-year-old girl interviewed by Rowntree and Lavers. 'Dancing is the best form of pleasure there is,' enthused a seventeen-year-old shop assistant. 'I can't really say I care for dancing. It's just a thing one has to do if one is going to have any social life at all,' stated a languid undergraduate.

What to the present young generation must appear to have been the truly remarkable feature of the Palais, is the fact of three million people getting onto the dance floor each week, with never a drop to drink or pill to swallow. But down the road and alternative to the Palais experience, there did exist a range of dance venues where drink was indeed available. 'I don't care for the Palais,' a twenty-five-year-old railway porter was reported as saying. 'I like a dance with a bar. I'm not all that keen on dancing really but if there is plenty of beer it's all right. It's a good place to pick up a girl.' Rowntree and Lavers were quick to point out the threat to decency contained in the porter's statement:

Modern ballroom dancing may easily degenerate into a sensuous form of entertainment, and if self-control is weakened with alcohol it is more than likely that it will do so, which might lead at least to unruly behaviour and not infrequently to sexual immorality.

The 1950s and three million people dancing sober, a young woman obeying her father's edict that she went out only twice a week, the subversive railway porter daring to hark back to the old formula of dance, drink and girls: not one of them knew that they were on the very edge of a changed world where people would dance to the music of drugs.

The 1960s and drugs partner the dance

For present purposes, it is unnecessary to chart in detail the revolution in the meaning of being young that came about in the 1960s. Whether you lived through it or not, that story is as familiar to most people as the sleeve of 'Abbey Road', and requires here no great retelling. Let's simply note that there developed at that time waves of change which redefined what it meant to be young in a Western society. Dance and music and fashion changed radically as the outer symbols of the new age, and a gulf opened between the tastes of the young and their elders – the young danced formless steps while those over twenty-five kept to their ballroom dancing or took up the Twist. The inward changes included emancipation of several kinds: the right to hedonism, sexual freedom, the partial breaking down of class barriers. That was the context in which leisure and the use of cannabis and LSD began to help define a mass youth culture, amphetamine mixed with dance and music, as a stimulant to keep the band playing and the young people on the floor dancing all night.

1968, a twenty-three-year-old man with very long hair, and wearing a resplendent antique military tunic, came to the clinic. He played a guitar with a well-known band. His private doctor would no longer give him the ration of 30 Dexedrine (dexamphetamine) tablets which he saw himself as requiring each 24 hours. The combination of sleeplessness and drugs has him drifting out of contact. 'Man, I can't do without it,' he says. He was offered a controlled reducing prescription of the tablets, but he went off not to be seen again.

In the 1960s, the amphetamine and music connection became widespread and far more extensive than anything seen with cocaine in the twenties (see Chapter 13). The 1960s were of historical importance as marking the start of a connection between drugs and the dance culture; this has continued to the beat of many different sorts of music, up to the present.

Dancing with drugs today

About 60 per cent of young people attending a present-day dance event in the UK will, that evening, use drugs. The whole night out will cost around £40 per head, with half that sum used to purchase drugs. The major source of supply will be friends, or a neighbourhood dealer from whom a purchase has been made ahead of the evening's fun. At some dance venues dealers will be in attendance, with the connivance of security staff, who will take a cut of the profits. Ostentatious gangster types are generally unwelcome, especially so if they expect free entry and drinks on the house.

These dancers take a wide spectrum of drugs. Top in popularity will still be alcohol and tobacco, with cannabis in third place. In varying order will then come Ecstasy, ketamine, GHB (gamma-hydroxybutyric acid, a sedative and intoxicant), amphetamine, LSD and amyl nitrite (poppers). Powdered cocaine may sometimes gain an entry low in the list, but crack and heroin are unlikely to feature in the dance drug menu. In the US, the mix will be much the same, but with PCP (angel dust, a stimulant and hallucinogen) more commonly available, and also Rohypnol, a rapid-acting sedative with an evil reputation as the facilitator of date rape.

The range of substances used by these dancers is, in outline, similar to that of their peers who devote their evenings to other pursuits. But the dancers use drugs much more frequently than other young people. Within the heavy-using habits of a generation where the majority of young men and women will have taken an illicit drug at least once by the age of twenty-five, the sector that regularly goes dancing stands out as one for whom drugs are a central part of their lifestyle. They are heavily drug involved, and drugs are highly valued by them. These are people who take drugs routinely when they dance, but they will also take them before and after dancing, and on other occasions too.

Dance venues are remarkably mixed. A rave organized by an entrepreneur in a warehouse may bring together hundreds or thousands of young people, in a setting which is a flashback to the dancing mania. These are events where the big crowd is an essential part of the experience. Dancing also goes on in clubs and pubs. Super clubs seek to echo, but at the same time sanitize, the ambience of the rave, and there will be tourists taking pictures. The dance form is amorphous, often seemingly solo, and does not at all look like what used to happen at the Palais. Dancing to drugs is a component part of the wider and intensely commercial entertainment scene.

As for the inner meaning, what it feels like, the why-do-it of this modern evening out: people are there to enjoy the music, socialize, look for sexual partners, have a good time, much as in any earlier dancing era. It is drink and drugs now, rather than just drink, which mixes with the dance and the music and the crowd to manufacture the modern moment.

Do the drugs in the mix really make the total brew of experience taste much different from the Dionysian flavour of any previous epoch? At times, it has been claimed that there is something special in Ecstasy and other popular drugs, in that they are 'empathogens' which will put on offer instant loving intimacy between strangers on the dance floor. Ecstasy has been described as a 'hug drug', and people who take it may claim that they feel 'loved up'. But it seems more probable that the experience is the product of setting and expectation rather than a specific effect of the drug on the brain cells. The Grateful Dead and Big Brother & the Holding Company out in California in 1966, the gigantic crowd, strobe lights, the beat of the music so strong that the floor vibrated, that was my personal introduction to something different from the Palais; we did not need drugs to tell us that the experience was amazing.

Normal is as normal does

Providing that the beat emanating from the warehouse does not wreck the just sleep of the citizens who still want to go to bed at a godly 11 o'clock, why should the state interfere with the pleasures of the large number of young people who in this post-Palais world choose to mix drugs with their dancing until dawn? Social scientists have described the use of drugs in this recreational way as a 'normalized' behaviour. They are not implying that the majority of young people in any country are taking illicit drugs with the determined frequency of the ravers and clubbers. Normalization is defined by the individual and group's own way of feeling about the behaviour. The dancers who are expecting to take drugs as a routine part of their leisure life do not regard themselves as freaks, sociopaths, criminals or people in any way alienated from mainstream society. They are not marching to the beat of a protest movement, but are consumers, albeit of an illicit product, in a consumer-led society. They are hedonists in a pleasure-seeking society, even if some of their instruments of pleasure are not approved by the law. Their self-definition is that of fully signed-up members of the larger culture, who happen to take drugs at the club when out dancing on Saturday and will wash the car on Sunday. They view themselves as not inhabiting the same planet as those alienated, ill, deviant, heroin users shooting up their drug on the same night in a mean quarter of town. Normal is as normal does, the sociologists insist.

Accept that definition of normality and the argument is won. Within this perspective, drug taking by young people who go dancing is as normal as abstinence ever used to be at the Palais, or beer for the railway porter out questing for girls. This type of drug taking is deviant in that it breaks the law, but in no other sense are the dancers a deviant sect.

Ecstasy

The drug

Ecstasy has a reputation as today's dance drug par excellence on account of its stimulant properties and its alleged capacity as an 'empathogen'. As already mentioned, it is far from the only drug likely to be employed in this setting. However, it deserves a heading of its own, both because of the worldwide popularity of its use and because of the possible long-term harm, when a generation experiences mass exposure to a chemical with the potential to compromise mental functioning.

Ecstasy's full scientific designation is extravagantly polysyllabic, 3, 4-methylenedioxymethamphetamine, but the abbreviation MDMA is commonly used. Ecstasy was first synthesized by Merck, the German pharmaceutical company, in the early part of the twentieth century and it was patented in 1912. There were no immediate medical applications for the drug, and for many years it had an orphan status. It was next heard of in the late 1970s, when it became popular among a small group of American psychotherapists as a chemical adjunct to psychotherapy. Ecstasy was being employed by them in much the same way that LSD and mescaline had earlier been used. However, the US Drug Enforcement Agency (DEA) become aware of the abuse potential, and in 1985 put Ecstasy under strict control as a Schedule 1 drug. That effectively prevented its further therapeutic exploitation in the US. In the UK, the drug was put under similarly stringent control in the same year.

That doctors resented the curtailment of prescribing rights when they believed the drug could benefit their patients was understandable. Recently, Dr Julie Holland, an American psychiatrist, has pleaded that the restrictions on the clinical application of Ecstasy should be eased. Her case is not helped by the extravagance of her claims: for instance, that a single MDMA experience is like 'a year of therapy in two hours', and that this hallucinogenic drug could be a treatment for schizophrenia. These kinds of claim leave one with a sense of relief that, in relation to this particular drug, the control authorities got ahead of further ill-advised medical experimentation.

In parallel with the small-scale, 1980s emergence of Ecstasy as a tool in psychotherapy, came its rapid and large-scale spread as an illicit drug favoured by the grateful young. In contrast to the usual sequence where America leads drug fashions, in this instance it was Britain out front. Customs and police seizures rocketed. The source of supply was bountiful: illicit manufacture coupled with much international cross-border trafficking.

Although Britain led the way, the US and other countries soon took up the drug enthusiastically. Ecstasy use has become 'normalized', within the sociological definition, in most developed countries. That happened very quickly, and everywhere there was a strong link to dance and music.

Is Ecstasy taking harmful?

Like the unwelcome guest at the dance, in the midst of all this fun a number of not too empathogenic side effects began to attract attention. These are broadly of two kinds: acute, toxic reactions with death the possible outcome, and the long-term possibility of brain damage.

Ecstasy can lead to hyperthermia (raised body temperature) due to an interaction between the drug's pharmacological impact and sustained physical activity in an over-heated environment. Body temperature can soar, with resulting distress, collapse, a rush by ambulance to hospital and little chance of recovery if it has reached a disaster threshold of 109° F. One way to avoid overheating and dehydration is to advise dancers to drink a lot of water. But the danger they may then paradoxically encounter is water intoxication and lowering of blood sodium (hyponatraemia), and that condition too can be fatal.

The first Ecstasy death was reported in 1988. Only a few such tragedies occur during any one year in any country, and the phrase 'only a few' will be much on the lips of those who regard talk of these deaths as got-up panic. Peanut butter causes more deaths than Ecstasy, the apologists insist. Furthermore, they will suggest that it is often the chemical contaminants in the illicitly manufactured product which do the harm: make Ecstasy legal, introduce quality control, there need be no deaths, the argument goes.

Health professionals are likely to take a less sanguine view. Within the usual formula, one would expect more casualties the more widely a potentially dangerous drug comes to be used. What is 'only a few' today may be quite a few tomorrow. And according to a recent report from St George's Hospital, London, that kind of upward drift in Ecstasy deaths seems perhaps now to be occurring in the UK. A recent year had forty of these deaths reported. Toxicologists will regard as dubious the claim that the contaminants are the major danger. No one wants to get up a panic, the annual number of deaths is still small compared to many other causes, it is too early confidently to predict trends, and chill-out rooms and sensible advice can reduce the risks. But for any parent whose child is added to the forty toll, talk of only small numbers will carry no comfort. Sadly, there is no getting away from the fact that Ecstasy can kill.

It is possible that Ecstasy can cause long-lasting impairment in certain kinds of mental functioning. The front-line reports are of young people who for a few days after taking Ecstasy are surprised to find themselves a little bit down in their mood and anxious, and perhaps also their memory is not too good. Those seemingly low-grade experiences may show the effect that Ecstasy is having on the brain's serotonin system.

Serotonin has featured at several previous points in this book. It is a chemical concerned with the regulation of feeling tone. Depletion of serotonin will lead to depression. There are cells concentrated in certain parts of the brain that store and then release serotonin so as to transmit messages across the gaps between cells. Experimental work on laboratory animals suggests that Ecstasy can damage the axons (nerve fibres) of these serotonin-rich cells, thus impairing their signalling capacity. There is a debate as to whether the doses employed in the animal experiments fairly reproduce the probable level of the dance-drug user's exposure. But it seems likely that, in the human subject, even a single, Saturday night dose of Ecstasy may leave a transient impairment in the brain's serotonin system lasting for a few days. The dopamine system is also involved, but it is the axons of the serotinergic brain cells that bear the brunt.

Add one dose of Ecstasy to another, pile up the little bits of chemical insult, and the result may be a still undramatic but none the less quite worrying kind and degree of permanent impairment. The risk of damage is related to dose. Someone who takes two or three Ecstasy tabs over a single evening is courting danger more than a person who takes a tablet only occasionally; but repeated 'safe' doses can add up to impairment. Various serotonin depletion effects have been described as the possible consequences of this type of nerve-cell toxicity, including panic attacks and feelings of unreality. But it is the mood disturbance and interference with memory which are the major causes for concern. Because at this age they have memory capacity to spare, some slight impairment in memory may go unnoticed in young people. But the long-term worry is how these decrements may come through to manifest themselves in the same individuals, years later, when they need all the memory function that the ageing brain can hold on to.

The interim appraisal
Ecstasy and its possible adverse impact on body and mind: what should be the balanced judgement on the evidence thus far? 'Thus

far' is an important part of that question in that new research on the topic is being published in the scientific journals all the time.

As regards mortality risk, the evidence seems firm and no impartial scientist could today say other than that Ecstasy carries some danger. The 'some' is small in statistical terms, but the abstract statistic translates into real-life tragedy. This danger should not be exaggerated, but neither should it be denied.

The difficulty for researchers lies more with interpretation of the work on brain damage. The results from animal research are suggestive, but proof positive that Ecstasy causes brain damage to humans is still not to hand. Interpretation of case series which compare the mental health of users and non-users is complicated by the fact that people who take drugs can be different from other people at the base point – more anxious perhaps or with a greater propensity for depression. Furthermore, among these young drug users, it is difficult to find people who have only ever used one type of drug, and that complicates the interpretation. And no investigator would see it as ethical to administer Ecstasy to human subjects as an experiment.

Most scientists with close knowledge of this area of research are likely to see the 'normalized' acceptance of Ecstasy as cause for some anxiety. Normal is as normal does, say social scientists, but that will not eliminate a drug's toxicity and the risk of substantial damage to the population riding on the coat-tail of the normalization.

And the K-hole

The discussion above has focused on Ecstasy. And yet all the other entries on the dance-drug menu, whether as familiar as alcohol or as recently arrived as any of the further polysyllabic designer drugs (MDA, MDE, MBDB), are substances where questions should be asked about safety. The questioning becomes all the more important when the drugs are often taken by young people on a pick-and-mix basis, with no clear knowledge as to what was picked last from the handful or how these chemicals will mix in their impact on the brain.

Ketamine has a place in medicine as a quick-acting anaesthetic. The drug has leaked sufficiently to the dance world for the expression 'K-hole' to have come into use to describe the state of intoxication it can induce. Here is a description of that experience as given by two researchers, Dr Valerie Curran and Dr Lisa Monaghan:

The diverse subjective experiences . . . termed the 'K-hole' . . . commonly include: the sensation of light through the body; novel experiences concerning 'body consistency' e.g. being made of wood or rubber; grotesque distortion of shape or size of body parts; a sensation of floating or hovering in a weightless condition; absence of sense of time; visions, hallucinations; insight into the riddles of existence . . . melting together with people or things; out of body experiences . . .

Some young people will find the K-hole a more interesting experience zone than was to be found on the alcohol-free dance floor at the Hammersmith Palais. Ketamine may offer all the special effects of film makers, but lived through in real time, and with a few additional experiences besides. Unfortunately, Curran and Monaghan's report goes on to suggest that Ketamine can result in persistent impairment of memory.

And Ketamine is only one drug in the commonly swallowed pick and mix.

Drug taking embedded in a commercialized culture

Popular music is a product of a vastly rich industry, and the leisure industry which gives it context is also hugely profitable. These legitimate enterprises now have an inextricable relationship with the very profitable, multinational enterprise relating to the manufacture and sale of drugs. It is drinking, drug taking and, more than anything, money which spins the commercialized dance world around. Removing drugs from that mix will not now be easy: the age of the rave has come, the dancing madness is here to stay, Dionysus is necking Ecstasy and probably getting his cut on the deal. It is difficult to believe that a normalized behaviour embedded in popular culture and in that nexus of cash will fade out as easily as the Palais.

Here is Dr Claudio Naranjo, a contributor to Julie Holland's recent book, rejoicing and unabashed and unworried:

MDMA (Ecstasy) . . . has been known and used widely for many years and despite accidents attributed to high blood pressure or inappropriate use it is remarkable for its lack of danger to healthy people. I would say it is the champagne of the feeling enhancers.

With dance drugs, society has fallen into a cash-hole and there will be no quick climbing out. But as a start one might do well to neutralize some of the misinformation which is peddled by the handful.

17

The Martian Calls Again

We have seen drugs of many kinds tasted over many centuries by many different countries, tolerance or intolerance of their presence, nil or ferocious control and positions in between, many inconsistencies, a plethora of experience.

What to make of the story thus far? My own sense of puzzlement in the face of all this material is such, at this stage, as to make me eager once more for a detached view. So I am again reaching for the Martian.

He emerges from his spacecraft. The reception committee stands ready to welcome him.

'Last time I touched down here,' he says, 'you told me about your planet's coexistence with licit drugs. "Fuddle and muddle," was the phrase I employed to encapsulate that encounter.'

'Exactly so,' says the spokeswoman. 'But do not forget that in characterizing that experience you added hypocrisy, venality, mendacity, stupidity and a tendency to denial, as further descriptors.'

'I did so,' replies the Martian. 'Now I need to put a big question to you. What is your advice – amazingly experienced as you are – on how to handle illicit drugs?'

Commotion erupts among the committee's members. Blows are randomly struck and there is much yelling. Some people fall weeping to their knees and pray for a quick victory in the War on Drugs, while others climb trees and make speeches through megaphones, favouring legalization across the board. Health-education material is being lavishly distributed but at the same time peddlers have moved in and are selling every kind of mind-acting substance, licit and illicit. Someone has collapsed with an overdose and several have been rendered psychotic. Scythians are seen heating their stones. A squad car arrives and people are arrested. Spontaneous dancing breaks out.

An effigy of Mr Anslinger is burned. A firing squad is seeking to locate dealers for summary execution. The police throw away their truncheons and join in the rave. Chaos reigns. Dionysus sways his way across the grass. The scene makes Platzspitz pale in comparison.

Eventually the spokeswoman succeeds in quelling the disorder. Addressing the Martian, she says:

Let me firstly assure you that we do indeed have a geographically vast and time-deep global experience with drugs, both those which are currently licit and those which are illicit. This is a drugged planet. If when you leave us you fly your craft low over the earth's land surface, you would have a fair chance of before long seeing below you some process of drug cultivation. You would see vineyards, coffee plantations, wide areas where the tobacco crop shaped the economy, fields of opium poppy, patches of lank Indian hemp flowering even on vacant city lots. The coca plant grows on the slopes of the Andes, so that 6 million peasants shall obtain their cocaine. Even the desert has the peyote cactus. As you looked down on the great industrial countries it would be the factories, however, rather than the fields which would properly catch your attention: modern technology spills out its tranquillizers, stimulants, analgesics and antidepressants by the billions, and the chemist much improves on cactus and mushroom. You would know that everywhere below varieties of actors were in the arena, and with an extraordinary changeability of roles. Sometimes the state would sell the drug and take the profit, sometimes the profit would go to the legally operating entrepreneur, sometimes that role would be played by the man with the mule train who makes his way over mountain paths. The money at stake is immense and countries might finance their treasuries to a large extent from drug revenue. Conflicts of opinion are violent, the state's response to unpermitted use draconian. The situation on which you looked down would, however, seem to be characterized by an unusual degree of confusion: a drug which was permissible yesterday might tomorrow be prohibited, a drug which for one society was of importance in religious sacrament might in another place be preached against. You could conclude that one of the main businesses of the world was to cultivate, manufacture, advertise, legislate on, tax, consume, adulate and decry mind-acting substances. The complexity of the matter is overwhelming, its ramifications endless.

So if you are looking for a planet that has wide and deep experience with mind-acting chemicals licit and illicit, you have landed in the right place. We have a vast base of experience from which to tell what living with drugs of any or all kinds feels like. But we think that all these substances make up one system and differentiation between licit and illicit categories is not for analytical purposes helpful. Fuddle and muddle binds all together.*

The Martian expresses his thanks, bids goodbye and flies off low over the earth's surface.

---

* The spokeswoman is quoting verbatim a passage from Edwards (1971), as given in 'Sources and Further Reading'.

Part Four

What To Do About Drugs?

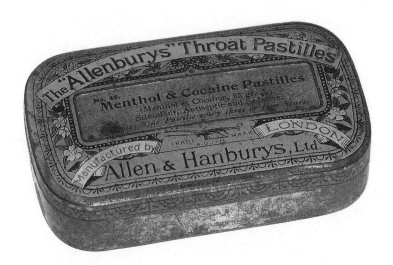

18

One Helluva Problem

In the Introduction to this book, I identified its two main and linked purposes, firstly a laying out of the facts on drugs, and secondly the application of that knowledge to better-informed responses to licit and illicit mind-acting substances. In the light of the world's astonishingly varied and protracted grapplings with the problem set by drugs, as chronicled in the preceding chapters, and with the book's first intention hopefully met, the focus in this final part of the book is on the second defined intention and how the problem can be better handled. What lessons are to be learnt from the store of experience? What successes are there on which to build? What dreadful errors can be identified, never again to be recycled?

Before looking for answers to these questions and going on to discuss (in Chapters 19 and 20) some ideas for the better handling of drugs, the present chapter will examine what it is about these substances which so often frustrates efforts at amelioration. For those who want to champion any new and radical remedy, the entry ticket to the debate should be the capacity to face the fact that society has, over centuries, failed to find a way of eliminating the damage done by drugs. The historical landscape is littered with devastating drug epidemics, many of which still run or smoulder. And new epidemics are breaking out even while the debate proceeds. What exactly is it about the drug problem which makes it one helluva problem?

One damned thing after another

The phrase 'the drug problem' might to the uninitiated suggest that what is problematic with drugs is at root one thing, a single behaviour to be targeted. Alas, nothing is further from the truth. The drug problem is intensely multiple and changeable in its manifestations, probably more so than any other medical or social problem we are ever likely to meet. A fixed enemy to be caught once and for all in the cross-wires, clearly defined battle lines – that absolutely is not the nature of the problem set by drugs.

The drug problem as a shifting, multiple mix of perplexities, and with awareness of the dangers always lagging behind the arrival of the next drug – that is its true nature.

A chronology of key drug-related events

14th century or earlier	Chewing of coca leaves a common practice in the Andes.
1492	Christopher Columbus ships tobacco back to Europe.
16th century	Distilled spirits spread across Europe.
17th century	Opium smoking emerges in the Far East.
1689	Gin epidemic hits London.
19th century	Smoked opium becomes a problem for the Chinese.
	In Europe and America opium preparations are used in medical practice and as over-the-counter remedies, and are misused.
1806	Morphine extracted from opium.
1860	Cocaine extracted from coca leaves.
1860s	Hypodermic syringe introduced to medical practice and employed for the administration of morphine.
1880s	Injected morphine recognized as a dependence threat.
	Cocaine becomes a popular medical drug and the first cocaine epidemic takes off. Sniffing becomes a route of cocaine taking.
1881	Bonsack patents a machine to roll cigarettes.
1898	Pharmaceutical heroin is promoted as a

	cough suppressant and a non-addictive substitute for morphine.
1903	Barbitone (Veronal) is the first barbiturate; over-prescribing of barbiturates becomes pernicious.
1910–20	America experiences a major problem with illicit drugs.
1943	LSD discovered.
1950s onwards	Cannabis becomes a Westernized drug.
1960s and 1970s	The psychedelic revolution.
	Heroin epidemic sweeps the US and somewhat later the UK.
1963	Benzodiazepines are a huge market success with consequent widespread dependence.
Early 1980s	Drug injection contributes to the epidemic spread of AIDS and hepatitis.
1980s	Ecstasy enters the dance-drug scene.
1984	Crack cocaine epidemic in the US and second cocaine epidemic takes off worldwide.
1990s	Dance drugs 'normalized'.
2001	The Taliban agree to ban illicit opium cultivation in perpetuity.
2002	Opium production in Afghanistan at its highest level ever.

What are the main truths to be extracted from this listing? For all the shifts, there are certain repeated themes that can be seen incessantly marching across the drugged landscape.

- Over the centuries, new drugs have time and again appeared over the horizon and made their entry. It is unbelievable that the list of inventions will now and henceforth be closed.
- Profound adverse health consequences have followed both from the extraction of alkaloids from plants, and from a sequence of synthetic mind-acting drugs. Never-ending pharmacological inventiveness has been part of the problem.
- The emergence of new techniques for getting an already available drug into the body is a constant theme. The cigarette and its mass

manufacture did the same for nicotine as the syringe did for opiates, and crack does for the coca leaf.

- Drugs introduced as medicines escape to uncontrolled use. Distilled spirits were initially a medicine, nicotine was medicine, the theme runs up to the minute with Ecstasy, a psychotherapeutic aid turned into a dance drug.
- Drugs breaking out from their previous geographical confines is a repeated element in the story. Nicotine has come out of the New World to invade the world entirely, opium and cannabis came in from the East, cocaine comes out of South America, and branded American cigarettes and high-technology lager spread from the rich North to the poor South.

It is a chronicle of multiple drugs sequentially springing endless, nasty surprises on an ever unwary world. There has always been yet another, nastier surprise waiting around the corner. The image that fits the case is not that of a single beast, 'the drug problem'. What walks through the landscape, prowling around the world's street corners, is a many-headed Hydra, that monster of Greek mythology capable of growing another head as soon as one was lopped off.

Embeddedness is the hell of it

When a drug arrives and is once taken up by a society, the likelihood is that it will not easily go away again. On the contrary, it will probably put down roots and be resistant to all efforts at eradication. Drugs are like invasive plants carelessly put in by a naïve gardener who does not realize their potential to spread. No amount of weeding will get that kind of pest out of the flowerbeds. Drugs very generally demonstrate the capacity to get bedded in.

One reason for mind-acting drugs having the capacity for embeddedness lies in their reinforcing potential. The fact that drugs are reinforcing was identified as a salient feature in the Introduction. People like taking a drug again because the effect was good the last time they took it, and the last experience proposes the next and the next, and thus the habit builds up and the learning trace becomes engrained.

A sniff or a puff or a gulp or a jab, and once more the user experiences the rewarding pleasure, the dullest day and the most disappointed life are lit by a positive chemical glow, and that is the reinforcing magic in the drug. Pleasure is immediate and pain postponed; a fundamental psychological truth is that immediate gratification will far more potently shape behaviour than delayed and uncertain pain.

To describe drugs as agents that provide quick pleasure is only incompletely to capture the magic they pack. Name a human need, and there will be a drug to meet it, however temporarily and spuriously. Cocaine and amphetamine for excitement, Ecstasy for intimacy and that loved-up feeling, opiates to dull-out psychic pain and cocoon the user emotionally, cannabis for a mellow mood, psychedelics as tickets to a Disneyland of the mind. Furthermore, as earlier chapters have repeatedly illustrated, one drug can produce different pleasures according to setting and circumstance. White wine sipped with polite company on the lawn helps build a sophisticated mood and make for light laughter, but it is the same drug with which other drinkers, when smashed out of their minds, will find aggressive pleasure wrecking the bar. Drugs can do so many happy, dark, wonderful, destructive things for the mind, it is no wonder their use becomes embedded.

But drugs, as well as being chemicals which act on the brain, are commodities traded within markets, and that embedment needs more than the dopamine system for explanation. The spending worldwide on illicit drugs runs at billions of dollars every year. The drug barons make their fortunes but a great number of small operators support themselves by working in drug agriculture or by petty selling on the streets. Money sticks to illicit drugs along every millimetre of the supply chain. That is equally true of alcohol and tobacco, where the money rubs off on fingers all the way from the multinationals who manufacture and market the drugs, to the corner tobacconist and the neighbourhood off-licence. With licit drugs, government sticks in its thumb to pull out the tax plum.

Besides the economic rootedness, drugs have the capacity to become culturally rooted, to enter into folkways and become symbols. Champagne is a symbol of good times and not just gassy wine. Give a cigar to a friend and that represents esteem and bonding. Cocaine in the Andes, the habit defines the *acullicador* as fully a person. With illicit substances, the embeddedness is in the rituals of the drug sub-culture, and being a heroin user is being someone. The cultural tying-in of drug use is pervasive and often very powerful. Drugs can be valued not only by the individual who uses them but by the society or section of society which gives them mutated meaning beyond pharmacology.

So no wonder that drugs do not yield as easily to public health measures as do classic infectious diseases. Plague was neither pleas-urable nor profitable, and it had no hint of addictive potential attached to it. However, there is a resemblance between the two classes of problem which is reasonably close: infectiveness. The transmission of microbes from one person to another is brought about by mecha-nisms very different from those operating in transmission from drug-taking friend to friend. Research shows that drug users are usually introduced to their drug by a family member or friend, rather than their reaching up for it from an impersonal shelf or going out to buy from an alien dealer. Over a five-year period, a hundred heroin addicts will, on average, each have turned on perhaps two further injecting users, thus swelling the pool by a total of about 200 new cases. Both cigarette-smoking parents and the adolescent peer group infect the young person with the tobacco habit. Wet societies make drinkers.

What can we do about the entrenchment of drugs? There are multiple reasons why it is extraordinarily difficult to weed drugs out of the garden once they have rooted.

The grip of globalization

Drugs of one kind and another have always exploited the available cross-national market opportunities and followed the trade routes, either by sail or steam. Coffee, opium, tobacco and alcohol have all been caught up in the tides of world commerce. Now it is often the aeroplane which is the carrier, and the availability of air transport has helped the dissemination of illicit drugs.

The progressive nature of the globalization of drugs is evident in the sheer physical fact of the dissemination of licit and illicit substances – such a strong and growing aspect of the present world situation.

The way these individual drugs have spread geographically has been a repeated theme in previous chapters. But what now needs to be brought into focus is how those individual histories come together to make the large and general fact of drug globalization.

The forces which drive the dissemination of drugs have many features in common, whatever the substance and whether the trade is licit or illicit. These are forces backed by enormous financial resources, driven by desire for profit, conducted by experienced operators with vast know-how and little scruple. They are charged with a certain kind of demonic energy. In common, and whether they are criminal entrepreneurs or a multinationals, they are machines designed to crash through national barriers.

However, the globalization of drugs means more than the mere physical fact of Carlsburg lager and Lucky Strike being available in provinces at the edge of the Arctic Circle, or dance drugs infiltrating Hong Kong. The geographical spread of commodities has been accompanied by the infiltration of Western lifestyles, by the dissemination of new cultural meanings given to drugs, as well as their physical presence. Western brands of tobacco and alcohol are sold as badges of modernity. Drugs are carried by the universal youth culture and are as much fashion accessories as an expensive pair of trainers. It is the attached meanings which aid dissemination and help root the substances.

Globalization of the drug markets accelerates by the day. The time has arrived when we can no longer hope to understand or respond effectively to drugs, whether they be licit or illicit, except within the total international frame. Where did that heroin come from, who invested in the brewery, what does Ecstasy mean in the New Territories? Drugged-up and listening to the music, can the young dancer tell in what country they are dancing tonight? It is the same music, the same drugs with the same coded meanings, North, South, East and West.

Within the global frame, one will of course still see village epidemics and need responses at the micro level, but in many settings previously unknown drugs are now available. What happens globally impacts everywhere.

All hell to pay

A problem of vast size and protean manifestations results, inevitably, in gigantic and diverse costs. The bill can be counted in cash losses, but it needs also to have entries for human suffering. As an illustration, a series of American cost estimates is given below.

Bill for damage done by alcohol
Dr Henrick Harwood and his colleagues have provided data for America on alcohol-related costs. They took the year 1992 as the base for their calculations and summed up the costs due to illness, social welfare payments, crime, motor vehicle accidents caused by alcohol, alcohol-related fires and various other debits to society. The total came to $148 billion for the year.

Bill for tobacco-related damage
A US report from the Center for Disease Control looked at disease-related tobacco costs for the years 1995–9. They estimated the averaged annual loss at approximately $157 billion. Some corresponding UK figures were given in Chapter 2.

Bill for controlling illicit drugs and the damage done by them
Here one can turn again to estimates offered by the Harwood team. They rounded up the 1992 figure for illicit drugs to a little over $97 billion.

Adding the costs across substances
To give meaning to strings of noughts is always difficult. A Victorian Temperance tract met this presentational challenge by converting the UK drinks bill into numbers of battleships that might otherwise have been put into commission by the British navy. Adding the three American component debits, which admittedly vary in their time base, the total comes to over $400 billion annually. That represents an enormous drain on national resources, even for the world's richest nation. Whatever the country from which the data come, the economic damage done by licit drugs substantially exceeds the figure for illicit substances.

There is then the question of who, year in and year out, is actually picking up the bill. Each one of us is not being asked to meet our share knowingly and directly, with itemized accounts popping through the letterbox. The costs for the most part are incurred indirectly. The demands land on the doorsteps of national and local government, and consume their assets. Insurance premiums for health, property and motor vehicles are pushed upwards. Losses in industrial efficiency are passed on to the consumer. It would thus be wrong to assume that costs fall only on the self-harming consumer: the losses are not so much billed to their addresses as to people up and down the road. There is no opt-out clause permitted for any citizen.

Damage done to the state

The damage that can be done to the state by illicit drugs has, at the extreme, been seen in the impact of narco-terrorism on governments in Latin America, particularly Colombia. Assassins in the pay of the drug syndicates have killed politicians, judges, lawyers and journalists. The activities of Pablo Escobar, the notorious Colombian drug criminal, for a time threatened to cripple the national government.

Far more common and geographically widespread than the insult to the body politic contained in narco-terrorism, is the gradual erosion of public confidence in state institutions, resulting from governmental failure to deal successfully with either the illicit or licit sectors of the drug problem. Why should anyone have confidence in the state's wider abilities for good governance when it has such a chronically poor track record for curbing the harm done by substances? Trust in government is damaged every time a politician utters the slogan 'War on drugs' but is seen to be empty of victories. With cirrhosis rates rising, it does not look good when government departments are found to be yielding to the pressure of the drinks industry, with increasing relaxation in control over public drinking. When a prominent politician leaves office and deftly moves to a lucrative directorship in the tobacco industry, trust in politicians is sullied. Fuddle and muddle over the drugs problem do not put government in a good light.

Summing the hurt done to individuals

Statistics on the personal consequences of substance misuse roll in endlessly, each set surprising or shocking and then quickly wiped from memory by another news story. Fifty per cent of injecting drug users in New York City are HIV positive. Alcohol contributes causally to twenty different diseases. In Australia, the number of deaths due to opiate overdose more than tripled between 1989 and 1999. In the summer of 2000 in Scotland, over a short period, thirty-four young people died, surprisingly and tragically, because the germ responsible for gas gangrene had contaminated their heroin. About 4 million people die worldwide from tobacco-related disease each year. In one week of 2001, the Chinese authorities executed seventy-four drug dealers.

No one image or statistic contains the sum of suffering caused at the individual level by mind-acting substances. We are dealing here with so many types of death. People are killed by substance-related diseases, but also by related accident, overdose, murder, suicide, the executioner's bullet. Short of death, there is an array of harm done to the individual's physical and mental health, or social well-being. Lives are made nonsense of, and people are hag-ridden by their life-long dependence. The hurt is not only to the users themselves but also to their families, strangers killed or crippled in a car crash, little bits of undramatic insult to public safety, people robbed or mugged or living in fear of any of these substance-related events.

The damage may be at the level of vivid tragedy, but it is often a matter of happiness and fulfilment undramatically eroded.

What substances do to individuals is not easily portrayed by a pound or dollar sign and rows of noughts; the human pain remains for the most part an invisible entry on the balance sheet, but it is one which needs to be given more salience in the audit.

Going forward

On the evidence of this chapter, an open-eyed look at the Hydra, otherwise known as the problem with mind-acting drugs, gives no cause for comfort. Drugs are one damn thing after another, they go on springing nasty surprises around every turn. For a variety of reasons, their use becomes embedded and they are increasingly entrenched across the globe. They cause large-scale and varied harm to society and individuals. The Hydra has heads beyond any ready counting on fingers.

If some readers find what is said here to be shocking, depressing, and even cause for despair, that would be understandable. The intention is not, however, to generate pessimism. The aim is to make plain that the starting point for consideration of what to do better about drugs must be the admission that we are confronted here by an unusually difficult problem. It is not likely to yield to anyone's facile, single slash of a masterstroke. The Hydra will all too easily respond with the growing of a new head.

19

The Legalization Debate

All developed nations have in place legislation which criminalizes the smuggling, illicit cultivation or manufacture, supply or possession of a wide range of mind-acting drugs. For major drug offences, the penalty levels reflect society's abhorrence of what are viewed as outstandingly heinous types of crime that are enormously profitable. The prison sentences imposed for the importing or selling of illicit drugs on a large commercial scale will in many jurisdictions equal those handed down for murder. Lesser offences will attract less draconian punishment and in some instances only a small fine or a caution, but large numbers of people engaged in petty dealing still go to prison. As with the law in general, drug laws are intended to deter, punish, remove dangerous people from circulation, protect the fabric of the state and carry an educative message. They may also be used to divert offenders in to treatment. People who are dissatisfied with the current legal response will point to its vast costliness, coupled with seeming inefficiency. The context for domestic legislation is each country's accession to powerful international drug-control treaties.

Should legal prohibition be kept in place or abandoned? This chapter will seek to identify the evidence and arguments which are likely to be advanced by the opposing sides. I hope to do this in an atmosphere of open and mutually respectful debate.

Britain's Misuse of Drugs Act of 1971

Here in outline is what Britain's Misuse of Drugs Act (MDA) of 1971 provides as a legal framework (the Drug Abuse Act constituted the parallel legislation in the US). Illicit drugs are divided by the MDA into three classes according to their perceived danger. Class A contains what are deemed to be the most dangerous substances, namely the opiates, cocaine and any Class B substance when prepared for injection. Surprisingly, Ecstasy and LSD are also lodged within Class A. Class B contains amphetamine, methamphetamine and the barbiturates. Until recently, cannabis was placed in B but it has been moved to C. Class C also embraces most of the benzodiazepines, low-potency amphetamine-type stimulants and buprenorphine (a drug used as a substitute for heroin in the treatment of opiate dependence).

With symmetry, penalty levels then vary according to designated category, with the most severe penalties attaching to offences involving Class A. Production or supply of any Class A substance has life imprisonment as the potential upper penalty level. Class B offences can incur up to fourteen years, while a Class C offence can receive up to five years. Penalties for simple possession, or possession with intent to supply, are similarly graded but lighter. For instance, simple possession of a Class A drug can result in up to a seven-year sentence, while the penalty for a similar Class C offence has two years as the upper limit.

So much for a brief outline of the statutory framework. The way the law is applied has a lot of flexibility built into it. The police can choose where they will target their enforcement, they can cut back on efforts directed at the pettier types of drug offence, and settle for no action rather than going for prosecution when a person is found with a few grams of cannabis on them suggestive only of personal use. And the courts have wide discretion in sentencing, with a compulsory treatment order an increasingly used alternative to a custodial sentence when the offence is a result of the individual's addiction. The courts, when dealing with drug-related acquisitive crime which is outside the terms of the MDA, will none the less have powers to impose a treatment order if the theft was to feed a drug habit. The legal framework for dealing with drugs is thus a good deal more subtle than the rather frightening tariff of penalties might at first sight seem to suggest. See a court in action, hear the probation officer give their pre-sentence report – it is not a fixed-schedule Napoleonic Code in operation.

But flexible or not, critics argue that the criminal law in this arena has become an intrinsic and ugly part of the drug problem, rather than its being part of the solution. They frame the debate fundamentally as taking place around a choice between two starkly contrasting formulae for the future handling of currently illicit drugs. Formula 1 is continuance of the present system, or in shorthand: the criminalized control formula or drug prohibition. Formula 2 would see the criminal law as instrument of control got out of the way and replaced by the model now used for the control of alcohol and tobacco: in short, the licit control formula. Some people may contend that drugs should be legalized outright, with the MDA shredded, while others will favour a halfway house in terms of decriminalization, rather than outright repeal of the law. Here, we will focus on the outright proposal; decriminalization will receive attention in the next chapter. The root-and-branch proposition is frequently advanced at chat-show level without much regard for the evidence, but it can also be heard coming from thoughtful and informed critics of good conscience. Their suggestion should not be dismissed as mere wild, liberal raving. Revolutionary? The idea of abolishing capital punishment for sheep stealing was no doubt in its time viewed as revolutionary.

Laying drug experiences end to end

Before getting into the details of the arguments for or against legalization, let us try to put end to end the main facts of the historical experience on the control of illicit drugs, as revealed in previous chapters. Put these separate stories together and what kind of large story emerges? Here is a history of that world experience in four and a half minutes.

Opium in China

What we may conclude from that saga is that drug wars can be lost as well as won. In the nineteenth century, despite determined attempts at prohibition, China lost its war against opium, with its defences overwhelmed by the superior economic and military power of the imperial British drug traders. Prohibition was broken by external forces, but one should also take into the reckoning that there was a vulnerable population ripe for the plucking. That vulnerability was exactly the reason why the British so mercilessly targeted China. Supply fuelled demand and the epidemic ran. A footnote is also important: when prohibition on imports ended and the trade became free trade consumption rocketed. Prohibition can be a partial success even when it is porous.

A Tale of Two Nations

To borrow the phrase which Norman Kerr employed when commenting on the origins of the Ulster ether epidemic (see Chapter 5), we have here America's 1914 Harrison Act as the *fons et origo* of criminalized drug control. Initially those controls seemed, in the US at least, to hold or ameliorate the national opiate problem, while in the UK there was not much of a problem to check. But come the post World War Two era and the prohibitory defences collapsed, first in the US and then in the UK, overwhelmed by the illicit supply.

Vietnam

What this story tells is that if heroin falls from the trees onto a population greedy for it, a lot of people will respond positively to the proffered opportunity. Drug use can run very high where there is ready supply, where there are no effective barriers to use, and where the population experiences the drug as meeting some kind of need.

The wide experience with opiates

There is so much contained in those short stories as to render dubious any single, simple reading of what they tell. But I am persuaded that the message comes through that, if control over non-injected opium is left to traditional cultures, more or less peaceful coexistence can be maintained, although even in those circumstances there can be problems. But that conclusion can not be generalized and applied to Zurich or any Western city where injected opiates are the mode. The syringe is a devastatingly malign change agent. Moreover, the intimate cultural controls which constrain opiate use in traditional societies are replaced only by a vacuum in the environment of modern inner cities.

On then from opiates to other illicit drugs.

Cannabis, cocaine and amphetamines etc.

Cannabis is, all the way from the Emir onwards, a story redolent of failed prohibition. Cannabis today seems to drop from the world's trees. Prevalence of use rivals Vietnam's opiates and the criminalized system of control has almost been abandoned.

Cocaine, too, can give no comfort to the champions of criminalization. Early on, curbs on pharmacy sales and on medical prescribing seemed to win the battle. Come, however, the 1980s and crack cocaine, criminal traders overthrew barriers and knocked prohibition flat, much as the British traders had done earlier for opium in China, and the criminal importers did for heroin across the US, the UK and many other countries. And again there were populations eager and waiting to consume the bountiful import. Seeming victory easily slides towards later messy defeat, and winning a battle is far short of winning the war: that is what cocaine seems to tell. As for *amphetamines etc.*, methamphetamine shows criminalized drug control of an alluring stimulant recently being knocked down across much of Asia.

Psychedelics and the dance to the music of drugs

Add these experiences to those with cannabis, and the idea of the police as regulator of pleasure seems to be laughed out of court. Young people will, in very large numbers, have their drug if that is their wish and intent, and the police will be left as clowns in the street theatre.

From this brief summary of what a set of chapters and a plethora of drug experiences have to tell about the efficacy of criminal controls on drugs, one can see two alternative and contrasting conclusions being favoured by the opposing sides in the debate. There are those who will draw the inference that nowhere across the vast experiential landscape can one identify a resounding and maintained instance of a victory gained against drugs by imposition of the criminal law. Little bits of amelioration, betterment at the margins or in the short term, it is not all bad news, but what stands out staringly, they will say, is the lack of evidence that a war on drugs, fought with the criminal law as bludgeon, has ever, anywhere, delivered a knock-down win. Would that it were otherwise, but, scanning the battlefield, there really is nothing that deserves to be rated as a glorious victory. That must be conceded.

Game over, a win to the legalizers? That is one possible inference to be drawn from the historical record, but a speaker on the opposite side can be counted on to fight back with a contrary interpretation. That person will argue that without prohibition the level of drug use would often have been much heavier, and the problems experienced with drugs even worse. Drug prohibition is always porous and they will admit it sometimes leaks like a sieve, but that does not prove that no legislative defences are better than imperfect ones.

An end-to-end review of a long history, two competing inferences drawn, and the debate is now truly underway rather than shut down by anyone's knockout blow delivered in the opening minutes.

The American experience with alcohol prohibition traduced

Sooner rather than later in this debate, one will expect a champion of the legalization case to quote the American experience of alcohol prohibition of 1920–33 as conclusive proof of the folly of drug prohibition of any sort. Everyone knows, they will aver, that Prohibition was a costly failure imposed on the country by moralistic cranks. The illicit trade in liquor flourished, America drank more heavily than ever before, Al Capone grew rich, gun-happy enforcement agents shot innocent citizens in the streets, no good was achieved, and the people themselves before long rose up to demand repeal and return to their quiet enjoyment of a drink or two. That is the history of Prohibition as commonly presented.

Anyone who has studied the historical record, rather than putting reliance on the myth commonly peddled of Prohibition as an unmitigated disaster, will wish to challenge the simplistic reading. Prohibition had its considerably negative side but its introduction was supported by state-wide plebiscites, while the later repeal was a politically motivated manoeuvre to help F. D. Roosevelt levy liquor taxes to fund the New Deal. And in health terms, far from Prohibition's failing, the cirrhosis death rate stayed at the remarkably low level that had been achieved during the preceding years when the creeping edge of Prohibition had seen some states prohibit alcohol. Prohibition succeeded in keeping the national alcohol consumption at a relatively low level: that is the message to be drawn from the cirrhosis figures. As for the alleged burgeoning of organized crime, that kind of blight had become a feature of the American Dream considerably prior to 1920, and it is unconvincing to blame Prohibition for the birth of the Mafia.

What one should take from this saga is therefore something other than the usual one-sided interpretation. Prohibition provides an example of a country moving towards a prohibitory drug policy when the damage done by that drug becomes intolerable. In the nineteenth century, the drink problem had became unacceptable to the American public. Prohibition of alcohol was, then, in its outcome a mixed bag, not all success nor all failure, and not a brickbat to be thrown heedlessly across the floor of the debating chamber.

The criminal law and its collateral damage

Now let us turn to what is a very substantial issue in this debate. Those who favour legalization will argue that even if drug prohibition achieves some benefit by curbing consumption, that is an achievement earned at the cost of a profoundly unacceptable degree of damage. The present scale of the collateral harm done by the deployment of the criminal law in the drugs arena is illustrated by the astonishing fact that in the US rather more than 300,000 people are serving prison sentences for drug offences at any one time. The great majority of those imprisoned will be there on crack or heroin offences. Very heavy penalties are appropriate for big-time drug dealers, and in those instances punishment should be commensurate with the potential profit and the harm done to society. In passing sentence on drug offenders, the courts will take note of aggravating features, such as involvement in organized crime, possession of firearms or sale to minors. But the truth is that, in every country, by far the greater proportion of individuals going to prison on a drug-related charge are not the criminal masterminds. They are the middle- or low-level operators in the supply chain, or addicts caught with drugs in their pockets. Any city council wanting to deal with the problem set by illegal parking will know that success depends more on drivers' perceived likelihood of being ticketed or clamped, than on escalating levels of penalty. A ten-year sentence for parking, even on a double yellow line, is on no one's agenda. Criminological research consistently shows that the detection rate is more important for deterrence than swingeing penalties. The problem with illicit drugs is that they have acquired a diabolical image which then tends to invite inflated punishment. Those Chinese dealers (Chapter 18) executed and the families forced to pay for the bullets show what can happen when the sensible message coming from deterrence theory is ignored.

Imprisoning young citizens is bad for their present and future well-being, and on the current scale of mass operation it can further damage already deprived communities, as young men in particular are taken out and incarcerated in their thousands. Jails are places where illicit drug use frequently continues, previously drug-free individuals can acquire a habit, and virus infection from shared injection equipment is a hazard. Gang warfare around prohibited drugs also damages neighbourhoods, and that at a stroke can be got out of the way by legalization, the legalizers will say.

Another argument frequently heard in this debate is that the criminalization of drugs means that they remain devoid of any kind of quality control. Any old dirt or contaminant can be part of the deal. The hapless addict on the street does not know the strength of the latest purchase of heroin and will therefore be at random risk of fatal overdose. Make drugs legal, goes the contention, and their content will be as reliable as branded alcohol. No one is at risk of accidental overdose from double-strength sweet sherry.

Not only is the criminalized control formula loaded with damage, but it largely focuses only on the soft underbelly of the illicit trade, its critics will assert. As already mentioned, it is the petty or middle-rank dealers who are apprehended, and earnings from that level of dealing are such that there will always be ready replacements in poor communities. Working as a crack dealer at the lowest point in the supply chain will give a better hourly rate than cleaning cars. The top-level dealers are meanwhile much more difficult to catch and their takings are enormous. Those in favour of legalization will then also point out that the allegedly failed, mistargeted criminalizing system, summed across all levels of police and customs, is an exercise costing billions each year in any currency. And meanwhile the state is denied the tax revenue which would accrue if currently illicit drugs became legally tradable and taxable commodities.

No heroic victories anywhere to be cheered, a failed, cruel and costly farce, that is the way the legalizers will sum up their debating position. How can any rational person, on the basis of the world's painful experience, resist the logic of the call for outright abolition, they will demand? The counter-argument is likely to be that, ugly and costly as the present system certainly is, and with much need for amelioration of its worst excesses readily admitted, there is no workable alternative in sight for at least some of these drugs. Legalization would mean increased access, increased access would result in increased use, and increased levels of use would result in increased harm, just as night follows day. Is it really possible to envisage a responsible government letting the full range of currently illicit drugs go up there, prettily branded, on the shelf next to the drinks? Actually, that is precisely what we have in mind, will say the outright legalizers. Let market forces rule.

Outright legalization: how workable a proposition is it?

We will continue here to focus on the going for bust proposition of absolute drug law repeal, and a call for the return to the days before the Harrison Act set the world out on what some debating voices will stigmatize as a disastrously wrong journey.

Let us deal with all currently proscribed drugs within more or less the same formula as alcohol and tobacco, that is the outright agenda fairly stated. Critics of that position will see it as predicated on the belief that the tried and tested formula for managing licit recreational drugs does indeed work rather well, and can provide an alternative to the crassness of prohibition. But the anti-legalization side in the debate will contend that the licit control formula is in fact appallingly ineffective in preventing the harm done to populations by the drugs they seek to control. Say those who oppose legalization, anyone who blithely recommends these failed systems as an alternative to the Misuse of Drugs Act, or any other national equivalent, can only be doing so from profound ignorance of the fuddle, muddle and venality which characterizes the workings of the licit control apparatus.

Among people who have studied the public health consequences of alcohol and tobacco control systems, there may even be a 'must need their heads seen to' kind of reaction to the proposal that those control approaches provide a model to be recommended confidently for handling drugs as dangerous as, say, heroin and cocaine. Just pause for a moment and look at the tobacco death statistics, they will say: offering tobacco control as an exemplary model for controlling currently illicit drugs is, well, lunatic. That epithet may be heard coming from reasonably balanced persons.

The downside of the licit mode of handling is most evidently seen in the escalating health damage and very great social costs, as detailed in the preceding chapter. Besides the toll of these harms is the institutional damage that can result from governments becoming dependent on licit drug-derived revenue, as is the case with alcohol and tobacco. And how would it affect the Chancellor's independence of judgement if heroin, crack, LSD, amphetamine, Ecstasy and ketamine taxes became intrinsic to balancing the budget? We will bet our bottom dollar that in those circumstances tax imperatives would take precedence over health, contend those who speak against legalization.

Anyone favouring the licit control system as template had better also consider the likely consequences of allowing free-market capitalism to take over the production, promotion, distribution and sale of these currently illicit substances. See what this has done for the pushing of alcohol and tobacco, and who would want to find that kind of demonic energy harnessed to a wider range of drugs, say those who are opposed to legalization.

The dangers of vested commercial interests in the drug field may indeed be of such potential concern as to make the opponents of abolition contend that the flaws and failings in the criminal law are a tolerable price to pay for keeping the power of the multinationals away from linkage with the drug trade. The Mafia, the Colombian drug barons and similar entrepreneurs have done quite well in difficult circumstances, but they have never enjoyed the advantage of the tobacco or alcohol industry's promotional prowess; that is a handicap of large worth to public health, will say people on the anti-abolitionist side in the debate. Furthermore, the tobacco interests, and to some extent also the drinks trade, have run campaigns to obfuscate the truths coming from research – the black-market entrepreneurs have never been able to do that. This kind of obfuscation would be wide open to the manufacturers of branded methamphetamine. Come the glad dawn of the abolitionist dream and Asia might be bombarded with messages that methamphetamine is not addictive, the psychosis is due to diesel fumes, ice is cool.

Those who oppose the abolition of drug prohibition will thus not only be worried about the immediate likely impact of decontrol on individual consumption, and on what may be slipped lawfully into the individual shopping basket when all barriers to access have been removed. They will, in addition, be concerned about the enlargement of the market and the encouragement of a demand which could be the most profoundly dangerous structural consequence of the free market. No one in these deregulatory days can safely expect that the profitable commodities which are drugs would be left for long to state monopolies and dreary brown packaging with the fun taken out. The multinationals would invent and market their alluring images and strive to conceal the nastier truths, and popular culture would be cajoled into supporting those images. For decades the tobacco industry denied that nicotine was addictive and that smoking could cause cancer, and popular culture invested smoking with images of romance. Same again, is that what we want?

Legalization: the imponderables

Sadly, the legalization debate cannot be settled by computer modelling of the likely consequences which would flow from the ending of drug prohibition. There are too many imponderables. For instance, the legalizers claim that there could be great economic savings for the Criminal Justice system, stemming from the elimination of drug offences as a category of crime. What is, however, inevitable is that people with large drug habits would still rob and steal to pay for their legalized supply. Big habits would soon cost more than can be paid for out of most people's legitimate wages or welfare benefits, and legalization would mean more people involved in heavy drug taking because of lowered price. It is likely that the Health Service costs would escalate as a consequence of the increased drug use resulting from legalization. The grateful Chancellor's new stream of revenue resulting from the tax mark-up on the licit sale of previously prohibited substances might rather easily be eroded by the increase in health and social welfare costs and the cost to the state of increased drug-related unemployment.

Projecting the impact of legalization on organized crime is problematic. If the criminal suppliers saw their profits undercut by a new licit market in drugs they could be expected to hit back by lowering their prices, with a consequent further increase in the population's use of these products. In any case, the lesson from history is that organized crime does not usually agree to fade out gracefully and dismantle its operations in response to adversity: it more often responds by diversification.

There is a clutch of yet other uncertainties with which it would be difficult for any computer programmer to grapple. It is not easy to project the consequences of having a range of highly toxic substances lying around in people's homes and within anyone's casual reach. How many children would accidentally overdose? What would be the impact on suicide rates? Would drugs be used rather commonly to overpower victims of crime, or even as instruments of murder? What would be the consequences of legalization for adolescent drug use and the development of peer-group norms? What harm would be done to the psychiatrically vulnerable members of the community? What would be the impact on the already drug-troubled inner cities? If the whole world did not legalize on the same day, what sort of drug tourism would result?

If in the light of this cloud of uncertainties anyone is willing to assert that the benefits of legalization five years down that road would outweigh the disbenefits, it would be a guess rather than a conclusion underpinned by a computer simulation. It is the uncertainties attaching to legalization that some people will find particularly worrying. Others will argue that if the experiment went wrong one could always go back to prohibition. In reality, reinstating controls after their abolition would probably be difficult if powerful commercial interests and the tax take had by then become written into the equations.

To describe the legalization suggestion as 'gambling with the nation's health' might be seen as a pejorative dismissal of an argument which merits dispassionate examination. But that seemingly dismissive phrasing does point to the fact that legalization is a proposal made in hope of public benefit but with the benefit uncertain. That kind of risk-taking is what in common parlance is called a gamble.

Value systems and the Drugs Debate

In the light of prevailing uncertainties as to what would be the outcome of eliminating the present controls, it is inevitable that the positions taken by the competing protagonists will often be a reflection of their fundamental value systems. Commonly there are three kinds of belief that are to be found lurking beneath the surface of the debate.

- *The Libertarian ethic* Champions of this position are likely to take a nineteenth-century philosopher, John Stuart Mill, as their founding authority. In his classic essay *On Liberty* (1859), he argued that the state had no right to interfere with the behaviour of its citizens, unless the behaviour impinged negatively on other individuals or on society as a whole. Those who honour Mill and the libertarian principle none the less usually accept that with drug use, freedom of choice can be compromised by the fact of addiction. They will also concede that the cost of use frequently falls on others than the user, and on the state. The attempt to apply Mill's thinking to the dilemmas set by drug taking is immensely worthwhile, but some types and degrees of substance use appear to be exceptions to the libertarian rule of a kind which Mill himself envisaged as possible.
- *The Free Market ethic* Free markets constitute a system of trade. For some people they also enshrine an ethic, and to remove all barriers to free trade is for them a moral imperative. Such was the value system which the British trumpeted to justify the Chinese Opium Wars – the opium trade was at that time a vanguard for free-market capitalism, and Chinese protectionism an evil to be overcome (Chapter 8). Within this ethical perspective the world will be made a better place by the World Trade Agreement and the

unimpeded Western export of tobacco and alcohol to developing countries. To open up free domestic and international markets involving every type of currently prohibited substance is for subscribers to this doctrine the necessary next step. But even as J. S. Mill allowed an escape clause from the libertarian imperative in certain instances, the free-market ethic may need to exempt some sorts of commodity from its general principles. Drugs, it can be argued, are not ordinary market commodities.

- *The ethic of Public Health* Public Health is objectively no more than a system which seeks to apply scientific principles to the betterment of the people's health, but it too has within it a covert value system. For Public Health campaigners the health of the people is the highest law. At worst a situation can develop where Public Health disdains liberty, and tries to force people to be healthy against their wishes. But at best it is a movement which will work in alliance with the people it seeks to serve, enhance their capacities for free and informed choice, and protect their health from any threat coming from vested interests which rate health a less salient priority than profit. The modern Public Health movement came to maturity in its struggle with the machinations of the international tobacco industry. If Public Health is self-questioning and respectful of public opinion, it is a movement that can contribute to the ethical underpinning of what society does about drugs. The touchstone becomes what this particular aspect of drug laws, what that alcohol tax, what this cigarette vending machine will do to support or negate the health that the people wish to enjoy.

In a free society every individual must, of course, make their own choices as to what ethical values they most esteem. In debating drugs we do however need to declare our underlying ideologies. As to the values which guide my own position in the drugs debate, they are an amalgam. I am likely to take the health of the people as a pretty high priority when dealing with drugs. But I want that position to be tempered and challenged by the libertarian ethic. While appreciating the benefits of free trade, globalization is not for me an ethical imperative when deciding how to deal with the very unusual commodities that are mind-acting drugs. It would be naïve to trust this latter ethic as unfettered guardian of the world's health – nurturing health is not the mainspring of global capitalism. But economic development will in the longer term decrease the need for the poor countries to produce and export cocaine and heroin. That should be admitted and the argument will be developed further in Chapter 20.

Voting

One side seems to prevail and then another speaker comes in and appears to carry the greater conviction. Opposing interpretations offered for the same facts, passion and counter passion; as with any good debate one is likely to feel pulled first in one direction and then the other, as the alternative cases are cogently argued. How will any of us vote if the motion before us is 'This house believes that all currently illicit drugs should forthwith be legalized'?

The purpose of this book is to make the evidence available, to feed the debate and identify the arguments. Its aim is not to stuff the ballot box. Everyone must cast their own free vote. But let me say which way my own vote goes.

I vote for keeping the criminal law in place as an instrument for drug control. But I will want to move amendments to the motion. My support for the status quo is conditional, not absolute.

Why does my support go in that direction? Well, I do not think there is a safe or ready alternative control system to which we can leap, that is the nub of the matter. Make illicit drugs licit across the board, more available and cheaper (they would have to be cheap to undercut the black market), let them be branded and aggressively marketed and permit the multinationals to lie about them, build favourable popular images, put the Chancellor in hock, and on a strong balance of probabilities I would expect more harm than good to come of it. That conclusion derives from everything that experience can tell us about how to unbalance drug ecologies and inflame drug epidemics. Within a historical perspective, the outright legalization of all currently illicit drugs is not an invitation to a brave new dawn, but a fearless leap into the past and a forgetting of history. Drug prohibition came about because people found the harm and threat of free access intolerable.

But as I have said, my support for the ugly, flawed, leaky system of criminal control is certainly not unconditional. The continuance of that system has my vote only if the following amendments are agreed:

- If the response to illicit drugs is to have credibility, far more attention must be paid to the problem set by licit drugs.
- The response to illicit drugs such as cannabis and dance drugs, which are today very widely used recreationally, must be rethought.
- Ways must be found of dealing with Class A drugs which as far as possible reduce the damage caused by the present laws.

Maybe with those three amendments in place, some people of good conscience who are horrified by the collateral damage done here by the criminal law (a view I share), will feel able to resist voting for the total shredding of the Misuse of Drugs Act. A debate round those amendments is the business of the next chapter.

20

Better Deals

Looking at the entire range of society's current attempts to deal with licit and illicit mind-acting drugs, there are tensions in the system wherever one's glance falls. Nowhere does it have the appearance of a splendidly settled, workable and unworried coexistence, likely to endure for a thousand years. Coffee is probably the only substance which deserves to be excepted from this assessment. It is a safe bet that the aroma of coffee will still be enchanting the world into the next millennium, with caffeine never likely to be a candidate for control under the Misuse of Drugs Act.

This final chapter will follow on from the debate around legalization, and examine broadly how we can better deal with all types of drug. Those three proffered amendments will be taken up in this chapter. They indicate the major areas of tension within the present handling: society is not dealing adequately with currently licit recreational drugs, it is making a bad hand at dealing with the new wave of recreationals, and it is also making something of a mess in its dealing with heroin and cocaine. But discussion of better deals cannot mean the promulgation of master strokes, and I want to retain here the spirit of open-minded debate and the entertaining of alternatives.

Alcohol and tobacco

Profiles
These two long-established recreational drugs have in common the fact that they are profitable and taxed commodities, licitly and widely used; society has for both of them virtually excluded drugginess from

the drug while sticking on the labels. But in other important respects there are differences.

A citizen can drink alcohol life long in moderate quantities without significant risk to health or social well-being. As mentioned in Chapter 1, in middle age and later life alcohol can give a degree of protection against heart disease and stroke, and possibly also some other conditions. Unfortunately, a lot of people do not stay with only a moderate intake or what might be deemed the prescribed dose. They drink at a level to incur disease or cause accident to themselves, to impair the happiness and welfare of their families, and to hurt or distress other people. The sum of the damage done across the population is appalling, but, because only a small minority of drinkers end up by being grossly impaired, society continues to take a benign view of this drug. Few people would see banning alcohol as a sensible move. In the current political climate of laissez-faire, governments have in many countries tended to loosen controls over access, not tighten them. So alcohol continues to enjoy a favourable public image, while we passively watch and deny the harm. We graze on, and avert our eyes when our fellow antelopes are taken by this drug.

Tobacco is, in contrast, the only drug which when taken in the socially prescribed dose is potentially lethal. Even at the level of a few cigarettes per day, the smoker will shorten their life, with the risk rising step-wise with heavier intake. The danger of the habit is summed up in a recent report from the Royal College of Physicians (2000): smoking-related disease is responsible for one in five deaths in the UK. Unlike alcohol, cigarettes offer no proven health benefits, and the claim sometimes heard that smoking protects against Alzheimer's disease is dubious. Smoking not only threatens the health of the smoker but second-hand smoke can damage anyone in the smoker's environment. Smoking is for these reasons viewed by government and public alike as a habit to be curbed, with its elimination the ideal long-term aim. Thirty per cent of the population go on smoking, but they are increasingly invited to see themselves as pariahs who must huddle in the office doorway or out in the street if they want to continue with their nasty indulgence. In comparison to alcohol, the only good thing that can be said for tobacco is that it does not render the user drunk, violent or at risk of accident.

These are the current profiles of two recreational substances with vast market penetration, but with one of them now much slipped in its image. They have some common features but their statuses differ sufficiently for it to be necessary to consider them separately when looking for better deals.

Alcohol: what better deal?

As described in Chapter 1, alcohol causes enormous health damage and vast costs to society. What should we do about it? Debate around this question easily descends into becoming a shouting match. I will try to represent as dispassionately as possible the positions likely to be taken by the contesting sides.

Here, firstly, is the case against making any strong attempt to strike a new deal on alcohol, as might be advanced by a director of corporate affairs from a drinks industry conglomerate. Hear what he has to say from the platform: alcohol is not for most people a drug at all; to call it a drug is misleading and pejorative. True, a small minority are damaged by it, but there are always some idiots who can take any behaviour you care to name to excess – people can die from drinking too much water. Alcohol has nothing to do with alcoholism; alcoholics are constitutionally predisposed to their sad illness and not made by drink. They will drink sottishly whatever the price of alcohol or the pub opening hours, you can't stop them. Restrictions on alcohol or higher prices will interfere with the rightful pleasures of the sensible mass of the population, while not impinging on the behaviour of the sottish few.

The speaker continues: not only are restrictions ineffective but they are to be condemned as manifestations of the nanny state, and as prohibition by stealth. Let's educate schoolchildren and the adult population about sensible drinking, let's stress the government's sensible drinking limits message; more education, yes, but do not listen to the health fascists and the neo-prohibitionists. If there is a better deal to be had on alcohol, it will centre on the inculcation of personal responsibility, not on strengthened regulation, that is my message to government. Cut back on the national consumption of alcohol and you will precipitate a surge in heart disease.

That is a statement which will be received with sympathy by many members of the public and may well chime with the present mood of government. The tills will keep ringing, the tax will keep coming, and we can all go merrily on our drinking ways while the egregious alcohol-related casualties inhabit a separate drinking planet than us responsible drinkers.

So what is the opposing side likely to say in answer to the drinks industry's lucid exposition of its case against state interference in the supply of this liquid consumer good? The person now taking a place on the platform and advancing the opposing case is unlikely these days to be a prohibitionist or a temperance worker. It is probably someone with health concerns, who recognizes that alcohol is here to stay, acknowledges that it gives much pleasure, but who is wishing to reduce the harm it does.

Which witness are we to trust more? My belief is that, under-standably, the drinks industry spokesperson is trying to protect their commercial patch, but with truth the casualty. The health scientist, in my view, is truthfully reporting what the data tell. The relevant research has been accumulating over at least the last thirty years, and today does not offer just hints and murmurs but can give confident advice that can help a government reduce the overall sum of alcohol-related harm, if any government so wishes. The conclusion, that the overall level of the population's alcohol consumption is related to the likely level of harm, is not likely to surprise the man or woman on the Clapham omnibus. Who would doubt the parallel logic as applied to cigarettes, fat in the diet, or handguns?

But the health scientist would be naïve and above their station if they expected the scientific truth to dictate public policy immed-iately. Other people may rate the cheap and easy access to drink higher than prevention of the great range of alcohol-related damage which is not in their thoughts on a congenial evening as they hold out their glasses for a refill. What is happening in the A and E depart-ment, the cirrhosis death rates, the contribution of alcohol to social and family problems: these are not in the party's consciousness. What seems historically to make society turn against excessive drinking is not usually personal damage but unseemly public drunkenness. That is what Lord Lonsdale found so distressing when he looked out of the window of his coach. Today, this kind of affront seems increas-ingly to be back in public spaces as the late-night entertainment districts of our cities are threatened by intolerable levels of intoxi-cation. The city centre is no longer a salubrious or safe place for a strolling couple when the lads of Britain have become 'lagered' up. Taunts, jostling, a beer can thrown, a fight spilling across the pavement, this scene may become a price higher than the electorate is happy to pay for 24-hour opening, seven days a week.

The science can bear witness and has a responsibility to keep speaking the truth, even if it is not likely to be politically acceptable immediately. If the second platform speaker were recalled and asked to provide a few concrete ideas to support a better deal on alcohol, these are the kind of points they might put into their memo to the Minister.

- *Curb consumption* Unlike the case of tobacco, the policy aim here should not be elimination but the pegging of national consumption at a publicly acceptable and agreed level. But rather than leaving consumption to commercial imperatives, it should be the health of the people that sets the national consumption benchmark. In 1965, an adult in the UK was drinking on average the equivalent of 6 litres of absolute alcohol annually, but by 1995 that figure had risen to 9 litres. The British have recently overtaken the Italians in the European drinking league, and if current trends are left unchecked they will before long nudge ahead of the French. Unsurprisingly, the indices of alcohol-related harm show escalations much in step with increased consumption.

- *Use taxation in the health interest* Consumption can be affected by intentionally varying tax levels in the light of consumption trends. Taxation employed in this way is an instrument which can reduce alcohol-related problems very broadly. Even if the result is that people drink less, they will pay more tax on each drink, so the Chancellor will not necessarily be out of pocket.

- *Regain control over access* During recent decades there has been a tendency in countries such as Britain, which previously had fairly strict controls over access to alcohol, progressively to dismantle these defences. The number and type of places selling alcohol have increased, opening hours for licensed premises have been extended to a virtual 24/7, city-centre night life revolves around drink with public drunkenness commonplace, drink is available in all supermarkets. It is time for government to rein back a situation which threatens to become scandalous.

- *Try to cut back on the duty-free allowances* In the EU duty-free allowances have been increased to a level which comes near to making nonsense of the UK's attempt to maintain a higher alcohol tax level than its neighbours. A country loses control over the drink supply if bottles are allowed to leak across borders in van-sized batches.
- *State retail monopolies could make sense* Too extreme a suggestion? Depends how seriously you want to tackle the problem. The driving force of private profit would be considerably curbed if off-licence sales became state monopoly: pubs, clubs, restaurants and so on would be exempted from such an enactment. This suggestion is supported by the experience of the Scandinavian countries and some individual states in the US. Most of such arrangements have over recent years been swept away by free-market enthusiasm, but any scheme which reduces the money sticking to fingers is likely to be pro-health. The state monopoly would sell branded products but would not push or promote them.
- *Curb advertising* Advertising of alcohol is directly about the creation of favourable images and what has been referred to in Chapter 1 as the 'packaging'. The billboards flood us with images of alcohol as essential to the good life; the downside is never mentioned at all.

A better deal on alcohol? It is there for the taking if that is what the people want and if government will then heed their wishes.

Tobacco: what better deal?

The political will to deal with tobacco is greater than with alcohol; many governments, for some time, have seemed willing to listen to the truth. This is good news. Yet the UK seems to be stuck at about a 26 per cent smoking prevalence in the adult population, and the developing world threatens to be ravaged by tobacco-related death and disease. Certainly, a better deal on smoking is still needed.

On this occasion, to invite an industry spokesperson on to the platform would not make good sense. The tobacco industry has long since lost credibility as any kind of reliable witness. Let us try briefly to identify what might go into a memo outlining a few crucial steps on the tobacco-policy front, building on what was said in Chapter 2.

- *Cut consumption by every means possible* That must be the prime aim, to which all other policies contribute.
- *Cut the private profit* Here is the money argument coming in again. To deal more effectively with tobacco, the important next step is to dent private profit. There is a strong case for advocating that the manufacture of tobacco and the wholesale trade in it should be handled within each country by a state monopoly, acting solely in the public interest.
- *Set taxation levels at arms' length from government* To bear down on consumption, tax levels should be set by a body independent of government financial interests, and in a manner similar to the independent setting of central bank rates in the UK and other countries. That might see single cigarettes priced up to the level of single cigars, and a cigarette a treat rather than one item in the large daily ration plucked from the pack.
- *Eliminate advertising and promotion of all kinds* That goes without saying.
- *Treat the addicted smoker* Nicotine replacement therapies using patches or gum, and with the addition of skilled counselling, are of proven worth. Recently, the UK government has acted on the research evidence and put additional money into supporting expansion in the treatment services available for the smoker who wants to quit. This type of support should be maintained and further expanded, and is a rather easy way of saving lives.
- *International trade agreements* The global aspects of the problem should be dealt with by taking tobacco out of international trade agreements such as the World Trade Agreement (WTA) and the General Agreement on Tariffs and Trade (GATT) that at present force a free trade in tobacco. Countries should be allowed to put in place any trade barriers against imported tobacco which they see as beneficial for health.
- *International collaboration* International collaborative initiative will be needed to help reduce, and ultimately phase out, tobacco production in countries at present heavily invested in that kind of agriculture. The fact that money sticks to the tobacco leaf, often

in poor countries which have much need of that money, must be faced up to. WHO has recently agreed with member states a new international protocol on tobacco, but it is too soon to tell whether this will have teeth.

There is a sense of a strong evolving deal on tobacco, but one which needs much further strengthening if the momentum is to be kept, further progress made and the world's worst-ever drug problem overcome. Why not criminalize tobacco, place it within the Misuse of Drugs Act, put it into Class C and have two years for simple possession of this dangerous drug? someone may ask. That kind of extreme attack on an established drug ecology is politically and culturally unfeasible, but it is an awkward question in the debate which needs to be asked. If we cannot stomach the idea of putting tobacco into the MDA and see that as such an impossibility, why do we accept putting the modern, alternative recreational drugs under that kind of penal control?

And so to the next issue for debate.

Dealing with the alternative recreational drugs

A proposal much in the air concerning cannabis is that it should be decriminalized. That word has somewhat different meanings for different people. What is most commonly being proposed is, however, that possession and sale of small quantities of the drug should cease to be a criminal offence. Thousands of people who currently fall foul of the law each year would be exempted from prosecution.

The best-known example of this formula is the Dutch coffee-shop scheme. Owners of the shops are allowed to hold stocks of cannabis up to a stated limit; cannabis can be sold to anyone who comes through the doors, up to a defined amount: the limits for both stock and retail are now more restrictive than initially permitted.

The Dutch authorities claim that the experiment has met all its intentions. People can use cannabis as a recreational drug without being made into criminals. The shops have not driven up the level of cannabis use. The sale of cannabis is entirely separated from the sale of more dangerous drugs and there is no peddler at the back of the shop ready to offer a deal in crack cocaine as a sideline.

The critics of the Dutch deal will suggest that before-and-after surveys in fact do suggest a moderate increase in use. The mere fact of the shops' existence is a kind of advertising. And, say the critics, there is a deep ambiguity in a system which allows personal use and small-scale sale and purchase, but still goes after the higher-level traders with the full force of the criminal law. What, logically, can be wrong, or criminal and worthy of a prison sentence, in growing cannabis plants on an industrial scale, or in importing kilos of Moroccan Gold, if down the road the honest Netherlander is rolling the stuff into a decriminalized joint? Such a formula, say the critics, fundamentally compromises the good sense and integrity of society, and is duplicitous.

Certainly no very manifest harm has thus far resulted from the Dutch experiment. Other varieties of the decriminalization formula are also talked about today in many countries. Shops or no shops, there is always the opportunity to cease prosecuting cannabis users for personal possession or small-scale dealing. This sort of experiment was recently tried in Brixton (London) with not entirely favourable results. Many local people did not like the open dealing they saw going on around them. But those in favour of decriminalization of cannabis will argue that, although it may have a few drawbacks, it is a much better deal than the unworkable absurdity of criminalization.

There are two further directions in which advocates of decriminalization may want to go. Firstly, there is the possibility of adding other currently illicit recreational drugs to the deal, with Ecstasy the next candidate but with the list potentially very expandable. Secondly, there is the suggestion that legalizing should be extended to cover all drugs – the going-for-bust formula discussed in the previous chapter and applied to all the latter-day recreationals.

Again, and as with so many other facets of society's dealings with drugs, there are choices in the ways of looking at the matter that not only reflect different interpretations of the facts, but also address fundamentally different value systems. Before offering a view on what to do with these latter-day recreational substances, whose use levels and popular acceptance have soared unimaginably since the

MDA's enactment in 1971, one does well to check one's personal pulse.

If pursuit of pleasure is viewed as taking precedence as an inalienable liberty, provided only that not too many other people are harmed along the way, then clearly the vote is likely to be for decriminalization of this clutch of drugs, probably as the first step to legalization. Feel another pulse: the free marketeers, with their particular value system, will inevitably favour relaxation or abolition of the present penal controls. And a person of conservative bent will instinctively resist any such changes because of their own value system. James Callaghan, as seen in Chapter 12 denouncing the Wootton Report, provides a fine example of a politician beating with that kind of pulse.

These recreational substances are a litmus to underlying personal values, and it is not reasonable to expect unanimity on what constitutes the best new deal for this group of drugs. Here follows a view which is no more value free than that of anyone else but seeks to respect the lessons to be learnt from what history generally tells about drugs. It is an approach influenced by the value system of the public health tradition as best I understand it.

This view is influenced by two linked considerations. Firstly, there is still a great deal that is not known about the danger in these drugs; secondly, although the danger of tea drinking may in the past have been exaggerated, the historical record has more often been of the danger in drugs being underestimated or ignored, with tobacco the all-time warning. Put those two arguments together and the resulting recommendation must be that we move forward on this front only with extreme caution. Public health experts often favour what they call 'the precautionary principle'. For them any presumptive threat to public health is likely to be viewed as guilty until proved innocent.

It may be, for instance, that in twenty years' time talk about cannabis as a cause of cancer, executive brain impairment or contributory risk for psychosis have all been shown by science to be false. Alternatively, it may have become evident that cannabis is very damaging. So why leap now? There really is no great disadvantage to waiting a little longer, provided penalty levels are reduced to the kind of sensible level which deterrence theory would recommend. Neither Ecstasy nor LSD is without dangers, but they should not be in Class A. They do not possess anything approaching the capacity of other Class A drugs to kill individuals or damage communities. Injection is not a mode of use and they do not give rise to dependence. Their current scheduling, with the implied exaggeration of their danger, is likely to diminish the credibility of the law in the eyes of young people, while their more reasonable classification would support a position which still acknowledged that these drugs are dangerous.

Waiting, of course, only makes sense if the research is actually being done. Research which determines whether widely used drugs do or do not carry a significant threat to health is the kind of investment which should be given very high priority. Knowing what drugs are safe to use in our world deserves a higher priority than landing a probe on any distant planet, some might say.

What to do about Class A drugs?

Having discussed in turn what we might do better about the old and the new mass recreationals, it is time to move on to the very hard question of how to deal with drugs such as heroin and cocaine. Even these drugs can be used casually with an element of personal control, but their linkage with acquisitive crime sets a very special kind of problem.

At the end of the previous chapter, it was suggested that one condition for accepting the continued criminalization of these drugs was that the collateral damage should as far as possible be reduced. Diversion of offenders from the penal system into treatment can contribute to that goal and it is a strategy which needs to be expanded. Treatment for heroin users has been shown to be effective in terms of both reduced drug use and risk of death, and also in reduced offending. Treatment services need to be extended so as to eliminate excessive waiting times; if possible, addicts should be reached before they have to be routed for treatment by a court appearance. Treatment for cocaine and crack cocaine is not yet so well developed or successful.

Perhaps about 10 per cent of patients fail to achieve stability when offered routine maintenance with synthetic opiate substitutes such as methadone or buprenorphine, the well-tried therapeutic substitutes for heroin. It is this minority of patients which experts may see as candidates for maintenance on injectable heroin. That is not an extreme proposition; it involves no more than limited reintroduction, under much stricter control, of methods that Britain and America experimented with in the past (see Chapter 9). One approach to treatment of heroin dependence, which has recently attracted attention, is to offer maintenance with medically prescribed heroin. Studies with positive findings have been reported from both Switzerland and Holland. Patients are given their drugs several times a day in a clinic, with no risk of diversion of their drugs to the black market. Such patients show improvements in health and social functioning. There is a decrease in the use of street drugs, and crime levels fall. Some patients maintained on heroin will, after an initial period of settling down, ask to come off the drug; prescribed heroin can paradoxically be a pathway off heroin.

What would, however, be unacceptable is for doctors to drift towards acting as agents for social control rather than as physicians. Giving out heroin to prevent acquisitive crime might appeal to the belief of the law enforcement world, but it may not accord with the Hippocratic oath. There is a dilemma here which ethicists need to resolve. Heroin maintenance is not cheap: it would probably cost about £15,000 per patient each year in contrast to £3,000 for a year of methadone.

Many doctors would rather stay with and confront the difficult or even seemingly hopeless heroin addict, than retreat to neutralizing them with heroin. A patient on oral methadone or buprenorphine can function fully as a human being, will need to swallow their supervised dose just once a day, and will not be intoxicated by the oral opiate. That is what is so positive about the established oral kind of maintenance regime. Heroin injected four times a day at the clinic not only neutralizes criminal tendencies but can impair being human. This kind of regime results in daily highs of drug intoxication, and lows of incipient withdrawal, and such frequent attendance at a clinic is not easily compatible with gainful employment.

The greater availability of treatment, court mandated or voluntarily, with or without a clinic prescription of heroin, is likely to reduce the collateral damage to a significant but not huge extent. Treatment is a humane necessity and a sound investment, but its limitations include the fact that somewhat fewer than 50 per cent of the people who are in need of treatment are at any time receiving it. Meanwhile, they will be infecting themselves with blood-borne viruses, overdosing now and then, introducing others to drugs and feeding their habits through a mix of theft, social security and perhaps prostitution. Furthermore, the success achieved with treatment seldom sees more than say 60 per cent of patients achieving abstinence or significant improvement over a twelve-month period, and improvement is often difficult to hold on to.

Treatment matters, but advocates of treatment will not want to be drawn into issuing a bogus prospectus. Some addicts gloriously recover and many in the middle ground achieve substantial benefit; but treatment of heroin and cocaine dependence – by itself – is never likely to empty prisons.

Prevention is better than cure runs the old adage, but the trouble with these very disruptive types of drug misuse is that other than through the use of criminal controls as an attempt to bear down on access (and with all that collateral damage), the prevention cupboard appears to be rather bare. There is no evidence that drug education in schools decreases the later use of these kinds of drugs. Confiscating criminal assets makes good sense as a means of taking the money out of the system, but the larger part of the profits from the higher levels of drug dealing escape the reach of the law. The most intensive customs efforts only seize about 10 per cent of the drugs that flow across borders.

Prevention: what new deal is imaginable?

I am going to argue that a crucial further way to prevent these types of drug misuse is to take more seriously the amelioration of poverty and social deprivation which breeds their use. The proposal is for an ecological approach to prevention. Go for causes rather than reacting only to consequences, that is the argument.

This question needs to be looked at under two sub-headings: firstly the possible link between a country's internal social deprivation and drug misuse; secondly, the possible relevance of world poverty and failure in global development to the drug problems of developed countries.

Drug problems in rich countries: the connection with social deprivation

What is contended here is that one type of social condition that can sometimes influence some types of drug taking is social deprivation. That is not taking an extreme position. The research base is admittedly still rather sparse but a picture can be built up from the pieces of available evidence.

In 1998, the Advisory Council on the Misuse of Drugs (ACMD), a group responsible for advising the British government on drug policy, concluded that certain kinds of drug taking are rooted in the soil of inner-city deprivation. Drug prevention, argued the report, had therefore, of necessity, to tackle social disadvantage:

deprivation is far from being the total explanation of drug misuse – we cannot stress this point too often or too hard. Yet the analysis of links between deprivation and drug misuse forces the conclusion that deprivation sets questions of major relevance to prevention of drug misuse at both the local and strategic levels. This connection has in the past too often been neglected when formulating the policy mix. We want now and in the future to see deprivation given its full and proper place in all considerations of drug prevention policy, held in that policy consciousness, and not let slip from sight.

I chaired the working group which drafted the report and saw the cumulative evidence supporting its position being passed around the committee table. This was the first occasion on which the ACMD had told the government that deprivation is a strongly relevant item on the drug policy agenda.

Why do drug policy makers generally find it difficult to acknowledge the links that can exist between drug taking and impairment in the quality of the human habitat? The roots of the denial are probably several, and include the fact that rich countries find it embarrassing to admit that their promises of limitless wealth, and opportunity and social justice for all, is in large tracts of their cities a promise betrayed. Those slogans begin to look tarnished if it is admitted that the most destructive and intractable sorts of drug taking are often symptoms of the sad fact that, for many socially disadvantaged citizens, life is not a dream, cool or lucky. There is the fear that if social disadvantage is acknowledged to be a contributor to antisocial behaviour, that will excuse the socially deprived from exercising self-responsibility. In America, the finding that poverty and ethnic-minority status are intertwined adds to the political awkwardness of the drugs and deprivation link.

A person who is socially deprived endures a cluster of disadvantages. Not everyone so categorized will be experiencing the same disadvantages to the same degree, but the core and common experience is impairment in the social infrastructure. Poverty is almost invariably part of the nexus, but deprivation is a concept which goes wider than lack of money. Sub-standard housing, impaired educational opportunities and narrow employment opportunities often contribute to the picture. Questionnaires employed to measure deprivation often include unemployment, overcrowded accommodation, low occupational status, low income and lack of access to a car. An individual's deprivation may be expressed by a simple score, or in terms of relative deprivation and their place within the national spectrum of advantage and disadvantage. Besides deprivation being a characteristic of individuals, scores can be applied to describe the deprivation status of geographical areas.

Deprivation has a broad negative impact on health. When health scientists have looked for a deprivation connection in a particular sphere, the findings have more often than not come back positive. Being deprived is likely on average to shorten life by as much as ten years. In the UK, the gap in life expectation between unskilled and professional workers more than doubled between 1930 and 1990; greater overall national wealth does not necessarily mean fairer distribution of health advantages. As well as being an outwardly observable cluster of disadvantages, deprivation is also an inner state – a chronic not feeling good about one's life position, a sense that other people are doing better and of there being no way out or up.

It is unusual to find a relationship between deprivation and occasional, non-destructive drug taking. There is thus no strong association between light, occasional, non-dependent use of heroin and cocaine, and deprivation. Cannabis and Ecstasy use are generally found thoughout the social-advantage spectrum. It is when the focus turns to heavy, dependent, harmful use that deprivation is seen most clearly. What is true over one period of time about any of these connections is easily turned on its head a few years later.

That there is not a bigger research literature on this topic is perhaps in part a reflection of the innate political sensitivity of the questions being asked. But there is enough evidence to establish a case. The findings are not of a marginal kind but leap out from the pages.

Some British research evidence

In 1987, Professor Howard Parker published an article in which he and his co-workers surveyed the Wirral district of Merseyside. By using multiple information sources they were able to identify most heroin addicts with an active habit. For the researchers, the Wirral constituted an attractive terrain because it is dotted with townships enjoying very different levels of affluence. Parker found the prevalence of heroin use per thousand subjects aged 16–24 years varied from zero in highly privileged areas to 162 for the most deprived.

These are findings of a magnitude truly to jolt one's eyes. Grow up in a privileged dormitory town in the Wirral peninsula and a young person will be highly unlikely to walk into a bad drug problem. Not too far away, but where the social infrastructure has broken down, there will be almost a one in six chance of a deprived young person's becoming heroin dependent. What luck for the privileged, what bad luck for others. Some adolescents will head straight for university, while others will be heading for unemployment, delinquency and heroin. The ability to exercise self-responsibility is empowered or impaired by conditions for which the young person is in no way responsible.

Here is a study from Scotland pointing to essentially the same conclusion as Howard Parker's research.

A Public Health group led by Dr Laurence Gruer examined all drug-related emergency admissions occurring in greater Glasgow over a three-year period commencing in 1991. Many but not all of these admissions were caused by accidental overdose among injecting addicts. The researchers recorded the postcode for each patient's home address and they had data which allowed each geographical area to be assigned a deprivation score. They found that admission rates per capita for drug-related emergencies coming from the most deprived areas of Glasgow exceeded those drawn from the least deprived by a factor of thirty.

Again, how is that for a startling observation? Gruer suggested that another way of looking at his findings was that if admissions for each area could be reduced to the level of the least deprived, Glasgow's drug-related emergency admissions would be reduced by 90 per cent. But however the statistics are interpreted, the chance of a person's having an emergency drug problem was strongly related to social disadvantage.

Some evidence from America

Now for some relevant American data taken from a number of different reports, and bearing on the deprivation connection.

State as opposed to Federal prisons are likely to hold most of the people incarcerated for middle or petty level of drug dealing activity. Dr Robert MacCoun and Dr Peter Reuter reported that in 1992, 66 per cent of people held in state prisons for drug-related offences were Afro-Americans, although only 10 per cent of the general population had that ethnic background. This implies that a factor of ethnicity inflated the likelihood of imprisonment on a drugs charge six- or sevenfold.

Dr William Brownsberger (1997) surveyed treatment admissions for heroin and cocaine across the state of Massachusetts. People living in the poorest areas were ten times more likely to have such an admission than people living in the wealthy areas.

Cocaine use among pregnant women has, in America, become a matter of public concern. Tests conducted on mothers attending for pre-natal care have shown less than 1 per cent of women from affluent areas test positive for cocaine, while in poor areas about 30 per cent test positive [these facts again derive from Brownsberger].

Several pointers thus illustrate the repeated finding that, in modern-day America, heroin dependence and dependence on crack cocaine are concentrated in areas of deprivation, and among ethnic-minority groups. But in line with the prevalent habit of denial, the comment that comes back from the Office of National Drug Control Policies is that drugs 'are not a problem just for inner city residents, or the poor, or members of some minority group – they affect all Americans from every social, ethnic, racial and economic backdrop'. The patchiness of the database should again be underlined but this official statement is less than the truth. Of course drug problems affect 'all Americans' but the most destructive drug problems concentrate in the most deprived sectors of that rich society.

In Chapter 2, reference was made to British data showing that tobacco is, in the UK, becoming a drug of poverty. Fifty or so years ago, and at a time when the public were beginning to be aware that cigarettes were dangerous, there was not much difference to be seen in levels of smoking across social groups. Since then, the poor and the deprived have found it more difficult to respond to the health warnings than have the socially privileged. In 1961, about 60 per cent of men in socio-economic group V (unskilled) were smokers and about 54 per cent in group I (professional and managerial) – not a big differential. Thirty years later there was a marked divergence: group V was stuck at about 50 per cent while group I had brought their smoking rate down below 20 per cent. The social gradient employed is not identical with a measure of deprivation but is a useful proxy.

In Chapter 4, evidence was presented on the relationship between deaths due to VSA (volatile substance abuse) and deprivation. This evidence is relevant to the argument being developed here. Even among a very young age group, deprivation encourages dangerous use of a mind-acting substance.

It is necessary here to underline a truth of the opposite kind. General population surveys conducted in the US and the UK suggest that consumption of alcohol is not associated with deprivation. On the contrary, the well off will on average probably drink more heavily than the poor. The ethnic connection with drinking in the US is complex but in general does not point to close linkage, and there is no strong linkage in the UK.

As for why the casual taking of illicit drugs and the use of alcohol should be distributed quite uniformly across the terrain of social advantage and disadvantage while destructive drug use is significantly related to deprivation, the explanation probably runs as follows. On the one hand, recreational substance use is perceived across all social groups as not too risky and as affording harmless enjoyment – the pursuit of such low-risk pleasure speaks to human needs which transcend wealth and poverty. When, on the other hand, the use is more evidently dangerous or rated as delinquent, the privileged will do their risk assessment and leave well alone. However, the underprivileged do not have much to lose; in fact, perhaps they have more to gain from this latter kind of use, in terms of relief of frustration and society-engendered bad feelings, acting out of anger, and the economic advantages which attach to neighbourhood dealing. The social and psychological soil of poverty thus favours destructive drug use. Putting these various considerations together, it becomes none too surprising that cigarette smoking, volatile substance abuse, injected drug use and heavy involvement with crack cocaine all tend to map in a different way from the more harmless chemical indulgences. Deprivation affects the way a person will assess the balance between the short-term rewards from drug use and the possible longer-term harm.

On the basis of this brief tour of the research output, a conclusion presents itself to anyone who cares to look. *Nothing is always*, and this tour has been of only two industrialized countries and not the world. But in these countries, destructive substance use is concentrated where people are socially deprived.

Drug problems and global poverty

Here is another truth that needs to be spoken if the world is to deal with drugs better. In the year 2000, in the US, for every thousand live births an average of 8.7 children died before their fifth birthday. The UK can enter a slightly more favourable statistic in that year, with just seven per thousand dying before the age of five. Afghanistan? In that same year, out of every thousand live-born children, 279 died before their first five years were out.

Comparative childhood mortality statistics: what has this to do with why the rich world has an intractable problem with the nastier kind of illicit drug? Enter another statistic: Afghanistan, in the year 2000, produced largely for the export trade a total of 3,276 tonnes of opium, according to UN estimates. Afghanistan is the world's biggest cultivator of opium and supplies 75 per cent of the world's heroin. Britain currently derives 90 per cent of its heroin from that country's poppy fields.

The bridge between the infant mortality statistics and the tonnage of opium is as follows. Poverty is the major cause of Afghanistan's high mortality rate. Twenty-five per cent of Afghan children suffer from malnutrition, according to the World Bank. Poverty, along with the profound lack of economic development from which it derives, invites impoverished farmers to feed their families by growing opium as a cash crop. For thousands of subsistence farmers, the choice is between growing and selling opium, and starvation.

The economic force driving the rich world's illicit heroin and cocaine supplies lies very generally in the economic situation of poor countries. If proof were still needed of the contention that we live in one world, the problems which rich countries encounter with heroin and cocaine provide that proof. The problems encountered with these agricultural products are, in the ultimate analysis, squarely a development problem. While vast differentials in wealth exist between nations, it is likely that a drug trade energized by that differential will continue to prosper.

To assume that all drug-exporting countries are at exactly the same level of economic development, or that poverty alone is the force that drives the international trade, would be too simple. The countries involved vary widely in their wealth and degree of development. They include a group of Asian opium-producing countries (Afghanistan, Myanmar, Laos, Pakistan and some smaller players); Peru, Bolivia and Colombia as the traditional exporters of cocaine, but with Colombia having recently diversified into heroin; and Mexico as a traditional supplier of cannabis to the US market, but which is now also exporting heroin to America. The conditions which drive the Afghan opium trade are, for example, different from those driving the Colombian coca business. Afghan opium comes out of dire poverty and an extreme lack of economic, legal and political infrastructure, whereas the Colombian situation is characterized by less extreme poverty but the astonishing ability of the drug cartels to threaten and corrupt political institutions. Whatever the country or the drug, probably only about 5 per cent of the profit from the drug trade goes to the farmers, with 95 per cent being taken by the chemists and the various intermediaries along the criminal lines of supply. But without the poverty-stricken agricultural base in the producer countries, there would not be the trade directed at the consumer countries.

In the 1960s, the West started to explore the feasibility of strategies which might move drug-producing countries away from reliance on drug crops, and towards substitutes such as coffee or red peppers. Experience soon began to show that substituting a new cash crop for the old was not something achieved simply by distributing bags of seeds. Farming methods might have to be revolutionized, pesticides and fertilizers supplied, irrigation provided, transport links established and a market guaranteed. Most importantly, the new profit margin per hectare must equal that previously obtained from the poppy plant or coca bush. Economic and technical aid in support of the good, new crops would often go hand in hand with the drizzle of defoliates sprayed from the air onto the bad old botany, with funding also supplied for the arming and training of local enforcement personnel.

What does it feel like on the ground when the helicopters have defoliated the poppy fields, and the enforcement agents have fired bullets at the traders who previously gave good credit terms and bartered radio batteries in exchange for the opium or coca? How does it feel to the farmer, who is invited to start out anew as a coffee producer? The profit margins for the substitute crops are often not attractive; although the price of opium can be unstable, coffee is notoriously prone to slump. Crop substitution programmes have become more sophisticated since their start in the late 1960s, but there is little evidence to suggest that the investment in such work has had a big impact on the flow of heroin and cocaine from the poor to the rich countries. The Peruvian and Bolivian coca supply was curtailed with an opening up of the Colombian cocaine trade as a consequence.

If officials in the developed world should feel tempted to blame the drug-exporting countries for their intransigence, they are likely to be met by the riposte that if it were not for the rich world's appetite for drugs, the trade would not be so buoyant. While the rich world wants cocaine and heroin by the ton, poor countries will, with no practical alternative in sight, continue to supply the tonnage.

No sensible person would suggest that righting the current international economic inequalities could instantly wipe out the rich world's problems with illicit drugs. It is, however, probable that economic and developmental advances in poor countries would considerably ameliorate these problems. And until such advances are achieved, it is inevitable that cocaine and heroin will pour vengeance on to the streets of the rich.

Dealing better deals in the long term

Drug use, this book has argued, is a dimension of human activity which cannot be abstracted from the surrounding play. Drug taking is carried forward, shaped, ameliorated, or thrown out of control, as a result of intersections with multiple other strands of history and present circumstance. No drug is ever a story unto itself. That is true of the old and the new recreational substances, and of the most evidently destructive drugs.

All this connectedness, what bearing does it have on the practical future of dealing with drugs? Without any promise that even Utopia rising on the global skyline would guarantee a drug-free landscape, without the assumption that even spiritual perfection will some day be downloaded from the Internet, there is none the less a ringingly clear conclusion to be taken from the matters discussed in this chapter. Dealing with drugs is partly about dealing with drugs direct, plain and simple, and it is about limiting access. It is also a matter of dealing with much else besides drugs. It must be about our choice of value systems, the wide world outside the window, the quality of the world seen with the inner eye, and what life can offer that is as good as, or better than, intoxication.

Postscript

This book has criss-crossed the face of the planet, travelled centuries, listened to diverse voices, and called on the wisdom of science. I want briefly to revisit the journey's starting point, the village where the vicar sipped sherry and all was innocence as far as drugs were concerned.

That was the place where, aged seven, I was introduced to the reality of death. There was a diphtheria epidemic and a small girl who lived up the road from us caught the infection and died.

Memory stretched over such a span notoriously plays tricks. The church spire was clad with wooden shingles and the woodpeckers incessantly hammered to get at the grubs. The vicar tetchily complained about damage done to church property by the delinquent birds. That much I clearly and confidently remember, and can recall precisely the note struck by the tapping beaks. But death from diphtheria and an epidemic sweeping into a remote rural community: is my memory inventive?

I recently checked out the public health records. In the 1930s, my childhood years, there were roughly 100,000 reported cases of diphtheria annually in the UK, with an average of 2,500 deaths from the infection each year. But when I was a medical student in the 1950s, we laughed at the physician who lectured at us on the several ways diphtheria might clinically present, the faces of the disease. He was talking about an antique plague we expected never to meet, and we doodled. The elimination of that one disease is only a small token of the astonishing improvement in health that occurred over a century. Someone born in the year 2000 will on average have an additional twenty years added to their life beyond that of a forebear born in 1900.

Yet there was no improvement anywhere in Europe in life expectancy until about 1750. The subsequent, slow, incremental gains were for a long time more the consequence of improvement in nutrition and sanitation than the fruits of technical advance in medicine. It was the ecology that gave the added years to life.

The sad paradox is that some parts of those health gains are today eroded by corrosive, modern, substance epidemics. Lives saved from diphtheria each year may soon be exceeded by lives lost to injected drug use, if the injection-related AIDS and hepatitis component is added to the overdoses.

The fever hospital where we students listened to a dreary lecture on diphtheria closed its doors years ago because it no longer had patients to admit. One might hope that medical students some day will glaze over as a professor bores them with talk of extinct epidemics of damage done by mind-acting chemicals. Did people, in large numbers, really collapse dead with self-injected heroin? how ghastly. Millions of men and women around the world died each year from inhaling carcinogenic smoke? utterly bizarre. Alcohol killed and maimed on a large scale while governments fuddled and muddled, that stretches credulity. Go on, are you telling us that in those days young people needed to swallow pills before they could get on to the dance floor? pathetic. And the idea that doctors in A and E departments would have to deal with bullet wounds as a side effect of crack cocaine, the dark ages surely?

Sadly, it is likely to be a long time before medical students fret at the irrelevance of such lecture material. For the problems discussed in this book, the equivalent of the year 1750 has yet to dawn.

Sources and Further Reading

All quoted sources are identified under the relevant chapter headings and some additional references are included for readers who may want to go deeper into certain matters. Key references are asterisked.

Introduction: Understanding Drugs

Courtwright, D. T. (2001) *Forces of Habit. Drugs and the Making of the Modern World.* Cambridge, Mass.: Harvard University Press.

Edwards, G. (ed.) (2003) *Addiction: Evolution of a Specialist Field.* Oxford: Blackwell Science.

Edwards, G., Arif, A. and Hodgson, R. (1981) Nomenclature and classification of drug and alcohol-related problems; a WHO memorandum. *Bulletin of the World Health Organization* 59, 225–42.

Edwards, G., Arif, A. and Jaffe, J. (eds.) (1983) *Drug Use and Misuse: Cultural Perspectives.* London: Croom Helm, and New York: St Martin's Press.

Ghodse, H. (2002) *Drugs and Addictive Behaviour. A Guide to Treatment.* 3rd edn. Cambridge: Cambridge University Press.

*Goldstein, A. (2001) *Addiction, from Biology to Drug Policy.* 2nd edn. Oxford: Oxford University Press.

Gossop, M. C. (2000) *Living with Drugs.* 4th edn. Aldershot: Ashgate.

Griffiths, P., Gossop, M. and Strang, J. (1994) Chasing the Dragon: The Development of Heroin Smoking in the United Kingdom, ch. 9, pp. 121–33 in Strang, J. and Gossop, M. (eds.) *Heroin Addiction and Drug Policy: The British System.* Oxford: Oxford University Press.

*Jaffe, J. H. and Martin, W. R. (1985) Drug Addiction and Drug Abuse, ch. 23, pp. 532–80 in Gilman A. G., Goodman, L. S., Rall, T. W. and Murad, F. (eds.) *Goodman and Gilman's The Pharmacological Basis of Therapeutics.* 7th edn. New York: Macmillan.

Lindford-Hughes, A. and Nutt, D. (2003) Neurobiology of addictions and implications for treatment. *British Journal of Psychiatry* 182, 97–100.

Royal College of Psychiatrists and the Royal College of Physicians (2000) *Drugs, Dilemmas and Choices*. London: Gaskell.

Schuckit, M. A. (2002) *Drug and Alcohol Abuse: a Clinical Guide to Diagnosis and Treatment*. 5th edn. New York: Plenum.

Shadwell, A. (1902) *Drink in the Past. Drink, Temperance and Legislation*. London: Longmans Green (source for Lord Lonsdale).

Vanyukov, M. M. and Tarter, R. E. (2000) Genetics of substance abuse. *Drug and Alcohol Dependence* 59, 101–23.

West, R. (ed.) (2001) Special Issue: Theories of Addiction. *Addiction* 96, 1–192.

Zinberg, N. E. (1984) *Drug, Set and Setting. The Basis for Controlled Intoxicant Use*. New Haven, Conn.: Yale University Press.

1   On the Drink

*Babor, T., Caetano, R., Caswell, S., Edwards, G., Giesbrecht, N., Graham, K. et al. (2003) *Alcohol: No Ordinary Commodity: Research and Public Policy*. Oxford: Oxford University Press.

Britton, A. and Marmot, M. (2004) Different measures of alcohol consumption and risks of coronary heart disease and all-cause mortality. 11-year follow-up of the Whitehall II cohort study. *Addiction* 99, 109–16.

Caetano, R. and Cunradi, C. (2001) Alcohol dependence: a public health perspective. *Addiction* 97, 633–46.

Cohen J. M. and Cohen, M. J. (1960) *The Penguin Dictionary of Quotations*. Harmondsworth: Penguin Books.

*Edwards, G. (2000) *Alcohol: The Ambiguous Molecule*. London: Penguin [Published in the US as Edwards, G. (2002) *Alcohol, the World's Favourite Drug*. New York: Thomas Dunne Books, St Martin's Press].

*Edwards, G., Anderson, P., Babor, T. F., Caswell, S., Ferrence, R., Giesbrecht, N. et al. (1994) *Alcohol Policy and the Public Good*. Oxford: Oxford University Press.

Edwards, G. and Gross M. (1976) Alcohol dependence: provisional description of a clinical syndrome. *British Medical Journal* 1, 1058–61.

Edwards, G., Marshall, J. and Cooke, C. (2003) *The Treatment of Drinking Problems: A Guide for the Helping Professions*. 4th edn. Cambridge: Cambridge University Press.

Holder, H. H. (ed.) (2000) The supply side initiative: international collaboration to study the alcohol supply. *Addiction* 95 (Supplement 4), S461–S640.

London, J. [Jack] (1903) *The People of the Abyss*. New York: Macmillan.

MacAndrew, C. and Edgerton R. R. (1970) *Drunken Comportment: A Social Explanation*. London: Nelson.

Raistrick, D., Hodgson, R. and Ritson, B. (eds.) (1999) *Tackling Alcohol Together: The Evidence Base for a UK Alcohol Policy*. London: Free Association.

Rehm, J., Room, R., Graham, K., Monteiro, M., Gmel, G. and Sempos, C. T. (2003) The relationship of average volume of alcohol consumption and patterns of drinking to burden of disease: an overview. *Addiction* 98, 1229–38.

Room, R., Jernigan, D., Carlini-Marlatt, B., Gurese, O., Mäkelä, K., Marshall M. et al. (2002) *Alcohol and the Developing World: A Public Health Perspective*. Helsinki: Finnish Foundation for Alcohol Studies.

Warner, J. (2003) *Craze: Gin and Debauchery in an Age of Reason*. London: Profile Books.

2 Tobacco

Ballard, F. (1902) *The Smoking Craze: An Indictment with Reasons and an Appeal to Christians*. London: S. W. Partridge.

Department of Health (1998) Smoking Kills. A White Paper on Tobacco. London: The Stationery Office.

Doll, R. and Hill, A. B. (1950) Smoking and carcinoma of the lung. Preliminary report. *British Medical Journal* ii, 739–48.

Glanz, S. A., Slade, J., Bero, L. A., Hanauer, P. and Barnes, D. B. (1996) *The Cigarette Papers*. Berkeley, Calif.: University of California Press.

*Goodman, J. (1995) *Tobacco in History*. London: Routledge.

Haustein, K. O. (2002) *Tobacco or Health? Physiological and Social Damages Caused by Tobacco Smoking*. Berlin: Springer.

Hilton, M. (2000) *Smoking in British Popular Culture, 1800–2000*. Manchester: Manchester University Press.

Joosens, L. (2000) From public health to international law: possible protocols for inclusion in the Framework Convention on Tobacco Control. *Bulletin of the World Health Organization* 78, 930–37.

Kluger, R. (1996) *Ashes to Ashes. America's Hundred-year Cigarette War: The Public Health and the Unabashed Triumph of Philip Morris*. New York: Knopf.

Lewin, L. (1931) Tobacco, pp. 286–320 in *Phantastica – Narcotic and Stimulant Drugs, Their Use and Abuse*. English tr. from the second German edn, Wirth, P. H. A. London: Kegan Paul, Trench, Trubner.

Marsh, A. and McKay, S. (1994) *Poor Smokers*. London: Policy Studies Unit.

Pollock, D. (2000) *Denial and Delay: The Political History of Smoking and Health, 1951–64. Scientists, Government and Industry as Seen in the Papers of the Public Records Office*. London: Action on Smoking and Health.

Rowntree, B. S. and Lavers, G. R. (1951) *English Life and Leisure: A Social Study*. London: Longmans Green.

Royal College of Physicians (2000) *Nicotine Addiction in Britain*. London: Royal College of Physicians.

US Environmental Protection Agency (USEPA) (1992) *Respiratory health effects of passive smoking. Lung cancer and other disorders*. Washington, DC: USEPA.

Webster, C. (1984) Tobacco smoking addiction: a challenge to the National Health Service. *British Journal of Addiction* 79, 7–16.

*World Bank (1999) *Curbing the Epidemic. Governments and the Economics of Tobacco Control*. Washington, DC: World Bank.

Wynder, E. L. and Graham, E. A. (1950) Tobacco as a possible etiologic factor in bronchogenic carcinoma: a study of 684 proved cases. *Journal of the American Medical Association* 143, 329–36.

3 Little Comforters

Burn, J. H. (1958) Abuse of barbiturates. *British Journal of Addiction* 53, 115–17.

Burroughs, W. (1958) Letter from a master addict to dangerous drugs. *British Journal of Addiction* 53, 119–30.

Cooperstock, R. and Lennard, H. L. (1979) Some social meanings of tranquilliser use. *Sociology of Health and Illness* 1, 331–47.

Gabe, J., Gustaffson, V. and Bury, M. (1988) Medicating illness: newspaper coverage of tranquilliser dependence. *Sociology of Health and Illness* 13, 332–53.

Gabe, J. and Williams, P. (eds.) (1986) *Tranquillisers. Social, Psychological and Clinical Perspectives*. London: Tavistock.

*Hallstrom, C. (ed.) (1993) *Benzodiazepine Dependence*. Oxford: Oxford University Press.

Kerr, N. (1894) *Inebriety or Narcomania: Its Etiology, Pathology, Treatment and Jurisprudence*. 3rd edn. London: H. K. Lewis.

Klee, H., Faugier, J., Hayes, C., Boulton T. and Morris, J. (1990) AIDS-related risk behaviour, polydrug use and temazepam. *British Journal of Addiction* 85, 1125–32.

Lader, M. (1978) Benzodiazepines – the opium of the masses? *Neuroscience* 3, 749–51.

——(1994) Biological processes in benzodiazepine dependence. *Addiction* 89, 1413–18.

Marks, J. (1978) *The Benzodiazepines: Use, Overuse, Misuse, Abuse.* Lancaster: MTP Press.

*Petursson, H. and Lader, M. (1984) *Dependence on Tranquillisers.* Maudsley Monograph 28. Oxford: Oxford University Press.

Ruben, S. M. and Morrison, C. L. (1992) Temazepam misuse in a group of injecting drug users. *British Journal of Addiction* 87, 1387–92.

Sternbach, L. H. (1980) *The Benzodiazepine Story.* Basle: Editiones Roche.

Strang, J., Seivewright, N. and Farrell, M. (1992) Intravenous and other novel abuses of benzodiazepines: the opening of Pandora's Box. *British Journal of Addiction* 87, 1373–5.

Trethowan, W. H. (1975) Pills for personal ills. *British Medical Journal* 3, 749–51.

Tyrer, P. (1974) The benzodiazepine bonanza. *Lancet* 2, 709–10.

4   Deadly Vapours

Beauvais, F. and Oetting, E. R. (1988) Indian youth and inhalants: an update, pp. 34–48 in Rider, R. A. and Rouse, B. A. (eds.) *Epidemiology of Inhalant Abuse: Update.* NIDA Monograph 85. Rockville, Md.: National Institute on Drug Abuse.

Brady, M. (1993) *Heavy Metal: The Social Meaning of Petrol Sniffing.* Canberra: Aboriginal Studies Press.

de la Fuente, R. (1980) Mexico: young inhalant abusers, pp. 63–71 in Edwards, G. and Arif, A. (eds.) *Drug Problems in the Sociocultural Context: A Basis for Policies and Programme Planning.* Public Health Papers 73. Geneva, WHO.

Dinwiddie, S. H. (1994) Abuse of inhalants: a review. *Addiction* 89, 925–30.

Esmail, A., Warburton, B., Bland, J. M., Anderson, H. R. and Ramsey, J. (1997) Regional variations in death from volatile solvent abuse in Great Britain. *Addiction* 92, 1765–71.

*Home Office (1995) Volatile Substance Abuse. A Report by the Advisory Council on the Misuse of Drugs. London: HMSO.

Lewin, L. (1931) Benzine, pp. 203–5 in *Phantastica – Narcotic and Stimulant Drugs, Their Use and Abuse.* English tr. from the second German edn, Wirth, P. H. A. London: Kegan Paul, Trench, Trubner.

Taylor, J. C., Field-Smith, M. F., Norman, C. L., Bland, J. M., Ramsey, J. D.

and Anderson, H. R. (2000) *Trends in Deaths Associated with Abuse of Volatile Substances 1971–98*. London: St George's Hospital Medical School.

5   All sorts

Coffee and Tea

*James, J. E. (1991) *Caffeine and Health*. London: Academic Press.

Johnson, S. [Samuel] (1757) Review in the *Literary Magazine*, Vol. 2, No. 13.

Macfarlane, A. and Macfarlane, I. (2003) *Green Gold: The Empire of Tea*. London: Ebury Press.

Richardson, B. W. (1883) *Diseases of Modern Life*. New York: Fowler and Wells.

Silverman, K., Evans, S. M., Strain, E. C. and Griffiths R. R. (1992) Withdrawal syndrome after the double blind cessation of caffeine consumption. *New England Journal of Medicine* **327**, 1109–13.

Smith, R. F. (1985) A History of Coffee, ch. 1, pp. 1–12 in Clifford, M. N. and Wilson, K. C. (eds.) *Coffee: Botany, Biochemistry, and Production of Beans and Beverages*. London: Croom Helm.

Strain, E. C., Mumford, G. K., Silverman, K., and Griffiths, R. R (1994) Caffeine dependence syndrome: evidence from case histories and experimental evaluations. *JAMA* **272**, 1043–8.

Van Dussledorp, M. and Katan, M. B. (1990) Headache caused by caffeine withdrawal among moderate coffee drinkers switched from ordinary to decaffeinated coffee: a 12-week double blind trial. *BMJ* **300**, 1558–9.

Ether drinking

*Connell, K. H. (1965) Ether drinking in Ulster. *Quarterly Journal of Studies on Alcohol* **26**, 629–53.

Kerr, N. (1894) ch. 9, pp. 128–38 in *Inebriety or Narcomania: Its Etiology, Pathology, Treatment and Jurisprudence*. 3rd edn. London: H. K. Lewis.

Lewin, L. (1931) Ether, pp. 198–203 in *Phantastica – Narcotic and Stimulant Drugs, Their Use and Abuse*. English tr. from the second German edn, Wirth, P. H. A. London: Kegan Paul, Trench, Trubner.

Khat

*Baasher, T. (1981) The use of drugs in the Islamic World. *British Journal of Addiction* **76**, 223–43.

Carothers, J. C. (1945) Miraa as a cause of insanity. *East African Medical Journal* **22**, 4–6.

Griffiths, P. (1998) Qat use in London: a study of qat use among a sample of Somalis living in London. Central Drugs Prevention Unit, Paper 26. London: Home Office.

Numan, N. (2004) Exploration of adverse psychological symptoms in Yemeni khat users by the Symptoms Checklist-90 (SCL-90), *Addiction* **99**, 61–6.

Bananas

The Banana Affair. http://www.countryjoe.com/banana.htm

7   Opiates Introduced

Berridge, V. (1999) Opium before the nineteenth century, pp. xxii–xxiv in *Opium and the People: Opiate Use and Drug Control Policy in Nineteenth and Early Twentieth Century England*. London: Free Association Books.

Gutstein, H. B. and Akil, H. (2001) Opioid Analgesics, ch. 23, pp. 569–620 in Hardman, J. G. and Limbird, L. E. (eds.) *Goodman and Gilman's The Pharmacological Basis of Therapeutics*. 10th edn. New York: McGraw Hill.

Jones, J. (1700) *Mysteries of Opium Reveal'd*. London.

Lewin, L. (1931) *Opium and Morphia as Euphorics: Their History, Production and Effect*. London: Kegan Paul, Trench, Trubner.

O'Brien, C. P. (2001) Drug Addiction and Drug Abuse, ch. 24, pp. 621–42 in Hardman J. G. and Limbird L. E. (eds.) *Goodman and Gilman's The Pharmacological Basis of Therapeutics*. 10th edn. New York: McGraw Hill.

Oppenheimer, E., Tobutt, C., Taylor, C. and Andrews, T. (1994) Death and survival in a cohort of heroin addicts from London clinics: a 22-year follow-up study. *Addiction* **89**, 1299–1308.

Rudgley, R. (1993) *The Alchemy of Culture*. London: British Museum Press.

Sydenham, T. (1680) *Epistolae reponsoriae duae. I. De morbis epidemicis annorum 1675–1680 [II. De luis venereae historia et curatione]*. London: 1680, 1685; Geneva: 1683.

8   Opium in China

Barbour, D. (1894–5) Vol. VI, p. 57 of *Report on the Royal Commission on Opium*. London: HMSO (7 vols.).

Berridge, V. and Edwards, G. (1981) 'Britain's Opium Harvest'. The Anti-Opium Movement, ch. 14, pp. 173–94 in *Opium and the People: Opiate Use in Nineteenth-Century England*. London: Allen Lane.

Choo Tsun (1836) Documents Relating to Opium etc. (1837) No. 5, 18–26, Memorial against opium from Choo Tsun. English tr. of the Chinese. London: The Chinese Repository.

Christlieb, T. (1879) *The Indo-British Opium Trade and its Effect: A Recent Study*. Authorized tr. from the German by Croom D. B. London: James Nisbet.

Dickens, Charles (1870) *The Mystery of Edwin Drood*, ch. 23. David Paroissien (ed.) 2002. London: Penguin Classics.

Didgeon [no initial] (1876) Appendix B, p. 250 in Turner *British Opium Policy*.

Emperor of China (c. 1839) Letter to the Queen of England Translated from the Chinese. Reprinted pp. 279–83 in Turner *British Opium Policy*.

Gladstone, W. E. (1840) Hansard 18, 709–10.

Goldsmith, M. (1939) *The Trail of Opium: The Eleventh Plague*. London: Robert Hale.

Hastings, W. (1778) Quoted p. 48 in Owen, D. E. (1934) *British Opium Policy in China and India*. New Haven, Conn.: Yale University Press.

Heu Naetse (1835) Documents Relating to Opium etc. (1837) No. 1, 1–6. Memorial to legalise the importation of opium. English tr. from the Chinese. London: The Chinese Repository.

Holt, E. (1964) *The Opium Wars in China*. London: Putnam.

Illustrated London News (3 May 1857) Progress of the Chinese Dispute, 339–400.

Inglis, B. (1975) The Opium Wars, ch. 6, pp. 72–95 in *The Forbidden Game: A Social History of Drugs*. London: Hodder and Stoughton.

John, G. (1876) Appendix A, XV, pp. 241–2 in Turner *British Opium Policy*.

*Kalant, H. (1997) Opium revisited: a brief review of its nature, composition, non-medical use and relative risks. *Addiction* 92, 267–77.

Little [no initial given] (1855) pp. 17–18 in Alexander, R. (1856) The Rise and Progress of British Opium Smuggling. London [pamphlet, no publisher given].

Lockhart, W. (1876) Appendix A, I, pp. 229–36 in Turner *British Opium Policy*.

*Lowes, P. D. (1966) *The Genesis of International Narcotics Control*. Geneva: Libraire Droz.

Mars, S. (1992) British Attitudes to the Chinese 1838–60: A Mirror for British Nationality. Undergraduate Dissertation submitted for BA (Hons) in History. University of Cambridge.

Martin, M. (1856) p. 55 in Alexander, R. (1856) The Rise and Progress of British Opium Smuggling.

Medhurst, C. M. (1855) Remarks on the Opium Trade Based on the Preceding View [pamphlet, no publisher given, pages not numbered].

Report on the Royal Commission on Opium (1894–5) London: HMSO (7 vols.).

Select Committee (1832) Quoted pp. 26–7 in Turner *British Opium Policy*.

Thelwall, Revd A. S. (1839) *The Iniquities of the Opium Trade with China; being a Development of the Main Causes which Exclude the Merchants of Great Britain from the Advantages of an Unrestricted Commercial Intercourse with that Vast Empire*. London: Wm H. Allen.

Trocki, C. (1999) *Opium, Empire and the Global Political Economy: A Study of the Asian Opium Trade, 1750–1950*. London: Routledge.

Turner, F. S. (1876) *British Opium Policy and the Results to India and China*. London: Sampson Low, Marston, Searle and Rivington.

Westermeyer, J. (1981) Opium availability and the prevalence of addiction in Asia. *British Journal of Addiction* **76**, 85–90.

9   Opiates: a Tale of Two Nations

Anonymous (1873) Notes on Madras as a Winter Residence. *Medical Times and Gazette*, **3**, ii, 73.

Anslinger, H. J. and Tompkins, W. F. (1953) *The Traffic in Narcotics*. New York: Funk and Wagnalls.

Ball, J. C. and Chambers, C. D. (eds.) (1970) *The Epidemiology of Opiate Addiction in the United States*. Springfield, Ill.: Charles C. Thomas.

*Berridge, V. (1999) *Opium and the People: Opiate Use and Drug Control Policy in Nineteenth and Early Twentieth Century England*. London: Free Association Books.

Chein, I., Gerard, D. L., Lee, R. S. and Rosenfeld, E. (1964) *Narcotics, Delinquency and Social Policy. The Road to H.* London: Tavistock.

*Courtwright, D. T. (2001) *Dark Paradise: A History of Opiate Addiction in America*. Cambridge, Mass.: Harvard University Press.

Delevigne, M. (1935) Some international aspects of the problem of drug addiction. *British Journal of Inebriety* **32**, 125–51.

Departmental Committee on Morphine and Heroin Addiction (1926) Report. London: HMSO [Rolleston Report].

De Quincey (1821) *Confessions of an English Opium Eater*, p. 31. Harmondsworth: Penguin, 1971.

Frankau, I. M. and Stanwell, P. M. (1960) The treatment of drug addiction. *Lancet* **2**, 1377–9.

Hawes, A. J. (1970) Goodbye junkies. *Lancet* **1**, 258–60.

Heyman, P. and Brownsberger, W. N. (2001) *Drug Addiction and Drug Policy: The Struggle to Control Dependence*. Cambridge, Mass.: Harvard University Press.

Hunter, C. (1865) *On the Speedy Relief of Pain and other Nervous Affections by means of the Hypodermic Method*. London: John Churchill and Sons.

Judson, H. F. (1974) *Heroin Addiction in Britain*. New York: Harcourt Brace Jovanovich.

*Massing, M. (1998) *The Fix*. New York: Simon and Schuster.

Ministry of Health (1961) Drug Addiction: Report of the Interdepartmental Committee. London: HMSO.

——(1965) Drug Addiction: The Second Report of the Interdepartmental Committee. London: HMSO.

*Musto, D. F. (1999) *The American Disease: Origins of Narcotic Control*. 3rd edn. New York: Oxford University Press.

——(ed.) (2002) *One Hundred Years of Heroin*. Westport, Conn.: Auburn House.

Parker, H., Newcombe, R. and Bakx, K. (1987) The New heroin users: prevalence and characteristics in Wirral, Merseyside. *British Journal of Addiction* 82, 147–57.

Spear, H. B. (1969) The growth of heroin addiction in the United Kingdom. *British Journal of Addiction* 64, 245–56.

——(1994) The early years of the 'British System' in practice, ch. 1, pp. 5–28 in Strang and Gossop *Heroin Addiction*.

——(2002) *Heroin Addiction Care and Control: The British System 1916–1984*, Mott, J. (ed.). London: Drugscope.

*Strang, J. and Gossop, M. (eds.) (1994) *Heroin Addiction and Drug Policy: The British System*. Oxford: Oxford University Press.

Terry, C. E. and Pellens, M. (1928) *The Opium Problem*. New York: Committee on Drug Addiction in collaboration with the Bureau of Social Hygiene.

10   The Vietnam War

Baskir, M. L. and Strauss, W. A. (1978) *Chance and Circumstances: The Draft, the War and the Vietnam Generation*. New York: Knopf.

Crystal, D. (ed.) (1990) Entry on the Vietnam War, p. 1269 in the *Cambridge Encyclopaedia*. Cambridge: Cambridge University Press.

Isaacs, A. R. (1997) *Vietnam Shadows: The War, its Ghosts and its Legacy*. Baltimore, Md.: Johns Hopkins University Press.

*Jaffe, J. H. (1987) Footnotes in the evolution of the American National Response to Drugs; some little known aspects of the first American Strategy for Drug Abuse and Drug Traffic Prevention. The Inaugural Thomas Okey Memorial Lecture. *British Journal of Addiction* 82, 587–600.

MacPherson, M. (1984) *Long Time Passing: Vietnam and the Haunted Generation*. Garden City, NY: Doubleday.

Massing, M. (1998) *The Fix*. New York: Simon and Schuster.

Robins, L. N. (1973) *A Follow-up of Vietnam Drug Users*. Special Action Office Monograph, Series A, No. 1. Washington, DC: Executive Office of the President.

——(1973) The Vietnam Drug User Returns. Final Report. Washington, DC: Government Printing Office.

*——(1993) Vietnam veterans' rapid recovery from heroin addiction: a fluke or normal experience? The Sixth Thomas James Okey Memorial Lecture. *Addiction* 88, 1041–54.

Robins, L. N. and Slobodyan, S. (2003) Post-Vietnam heroin use and injection by returning US veterans: clues to preventing injection today. *Addiction* 98, 1053–60.

Westmoreland, W. C. (1986) *A Soldier Reports*. New York: Da Capo (originally published in 1976. Garden City, NY: Doubleday).

11 Opiates: the Wide Experience

*Ganguly, K. K., Sharma, H. A. and Krishnamachari, K. A. U. R. (1995) An ethnographic account of opium consumers in Rajasthan (India): socio-medical perspective. *Addiction* 90, 9–12.

*Huber, C. (1994) Needle Park: what can we learn from the Zurich experience? *Addiction* 89, 513–16.

Kerimi, N. (2000) Opium use in Turkmenistan: a historical perspective. *Addiction* 95, 1314–34.

*McIntosh, J. and McKeganey, N. (2002) *Beating the Dragon: The Recovery from Dependent Drug Use*. Harlow: Prentice Hall.

Poshyachinda, V. (1995) Indigenous opiate use: the Thai experience. *Addiction* 90, 14–15.

Wille, R. (1980) United Kingdom: processes of recovery among heroin users, pp. 103–14 in Edwards, G. and Arif, A. (eds.) *Drug Problems in the Sociocultural Context: A Basis for Policies and Programme Planning*. Public Health Papers 73. Geneva: WHO.

12 Cannabis

Anslinger, H. J. and Tompkins, W. F. (1953) *The Traffic in Narcotics*. New York: Funk and Wagnalls.

Arsenault, L., Cannon, M., Witton, J. and Murray, R. M. (2004) Causal association between cannabis and psychosis: examination of the evidence. *British Journal of Psychiatry* **184**, 110–17.

Bromberg, W. (1934) Marijuana intoxication: a clinical study of Cannabis Sativa intoxication. *American Journal of Psychiatry* **91**, 302–30.

Brown, K., Pan, L. and Rexed, I. (1975) *The Gentlemen's Club. International Control of Drugs and Alcohol.* Chicago, Ill.: University of Chicago Press.

Budney, A. J., Novy, P. L. and Hughes, J. R. (1999) Marijuana withdrawal among adults seeking treatment for marijuana dependence. *Addiction* **94**, 1311–21.

Cannabis: Report of the Advisory Committee on Drug Dependence [Wootton Report, 1968]. London: HMSO.

Edwards, G. (1974) Cannabis and the criteria for legalisation of a currently prohibited recreational drug: groundwork for a debate. *Acta Psychiatrica Scandinavia Supplementum* **251**. Copenhagen: Munksgard.

Fergusson, D. M. and Horwood, J. (2000) Does cannabis use encourage other forms of illicit drug use? *Addiction* **95**, 505–20.

Fuchs, L. (1542) *The Great Herbal of Leonhart Fuchs.* Facsimile edn (1999). Stanford, Calif.: Stanford University Press.

Gautier, T. (1843) Hashish. English tr. by Maurice Stang in *Hashish, Wine, Opium: Theophile Gautier and Charles Baudelaire* (1972). London: Calder and Boyars.

Gledhill-Hoyt, J., Lee, H., Strote, J. and Wechsler, J. (2000) Increased use of marijuana and other illicit drugs at US colleges in the 1990s: results of three national surveys. *Addiction* **95**, 1655–68.

Government of India (1894) *Indian Hemp Drugs Commission Report.* Simla: Government Central Printing Office. 7 vols.

Hall, W. and Babor, T. F. (2000) Cannabis use and Public Health: assessing the burden. *Addiction* **95**, 485–90.

*Hall, W., Degenhardt, L. S. and Lynskey, M. (2001) *The Health and Psychological Consequences of Cannabis Use.* Canberra: Australian Publishing Service.

Hall, W. and Macphee, D. (2002) Cannabis and cancer. *Addiction* **97**, 243–8.

Hall, W. and Pacula, R. L. (2003) *Cannabis Use and Dependence: Public Health and Public Policy.* Cambridge: Cambridge University Press.

Hansard (27 January 1969) House of Commons, col. 959 [Mr James Callaghan].

Home Office (2000) *Drug Seizure and Offender Statistics, United Kingdom, 1998.* London: Government Statistical Service.

House of Lords (1998) *Cannabis: The Scientific and Medical Evidence.* Select Committee on Science and Technology. London: The Stationery Office.

Hughes, P. (1977) *Behind the Wall of Respect: Community Experiments in Heroin Addiction Control*. Chicago, Ill.: University of Chicago Press.

*Kalant, H., Corrigall, W., Hall, W. and Smart, R. (eds.) (1998) *The Health Effects of Cannabis*. Toronto: Addiction Research Foundation.

Kandel, D. B. and Faust, R. (1975) Sequences and stages in patterns of adolescent drug use. *Archives of General Psychiatry* 43, 746–54.

Kendell, R. (2003) Cannabis condemned: the proscription of Indian hemp. *Addiction* 98, 143–51.

Lewin, L. (1931) Indian hemp: Cannabis Indica, pp. 107–23 in *Phantastica – Narcotic and Stimulant Drugs. Their Use and Abuse*. English tr. from the second German edn, Wirth, P. H. A. London: Kegan Paul, Trench, Trubner.

Lynskey, M. and Hall, W. (2000) The effects of adolescent cannabis use on educational attainment: a review. *Addiction* 95, 1621–30.

Mayor's Committee on Marihuana (1944) [La Guardia Report] The marihuana problem in the city of New York. Sociological, medical, psychological and pharmacological studies. Lancaster, Pa.: Cattell Press.

Musto, D. F. (1973) *The American Disease: Origins of Narcotic Control*. New Haven, Conn.: Yale University Press.

O'Shaugnessy, W. B. (1842) On the preparations of the Indian hemp, or Gunjah; their effects on the animal system in health and their utility in treating tetanus and other convulsive diseases. *Transactions of the Medical and Physical Society of Calcutta* 8, 421–61.

Pertwee, R. G. (1998) Pharmacological, physiological and clinical implications of the discovery of cannabinoid receptors. *Biochemical Society Transactions* 26, 267–72.

——(1999) Medical uses of cannabinoids: the way forward. *Addiction* 94, 317–20.

Rottanburg, D., Robins, A. H., Ben-Arie, O., Teggin, A. and Elk, R. (1982) Cannabis-associated psychosis with hypomanic features. *Lancet* 2, 1364–6.

Smiley, A. (1999) Marijuana: on road and driving-simulator studies, ch. 5, pp. 171–94 in Kalant et al. *The Health Effects of Cannabis*.

Solowij, N. (1998) *Cannabis and Cognitive Functioning*. Cambridge: Cambridge University Press.

Spear, H. B. (1969) The growth of heroin addiction in the United Kingdom. *British Journal of Addiction* 64, 245–55.

Tashken, D. P. (1999) Cannabis effects on the respiratory system, ch. 9, pp. 311–46 in Kalant et al. *The Health Effects of Cannabis*.

Taylor, D. R., Poulton, R., Moffitt, T. E., Ramankutt, P. and Sears, M. R. (2000) The respiratory effects of cannabis dependence in young adults. *Addiction* 95, 1669–78.

Tennant, F. S. and Groesbeck, C. J. (1972) Psychiatric effects of Hasheesh. *Archive of General Psychiatry* **27**, 133–6.

'W. W.' (1890) *Lancet* **2**, 621.

Wilkinson, P. B. (1929) Cannabis Indica: an historical and pharmacological study of the drug. *British Journal of Inebriety* **27**, 72–80.

Zammit, S., Allebeck, A., Andreasson, S., Lundberg, I. and Lewis, G. (2002) Self-reported cannabis use as a risk factor for schizophrenia in Swedish conscripts of 1969: historical cohort study. *BMJ* **325**, 1199–1201.

13 Cocaine

Anonymous (1877) A new use for cocaine. *Lancet* **2**, 449.

Bock, G. B. and Whelan, J. (eds.) *Cocaine: Scientific and Social Dimensions.* Ciba Foundation Symposium 166. Chichester: John Wiley and Sons.

Carter, W. E., Parkerson, P. and Mamani, M. (1980) Traditional and changing patterns of coca use in Bolivia, pp. 159–64 in Jeri *Cocaine.*

Collins, W. J. (1916) War measures against inebriety. *British Journal of Inebriety* **14**, 41–4.

Denison, M. (1986) Entry on Sir Noël Peirce Coward, pp. 186–9 in Blake, Lord and Nicholls, C. S. (eds.) *The Dictionary of National Biography, 1971–80.* Oxford: Oxford University Press.

Dixon, W. E. (1924) Drug addiction. *British Journal of Inebriety* **22**, 149–54.

——(1925) Cocaine addiction. *British Journal of Inebriety* **23**, 103–12.

'Dope Head Blues' (1928) Reprinted pp. 39–40 in Shapiro, H. (1999) *Waiting for the Man: The Story of Drugs and Popular Music.* London: Helter Skelter.

Grinspoon, L. and Bakacar, J. B. (1985) Drug dependence: non-narcotic agents, in Kaplan, H. I. and Sadock, B. J. (eds.) *Comprehensive Textbook of Psychiatry*, Vol. 1, pp. 1614–28. Baltimore, Md.: Williams and Wilkins.

Jeri, F. R. (ed.) *Cocaine 1980: Proceedings of the Interamerican Seminar on Medical and Sociological Aspects of Coca and Cocaine.* Lima: PAHO/WHO and International Narcotics Management.

Jones, E. (1953) *The Life and Work of Sigmund Freud.* 3 vols. New York: Basic Books.

*Kleber, H. D. (1988) Epidemic cocaine abuse: America's present, Britain's future. *British Journal of Addiction* **83**, 1359–71.

Kleiman, M. A. (1998) Cocaine, ch. 10, pp. 286–316 in *Against Excess, Drug Policy for Results.* New York: Basic Books.

Kohn, M. (1992) *Dope Girls: The Birth of the British Drug Underground.* London: Lawrence and Wishart.

Kuhar, M. J., Ritz, M. C. and Boja, J. W. (1991) The dopamine hypothesis of the reinforcing properties of cocaine. *Trends in Neuroscience* **14**, 299–302.

Maier, H. W. (1926) *Der Kokainismus.* Leipzig: Georg Thieme Verlag (English tr. Kalant, O. J. 1987. Toronto: Alcohol and Drug Addiction Research Foundation).

Massing, M. (1998) *The Fix.* New York: Simon and Schuster.

Mortimer, W. G. (1901) *History of Coca 'the Divine Plant of the Incas'.* New York: J. H. Vaile and Co. (Fitz Hugh Library edn, 1974, San Francisco).

Musto, D. F. (1992) Cocaine's history, especially the American experience, pp. 14–19 in Bock and Whelan *Cocaine.*

*Negrete, J. C. (1992) Cocaine problems in the coca-growing countries of South America, pp. 40–50 in Bock and Whelan *Cocaine.*

Reuter, P., MacCoun, R. and Murphy, P. (1990) *Money from Crime: A Study of the Economics of Drug Dealing in Washington, DC.* Santa Monica, Calif.: Rand/Drug Policy Research Center.

Rydell, C. and Everingham, S. (1994) *Controlling Cocaine: Supply versus Demand Programs.* Santa Monica, Calif.: Rand/Drug Policy Research Center.

Sandagorda, A. (1980) Socio-cultural aspects of coca use, pp. 150–53 in Jeri *Cocaine 1980.*

Spillane, J. F. (1999) Making a modern drug: the manufacture, sale, and control of cocaine in the United States, 1880–1920, pp. 21–45 in Gootenberg, P. (ed.) *Cocaine: Global Histories.* London: Routledge.

*——(2000) *Cocaine: From Medical Marvel to Modern Menace in the United States, 1884–1920.* Baltimore, Md.: Johns Hopkins University Press.

Stoddart, W. H. B. (1925) Comments on W. E. Dixon's 'Cocaine Addiction'. *British Journal of Inebriety* **12**, 120–21.

Sturge, M. D. (1913) Medicated wines. *British Journal of Inebriety* **10**, 74–80.

Williams, E. J. (1914) The drug habit in the South. *Medical Record* **85**, 247–9.

Woolverton, W. L. (1992) Determinants of cocaine self-administration by laboratory animals, pp. 149–61 in Bock and Whelan *Cocaine.*

14   Amphetamines etc.

Brandis, B., Sproule, B. and Marshman, J. (eds.) (1998) Amphetamines, pp. 153–63 in *Drugs and Drug Abuse.* 3rd edn. Toronto: ARF.

Buncombe, A. (2 January 2003) US pilots in friendly fire case were given amphetamines. *Independent*, p. 13.

*Connell, P. H. (1958) *Amphetamine Psychosis*. Maudsley Monographs 5. London: Oxford University Press.

de Alarcon, R. (1972) An epidemiological evaluation of a public health measure aimed at reducing the availability of methamphetamine. *Psychological Medicine* 2, 293–300.

Dimsdale, J. H. (1998) Review of Klee, H. (ed.) (1997) *Amphetamine Misuse: International Perspectives on Current Trends. Addiction* 98, 290.

Farrell, M. and Marsden, J. (2002) Methamphetamine: drug use and psychosis becomes a major public health issue in the Asia Pacific region. *Addiction* 97, 771–2.

Hawks, D., Mitcheson, M., Ogborne, A. and Edwards, G. (1969) Abuse of methylamphetamine. *British Medical Journal* 2, 715–21.

Klee, H. (ed.) (1997) Amphetamine Misuse: International Perspectives on Current Trends. Amsterdam: Harwood Academic.

McGurk, J. (28 January 2003) Thailand school children fall prey to chocolate-coated drug pastilles. *Independent*, p. 14.

World Health Organization (1997) Amphetamine-Type Stimulants. A Report from the WHO Meeting on Amphetamines, MDMA and Other Psychostimulants. Geneva, 12–15 November 1996. Geneva: WHO.

15 Psychedelics

Aaronson, B. and Osmond, H. (eds.) (1971) *Psychedelics: The Use and Implications of Hallucinogenic Drugs*. London: Hogarth Press.

Davidson, R. S. (1961) Introduction: a psychologist explains, pp. 3–10 in Dunlap, J. *Exploring Inner Space: Personal Experiences Under LSD*. London: Victor Gollancz.

De Bold, R. C. and Leaf, R. C. (1969) *LSD, Man and Society*. London: Faber and Faber.

Einhorn, I. (1971) From data collection to pattern recognition, pp. 439–57 in Aaronson and Osmond *Psychedelics*.

Ellis, H. [Havelock] (1902) Mescal: A New Artificial Paradise. Annual Report of the Smithsonian Institute, pp. 537–48. Washington, DC.

Hoffman, A. (1994) History of the discovery of LSD, ch. 1, pp. 7–18 in Pletscher and Ladewig *50 Years of LSD*.

*Huxley, A. [Aldous] (1954) *The Doors of Perception*. New York: Harper and Brothers.

——(1980) *Moksha: Writings on Psychedelics and the Visionary Experience (1931–1963)* Horowitz, M. and Palmer, C. (eds.). London: Chatto and Windus.

Lewin, L. (1931) Hallucinatory Substances, pp. 89–146 in *Phantastica – Narcotic and Stimulant Drugs, Their Use and Abuse*. English tr. from the second German edn, Wirth, P. H. A. London: Kegan Paul, Trench, Trubner.

Masters, R. E. L. and Houston, J. (1971) Towards an individual psychedelic psychotherapy, pp. 323–42 in Aaronson and Osmond *Psychedelics*.

Mitchell, S. W. (1896) Remarks on the effects of Anhelonium Lewini. *British Medical Journal* ii, 1625–8.

Osmond, H. (1957) A review of the clinical effects of psychomimetic agents. *Annals of the New York Academy of Sciences* **66**, 418–34.

*Pletscher, R. A. and Ladewig, D. (eds.) (1994) *50 Years of LSD: Current Status and Perspectives of Hallucinogens*. New York: Parthenon.

Porta, J. B. (1999) To make a man out of his senses for a day, pp. 29–31 in Rudgley, J. (ed.) *Wildest Dreams: An Anthology of Drug-related Literature* [*Natural Magik*, London 1658].

16   Dance to the Music of Drugs

*Baggot, M. and Mendelson, J. (2001) Does MDMA cause brain damage?, ch. 9, pp. 110–45 in Holland *Ecstasy*.

Boot, B. P., McGregor, I. S. and Hall, W. (2000) MDMA (Ecstasy) neurotoxicity: assessing and communicating the risks. *Lancet* **355**, 1818–21.

Curran, H. V. and Monaghan, L. (2001) In and out of the K-hole: a comparison of the acute and residual effects of ketamine in frequent and infrequent ketamine users. *Addiction* **96**, 749–60.

Forsyth, A. J. M., Barnard, M. and McKeganey, N. P. (1997) Musical preference as indicator of adolescent drug use. *Addiction* **92**, 1317–25.

Gray, C. (30 July 2002) Ecstasy deaths double as price of drugs halve. *Independent*, p. 5.

Holland, J. (2001) *Ecstasy: The Complete Guide*. Rochester, Vt.: Park Street Press.

Larousse (1959) *Larousse Encyclopaedia of Mythology*. London: Batchworth Press.

Leshner, A. L. (2000) Using science to counter the spread of Ecstasy abuse. *NIDA Notes* **16**, 5, 1–6.

McElrat, H. K. and McEvoy, K. (2001) Fact, fiction and function: myth-making and the social construction of ecstasy use. *Substance Use and Misuse* **36**, 1–22.

*Measham, F., Aldridge, J. and Parker, H. (2001) *Dancing on Drugs*. London: Free Association Press.

Naranjo, C. (2001) Experience with interpersonal psychedelics, ch. 13, pp. 208–21 in Holland *Ecstasy*.

Parker, H., Aldridge, J. and Measham, F. (1998) *Illegal Leisure: The Normalisation of Adolescent Recreational Drug Use*. London: Routledge.

Ricaurte, G. A., Yvan, J., Cord, B. J. and McCann, U. D. (2002) Severe recreational dose regimen of MDMA (Ecstasy). *Science* **297**, 2260–63.

Riley, S. C. E., James, C., Gregory, D., Dingle, H. and Cadger, M. (2001) Patterns of recreational drug use at dance events in Edinburgh, Scotland. *Addiction* **96**, 1035–48.

Rowntree, B. S. and Lavers, G. R. (1951) *English Life and Leisure*. London: Longmans Green.

Rust, F. (1969) *Dance in Society*. London: Routledge and Kegan Paul.

Steele, T. D., McCann, U. D. and Ricaurte, G. A. (1994) 3, 4-methylenedioxymethamphetamine (MDMA, 'Ecstasy'): pharmacology and toxicology in animals and humans. *Addiction* **89**, 539–51.

17   The Martian Calls Again

Edwards, G. (1971) Unreason in an Age of Reason. Edwin Stevens Lecture for the Laity. London: Royal Society of Medicine.

18   One Helluva Problem

Center for Disease Control (2002) Annual smoking-attributable mortality, years of potential life lost, and economic costs – United States 1995–1999. *Morbidity and Mortality Weekly Report* (12 April), **51**, 300–303.

Giesbrecht, N. (2000) Role of commercial interests in alcohol policies: recent developments in North America. *Addiction* **95**, 5581–96.

Harwood, H. J., Fountain, D. and Livermore, G. (1999) Cost estimates for alcohol and drug abuse. *Addiction* **94**, 631–47.

MacLeod, C. (28 June 2000) Executions hit new high in China's drugs war. *Independent*, p. 18.

*Reuter, P., MacCoun, R. and Murphy, P. (1990) *Money from Crime: A Study of the Economics of Drug Dealing in Washington, DC*. Santa Monica, Calif.; Rand/Drug Policy Research Center.

Warren, K. E., Hodgson, T. A. and Carrol, C. E. (1999) Medical costs of smoking in the United States: estimates, their validity, and their implications. *Tobacco Control* **8**, 290–300.

19 The Legalization Debate

Caulkins, J. P. and Reuter, P. (1997) Setting goals for drug policy: harm reduction or use reduction. *Addiction* **92**, 1143–50.

Drug Policy Foundation (1992) *The Andean Strategy Reconsidered: Toward a Sensible International Drug Policy*. Washington, DC: Drug Policy Foundation.

*Heyman, P. and Brownsberger, W. (2001) *Drug Addiction and Drug Policy: The Struggle to Control Dependence*. Cambridge, Mass.: Harvard University Press.

*Kleiman, M. A. R. (1992) *Against Excess: Drug Policy for Results*. New York: Basic Books.

*MacCoun, R. J. and Reuter, P. (2000) *Drug War Heresies: Learning from Other Vices, Times and Places*. Cambridge: Cambridge University Press.

Mill, John Stuart (1859) *On Liberty*. London, John W. Parker and Son (Penguin edition 1974, edited with an introduction by Gertrude Himmelfarb. Harmondsworth: Penguin Books).

Natarajan, M. and Hough, M. (eds.) (2000) *Illegal Drug Markets: From Research to Prevention Policy*. Crime Prevention Studies Vol. 11. Monsey, NY: Criminal Justice Press.

*National Research Council Committee on Data and Research on Policy on Illicit Drugs (2001) *Informing America's Policy on Illegal Drugs: What We Don't Know Keeps Hurting Us*. Manski, C. E., Pepper, J. V. and Petrie, C. V. (eds.). Washington, DC: National Academy Press.

Reuter, P. (2001) *The Limits of Supply Side Control*. Santa Monica, Calif.: Rand.

Stimmel, B. (1996) *Drug Abuse and Social Policy in America: The War that Must be Won*. New York: Haworth Press.

Weatherburn, D., Jones C., Freeman, K. and Makkai, T. (2003) Supply control and harm reduction: lessons from the Australian heroin 'drought'. *Addiction* **98**, 83–91.

20 Better Deals

Academy of Medical Science (2004) *Calling Time*. London.

*Advisory Council on the Misuse of Drugs (1998) *Drug Misuse and the Environment*. London: Home Office.

Afghanistan (12 June 2002) http://devdata.worldbank.org/external/CPProfile.asp

Brownsberger, W. (1997) Prevalence of frequent cocaine use in urban poverty areas. *Contemporary Drug Problems* **24**, 349–71.

——(1997) *Profile of Anti-drug Law Enforcement in Massachusetts.* Princeton, NJ: Robert Woods Johnson Foundation.

——(2001) Drug users and drug dealers, ch. 2, pp. 51–80 in Heymann, P. and Brownsberger, W. *Drug Addiction and Drug Policy: The Struggle to Control Dependence.* Cambridge, Mass.: Harvard University Press.

Brundtland, G. H. (2002) World summit on sustainable development: importance of health in economic development makes it a priority. *BMJ* **325**, 399–400.

Central Committee on the Treatment of Heroin (CCBH) (2002) *Medical Co-prescription of Heroin: Two Randomized Controlled Trials.* Utrecht: CCBH.

Chouvy, P. A. (7 September 2002) Trafic de Drogue et consequences sanitaires en Afghanistan et en Asie Centrale. *Revue Toxibase*, 1–13.

Commission on Macroeconomics and Health (2001) *Macroeconomics and Health: Investing in Health for Economic Development.* Geneva: WHO.

Department of Health (2003) *Tackling Health Inequalities: A Programme for Action.* London: Department of Health Publications.

Esmail, A., Warburton, B., Bland, M., Anderson, H. R. and Ramsay, J. (1997) Regional variations in death from volatile solvent abuse in Great Britain. *Addiction* **92**, 1765–71.

Fischer, B., Rehm, J., Kirts, M., Casas, M., Hall, W., Drausz, M. et al. (2002) Heroin assisted treatment as a response to the public health problem of opiate dependence. *European Journal of Public Health* **12**, 228–34.

Foxcroft, D. R., Ireland, D., Lister-Sharp, D. J., Lowe, G. and Breen, R. (2003) Longer term primary prevention for alcohol use in young people. A systematic review. *Addiction* **98**, 397–412.

*Giddens, A. (1991) *Modernity and Self-identity: Self and Society in the Late Modern Age.* Cambridge: Polity Press.

Gossop, M., Marsden, J., Stewart, D. and Kidd, T. (2003) The National Treatment Outcome Research Study (NTORS); 4–5 year follow-up results. *Addiction* **98**, 291–304.

Grieshaber-Otto, J., Sinclair, S. and Schacter, N. (2000) Impacts of international trade, services and investment treaties on alcohol regulation. *Addiction* **95** (Supplement 4), S491–S504.

Gruer, L., Murray, S. and Boyd, A. (1997) Extreme variations in the distribution of serious drug misuse-related morbidity in Greater Glasgow. Reported in Advisory Council on the Misuse of Drugs (see above), pp. 108–9.

Hennesy, J. J. and Fallone, N. J. (eds.) (2002) *Drug Courts in Operation: Current Research.* Binghamton, NY: Haworth Press.

Holder, H. D. and Edwards, G. (eds.) (1995) *Alcohol and Public Policy: Evidence and Issues.* Oxford: Oxford University Press.

Hser, Y. L., Hoffman, V., Grella, C. E. and Anglin, M. D. (2001) A 33-year follow-up of narcotic addicts. *Archives of General Psychiatry* 58, 503–8.

Jernigan, D. H. (1997) *Thirsting for Markets: The Global Impact of Corporate Alcohol.* San Rafael, Calif.: Marin Institute.

——(2000) Implications of structural changes in the global alcohol supply. *Contemporary Drug Problems* 27, 163–87.

——(2002) Global ramifications of European alcohol policies. *Addiction* 97, 615–18.

Jha, P. and Chaloupka, F. J. (2000) The economics of global tobacco control. *BMJ* 321, 358–61.

——(2000) *Tobacco Control in Developing Countries.* Oxford: Oxford University Press.

Lancaster, T., Stead, L., Silagy, C. and Sowden, A. (2000) Regular review: effectiveness of interventions to help people stop smoking: findings from the Cochrane Library. *BMJ* 321, 355–8.

Lemmens, P. H. (2003) Dutch government backs down on heroin prescription despite successful trial. *Addiction* 98, 247–9.

Lemmens, P. H. H. M. and Garretsen, H. F. L. (1998) Unstable pragmatism: Dutch drug policy under national and international pressure. *Addiction* 93, 157–62.

MacCoun, R. J. and Reuter, P. (2000) *Drug War Heresies: Learning from Other Vices, Times and Places.* Cambridge: Cambridge University Press.

Marzak, P. M., Tardif, K., Leon, A. C., Hirsch, C. S., Stajic, M., Porter, L. et al. (1997) Poverty and fatal accidental drug overdose of cocaine and opiates in New York City: an ecological study. *American Journal of Drug and Alcohol Abuse* 23, 221–8.

Mattick, R. P. and Degenhardt, L. (2003) Methadone-related and heroin-related deaths among opiate users: methadone helps save lives. *Addiction* 98, 387–8.

Painter, J. (1994) *Bolivia and Coca: A Study in Dependence.* London: Lynne Reinner.

Parker, H., Newcombe, R. and Bakx, K. (1987) The new heroin users: prevalence and characteristics in Wirral, Merseyside. *British Journal of Addiction* 82, 147–57.

Police Foundation (2001) *Drugs and the Law: Report of the Independent Inquiry into the Misuse of Drugs Act 1971.* London: Police Foundation.

Prabbat, J., Chaloupka, F. J. (eds.) (1999) *Curbing the Epidemic: Governments and the Economics of Tobacco Control.* Washington, DC: World Bank.

Prowse, M. (7 December 2002) Is inequality good for you? *Financial Times*, pp. 1–2.

*Room, R. (2003) Rethinking alcohol, tobacco and other drug control. *Addiction* 98, 713–16.

Royal College of Physicians (2000) *Nicotine Addiction in Britain*. London: Royal College of Physicians.

Tomlinson, J. (1999) *Globalisation and Culture*. Cambridge: Polity Press.

Townsend, J., Roderick, P. and Cooper, J. (1994) Cigarette smoking by socio-economic group, sex and age: effects of price, income, and health publicity. *BMJ* 302, 923–7.

Uchtenhagen, A., Gutzwiller, F., Dobler-Mikola, A., Steffen, T. and Rihs-Middel, M. (1999) *Prescription of Narcotics for Heroin Addicts*. Basle: Karger.

United Nations Office of Drug Control and Crime Prevention (2002) *Global Illicit Drug Trends 2002*. New York: UN ODCCP.

Van Den Brink, W., Hendriks, V. M., Blanken, P. and Van Ree, J. W. (2003) Medical prescription of heroin in treatment resistant heroin addicts: two randomised controlled trials. *BMJ* 327, 310–12.

Vecchi, G. M. and Sigler, R. T. (2001) *Assets Forfeiture: A Study of Policy and its Practice*. Durham, NC: Carolina Academic Press.

Wallace, R. and Wallace, D. (1997) Community marginalisation and the diffusion of disease and disorder in the United States. *BMJ* 314, 1341–5.

White, D. and Pitts, M. (1998) Educating young people about drugs: a systematic review. *Addiction* 93, 1457–87.

*Wilkinson, R. G. (1996) *Unhealthy Societies: The Afflictions of Inequality*. London: Routledge.

Yi-Mak, K. and Harrison, L. (2001) Globalisation, cultural change and the modern drug epidemics: the case of Hong Kong. *Health, Risk and Society* 3, 39–57.

Postscript

Omran, A. R. (1971) The epidemiologic transition: a theory of the epidemiology of population change. *The Milbank Memorial Fund Quarterly* 49, 500–538.

Index